T0064940

DREAMS

To Paul M, for inspiring me to follow my dreams.

A Rockpool book
PO Box 252
Summer Hill
NSW 2130
Australia

rockpoolpublishing.co
Follow us! **f** 📷 rockpoolpublishing
Tag your images with #rockpoolpublishing

ISBN: 978-1-925924-48-0

First published in 2015 under ISBN 978-1-925017-17-5
This edition published in 2020
Copyright Text © Rose Inserra 2015
Copyright design © Rockpool Publishing 2020

A catalogue record for this
book is available from the
National Library of Australia

Design by Sara Lindberg, Rockpool Publishing
Edited by Katie Evans
Printed and bound in China
10 9 8 7 6 5 4 3 2 1

Every effort has been made to locate the copyright holders of printed material. The publisher welcomes hearing from anyone in this regard.

DREAMS

What Your Subconscious Wants To Tell You

ROSE INSERRA

ROCKPOOL

Contents

Introduction

WE ALL DREAM. That's a fact. It's one thing we have in common with the entire human race – and mammals, as research suggests. The ancient Greeks believed that when you fell asleep you'd fall into the arms of Morpheus, the god of dreams, where you would surrender to the divine messages given to you through your dreams in forms of symbols, images and prophecies. Indigenous peoples have held strong beliefs in dreams as a spiritual connection to spirits, guides and their ancestors. Dreams have featured in holy texts, such as the Bible, and across traditional religious beliefs from all nations. And modern science has made enormous progress in the understanding of our dreaming mind and its purpose and function in our lives. Both Carl Jung and Sigmund Freud conducted extensive research on the topic of dreams and provided valuable information that has increased our awareness and understanding of dream interpretation. Their findings on the purpose and messages of the subconscious have shaped our view on what dreams mean as a tool in helping us navigate our waking-life issues.

My belief is that dreams are a gateway to understanding yourself. Images you see in a dream highlight parts of your personality – what's going on at an 'ego' level and episodes in your life that may need to be examined or analysed.

In my experience, analysing our dreams is not simply a problem-solving device, even though dreams in fact help us with solutions. The magic that dreams provide is that they reveal feelings that need to be dealt with. They are a wake-up call from your soul or subconscious self. But how do you enable the emotions that surface in your dreams to transfer into your consciousness?

For those who want to understand their dreams but cannot remember them, *Dreams: What Your Subconscious Wants to Tell You* will motivate you to want to recall your dreams. For those of you who remember your dreams, this book will help you to take an active role in interpreting them and discovering the layers of meaning from their symbols and images. As dreams are a reflection of your inner world it's essential that *you*, and only *you*, are the final authority on what your dreams mean.

As a creative writer I love using metaphors and vivid imagery in my prose, and it became my mission to search for the perfect metaphor to encapsulate my own personal connection to the study of understanding dreams.

After a number of concepts that led to a dead-end, I finally discovered the thread metaphor. Comparing our existence to threads is closely associated with the thread of life spun for us by the Three Sisters of Fate from Greek mythology, the Moirae, who determine the life and death of all mortals. Clotho weaves the threads at the beginning of our life; Lachesis determines the shape and length of it and decides which events should occur in everyone's life; and Atropos cuts the thread when the time has come for death.

These threads represent the parts of ourselves that make up the greater tapestry of our life's experiences – and that includes the six years we spend dreaming during our lifetime.

I have also used the symbolism of 'thread' in the three parts of the book to represent our connection to one another as fellow dreamers. Dreams are threads given to us by our conscious to hang on to – they are everyday threads. We usually hold on by a thread to our reality when life gets too challenging, as we hang on by that invisible thread when we are desperately lost in our nightmares.

Dreams help us enter our subconscious and ensure we return back safely.

The thread is also a metaphor for the process we use as we wind our way through the labyrinthine dreamworld – holding on to an invisible thread of hope that we will be able to interpret the extraordinary dreams we weave. This process is made up of three parts:

1. Knowledge

2. Intuition

3. Application

Once applied, the three parts will provide you with tools that I believe will enable you to understand your dream messages more fully and empower you to make changes in your waking life.

The case studies used throughout the book reinforce the success of this process and I'm very grateful to have had the permission of the dreamers, whose names have been changed for confidentiality, to use their dreams to encourage insightful dream interpretation.

By viewing dreams as a wealth of resources rather than possessing rigid meanings, you can make the most of their gifts of wisdom. Then watch for magic to happen.

PART 1

Knowledge

WE ARE ALL connected to each other through the magic thread of dreams that we share as humans. This part of the book looks at the knowledge we can gain from how symbols work in our dreams and their magic in bringing to light all that you need for self-understanding.

There is an ancient Chinese proverb that says:

> *'An invisible red thread connects those who are destined to meet, regardless of the time, the place or the circumstance. The thread may stretch or tangle, but it will never break.'*

According to ancient Eastern beliefs, when a child is born, an invisible red thread extends from the child's spirit and connects him or her to all the significant people – present and future – who will play a part in his or her life. As the child grows, the thread shortens; this draws those people who are destined to be together closer.

The concept of destiny and the red thread extends to the folklore of the old lunar matchmaker god, who ties an invisible red string around the ankles of men and women who are destined to become soul mates and will one day marry each other. This magical thread, too, may stretch or tangle, but will never break. And so it is with the dream thread. You don't know why a theme or a piece from a scene is carried through the dreamer to the waking world, but you trust it because it will reveal itself to be significant.

The magic of understanding our dreamscape is all about the journey we take into our dreaming world and how we bring it back into our conscious lives. You may ask, what do I do with these dreams? How do I journey safely? How do I retrieve the symbols and meanings so that my life's better? What does it require?

Trust the red thread of connection. The thread will never break. Your dreams hold the answer. Use the knowledge from this first part of the book to understand your personal symbols and to interpret the code of what your subconscious is trying to tell you.

CHAPTER 1

What You Need to Know About Dreams

'A dream is a microscope through which we look at the hidden occurrences in our soul.'
— **Erich Fromm**

DREAMING REPRESENTS AN important part of our lives – whether you remember your dreams or not, we do it every single night. It is a universal experience and more than just a biological function. In ancient civilisations, dreams were considered a sacred connection with the divine (the gods), who provided healing and predicted the future through omens sent from dreams.

People created shrines and built temples where dreams were incubated for healing purposes. The most famous dream-incubating shrines were dedicated to the Greek physician Asklepius, who is thought to have lived in the 11th century BCE and was later worshipped as a god. Over time, more than 400 temples were built in his honour. Followers of the dream cult slept overnight in the shrines in the hope of a visit from the gods to bring them healing for their ailments. In the morning, priests would interpret the dream and recommend a cure. Dreams were held in high regard as a means of finding cures for illness, foretelling the future, receiving guidance from divine sources, a precognitive device and speaking with the dead.

Throughout history, many cultures such as the ancient Egyptians were said to have written the oldest dream dictionary on papyrus, which dates back to 1250 BCE, known as the Dream Book from the Chester Beatty papyrus on dreams, which contains records of 200 dreams and their interpretations according to the priests of Horus. In Babylonia, temples existed to the goddess Mamu. Ancient Chinese visited temples and performed dream incubation, and to understand the dream was therapeutic. Ancient India's book on wisdom, the Atharva Veda, contains many early beliefs about dream symbols. The Bible refers to dreams and interpretations. Native American Indians and the Indigenous peoples of Australia believed in the healing power of dreams and guidance obtained by a vision or vision quest. Dreams, however, were not taken seriously for a long time in the Western world until psychologist Sigmund Freud (1856–1939) began to study them as part of psychoanalysis. He analysed and interpreted dreams as the place where unconscious fears, desires, sexual urges and repressions resided. His theory was that our conscious minds are so repulsed by our hidden urges that we repress them in the unconscious. For Freud, dreams were about the hidden parts of ourselves that we try to repress or reject. His work focused a great deal on finding the causes of dreams, using an analytical approach of free association in which the dreamer described thoughts and feelings as they came to mind. This technique was used to discover the real issue behind the dream. Freud, however, as an early pioneer, put too much emphasis on the motives behind dreams as being sexual repressions and wish fulfilment. Today, dream therapists do not follow Freud's teachings but are more often aligned with other later dream experts, such as Carl Jung and his philosophy of looking to the purpose of dreaming rather than the causes.

Carl Gustav Jung (1875–1961) was Freud's student, as well as a psychotherapist, a scholar of mythology and a mystic. He regarded the unconscious as a spiritual aspect of the self and dreams as a way to understand the unconscious. Dreams were a guide for becoming a whole person and providing solutions to waking-life issues. This process was called *individuation*. Jung's theories on the collective unconscious – universal symbols or archetypes that everyone in the world recognises and which can come through dreams and stories – have contributed significantly to current dream work.

Friedrich Perls (1893–1970) was the founder of Gestalt therapy, and believed that dreams contained the unwanted or rejected parts of ourselves.

In general, new theories suggest that dreams act as a safe place where we confront primal threats to our livelihood and survival. By confronting these fears in dreams, we rehearse how we deal with our waking-life challenges.

For me, dreaming is a space where magic happens. It's a transformative experience, as it has personal meaning and gives me direct guidance about what is going on in my world. It is the territory of my intuition, where anything is possible without restrictions. It is the world where my subconscious can express itself freely and where I can speak directly with my intuition.

Our dreams can reveal many truths about our lives, giving us amazing insights that can provide information on health, relationships, work and our overall emotional state. Our subconscious is like a personal therapist. Understanding our dreams can bring self-awareness and a strong connection to our soul.

Sleep States

We all experience five stages or cycles of sleep each night, from the lightest sleep (stages 1-2) to the very deep sleep (stages 3-4) where it's difficult to wake someone up. Stage 5 sleep is known as REM sleep – the sleep period where we dream most vividly. During REM (rapid eye movement) sleep, when we dream the brain is thought to be processing stored memory.

For most adults, the REM sleep cycle occurs every ninety minutes. The first cycle usually lasts for only three minutes, but the duration increases with each cycle, so by early morning the last cycle can last up to fifty-five minutes. That's why we can remember our dreams more easily, as we've stayed longer in this cycle and it's just before we wake up. Most people experience three to five intervals of REM sleep each night. In total we may dream up to two hours and have up to ten dreams on average in each cycle.

During REM sleep, our muscles are temporarily paralysed. That is so that we are protected from physically acting out our dreams with our bodies. During dreaming your eyes move rapidly, your heart beats faster, your breath accelerates, blood pressure rises and your brain waves are activated. In fact, brain waves are increased to the same levels as when you are awake.

Infants spend almost fifty per cent of their time in REM sleep, while adults spend about twenty per cent in REM sleep. REM sleep is thought to be vital for memory and learning.

Dreams facts

We sleep for about one third of our lives, and we have REM-sleep dreams for roughly one quarter of that time. It is estimated that we sleep for about twenty-five years and we dream for six of those years. In one year we have, on average, up to 1800 dreams, of which we will only remember a few, if any.

If disturbed or aroused from the REM sleep phase on a regular basis, a person may experience difficulty in concentration, irritability, mood swings, anxiety and even hallucinations.

Parts of the brain used in dreaming

Sleep studies show that dreams occur mostly in rapid eye movement (REM) cycles, but they can happen in other non rapid eye movement (NREM) sleep phases as well, although they are not as vivid. This explains people being able to sleepwalk, which cannot happen in REM sleep because, as mentioned previously, a person's muscles become temporarily paralysed – a phenomenon which takes place in the *pons* areas located in the brain stem and which travels upward through to certain sections of the brain.

After the pons paralyses that section of our brain, dream activity begins in the *lateral geniculate nucleus* and the *occipital cortex* – the two parts vital for our vision, which makes sense as dreams are predominantly visual. Once the occipital cortex is activated, other areas including the *cerebral cortex* and the *thalamus* begin to show signs of activity. These areas are connected with our other senses such as hearing, touch and movement; however, the parts of the brain that arouse smell and taste do not become activated during REM sleep.

Another part of the brain that is highly active during REM is the *limbic system*, which helps to regulate emotions, in particular two areas of the limbic – the *hippocampus* and *amygdala*, which are involved in memory and instincts. So if you feel any level of emotion during your dream, your brain processes it in the same way as if you were awake. It does not distinguish between your dreaming state and your waking state.

Our logical, problem-solving and planning part of the brain, the *prefrontal cortex,* is quiet during our dreaming sleep. It is not surprising, therefore, that as we dream our way through impossible, illogical and bizarre dream scenarios, we are able to participate in the dream freely without judgement. That is why we dream of doing things we would not normally do in real life, which seem perfectly natural to do in our dream world.

How we see our dreams

People who become blind after birth can see images in their dreams, however if one is born blind, they may not be able to dream in images but their dreams are equally vivid. Other senses such as sound, touch, smell and emotions compensate for the lack of visionary stimulation.

Even foetuses in the womb dream, despite the lack of visual stimuli. Research suggests that they enter REM and NREM sleep cycles, depending on the stage of their development, and their dreams are made up of sound and touch sensations.

The majority of people, approximately seventy-five per cent, dream in colour.

Why We Dream

> *'The general function of dreams is to try and restore our psychological balance by producing dream material that re-establishes, in a subtle way, the total psychic equilibrium.'*
>
> **– Carl Jung**

There is plenty of evidence to support the mental and physiological benefits of dreams. We need to be aware of these benefits in order to understand how they relate to our present state of being.

Biological necessity

Our bodies need a specific amount of REM sleep to assist with recovery and repair. Sleep also restores functions such as memory and learning. Dreaming, therefore, reduces stress and gives our busy, conscious mind a break while our brain and body regenerate.

To release, cleanse and process

Dreams help us get in touch with our emotions and bring imbalances to our attention. Our subconscious mind processes input from our everyday problems – stresses, anxieties, fears, self-doubt and repressed feelings – which can be filtered, sorted and then brought to the surface where healing can take place. Dreams provide a safe outlet where we can discharge or relieve our emotional build-up.

To investigate and problem solve

Dreams can help us pinpoint health problems, address major life issues and help us to solve problems by shutting out the busy-ness of our waking brain and allowing our subconscious mind to explore solutions and possible scenarios without restrictions.

In preparation for future events

Dreams allow us to rehearse or practise for future events, as we dream up scenarios of potential real-life scenes. Nightmares help us prepare for possible traumatic events in our lives. Haven't we heard ourselves say, 'This is a nightmare'? Chances are that it probably was, as our psyche protects us from the shock, because we've already experienced the emotions in our dream.

For creativity and inspiration

Dreams have had a huge impact on our inventions, creativity and inspiration. Recording artist Paul McCartney heard the tune of *Yesterday* in a dream. Author Stephen King dreamt the idea for his best-selling book *Misery*, as well as other characters and plots in his novels. Chemist Friedrich Kekule credited a dream to his discovery of the structure of the benzene molecule. In the dream he saw snake-like formations writhing and twirling in a dance-like manner. One of the snakes seized its own tail.

His discovery became known as the benzene ring. The alchemical symbol of the snake swallowing or eating its own tail is known as the *ouroboros*.

Spirituality

Dreams can be insightful and spiritually uplifting, as dreamers receive messages from their departed loved ones, spiritual guides or their own inner wisdom and use these lessons in waking life.

Layers of Consciousness

Dreams are a biological necessity that keep us healthy by identifying patterns of behaviour, and releasing old and unhelpful belief systems and thoughts. It's important, therefore, to understand the function of the conscious, the subconscious and the unconscious mind when working out the layers of the dream meanings and each type of dream.

The conscious

The conscious mind consists of all the mental processes of which we are aware. It gathers information from your five senses and makes all the decisions. It is the only part of your mind that thinks and, as such, solves problems – the outcome depends on whatever information it receives. In short, our aware mind, or awake mind, is the conscious.

The unconscious

According to Freud, the unconscious mind is described as being a reservoir of feelings, thoughts, urges and memories that are outside of our conscious awareness. Most of what's in the unconscious is unacceptable or unpleasant, such as feelings of pain, anxiety or conflict. Many of these feelings, desires or emotions are repressed and out of our awareness because they are too threatening or unacceptable to us. It's through dreams that sometimes these secret desires and unacceptable feelings make themselves known. In waking life they are also known as 'Freudian slips' or slips of the tongue.

Freud described the unconscious mind as an iceberg. Everything above the water represents conscious awareness, while everything below the water represents the unconscious. Somewhere in between the two is the subconscious.

The subconscious

The subconscious, sometimes called the pre-conscious, can be defined as just outside of awareness but within our reach, while our unconscious is the deeper materials that haven't yet emerged into subconscious awareness – the rejected, forgotten, devalued or ignored parts of ourselves. I personally prefer to use the term 'subconscious' when discussing dreams as I feel that it is more intuitive to the reader and has a less negative connotation. When we talk of someone being unconscious or in an unconscious state, it brings to mind a lack of control, or passivity. The subconscious is much more animated – it contains thoughts and feelings that a person is not currently aware of, but which can easily be brought to consciousness. The subconscious is where dreams emerge, and thoughts, emotions, feelings and forgotten memories can be accessed and brought to waking-life consciousness.

The superconscious

The superconscious mind is not connected with our physical shell or body. It exists at a level beyond time and space. It is known as the infinite intelligence or the universal mind – one that we are all connected to. It is like the internet, which allows us to connect to every other computer in the world as well as people using these computers. Some call it our Higher Self – one that extends beyond our birth and death and one which holds the blueprint for what we've set out to achieve in our lifetime. We can access this superconscious mind through spiritual dreams and precognitive or prophetic dreams.

Types of Dreams

Anxiety. Most dreams are anxiety based – that is, they highlight our waking-life anxieties that we mostly ignore or are not aware of. That knot in your stomach when you walk past the boss's office can very well turn into a real knot in a dream, where you are tied up and cannot undo the ties. This type of dream is therefore a reflection of our everyday life situation, where our attitudes and emotions are highlighted and exaggerated in our dreams. Our anxiety dreams often turn into recurring dreams or nightmares unless we deal with the ongoing issue.

Creative. Those working in creative fields such as art, music or literature are more directly impacted by creative dreams, which are a deep source of inspiration. Many an invention, work of art or musical piece has been a result of dreaming it first.

Compensatory. Whatever hasn't been given a healthy outlet or expression in your waking life has the potential to manifest as a negative, compensatory dream. Feeling angry? You may dream of angry characters trying to attack or chase you.

Wish fulfilment. The purpose of a wish-fulfilment dream is not to show the dreamer what is missing in their life, but rather to show the potential that is in each of us to achieve our goals and dreams.

Precognitive. Dreaming of something before it happens (a future event) can be a confusing dream type as the dreamer has not much indication if it's a symbolic dream or a precognitive/prophetic dream until after the future event happens.

Warning. Warning dreams show us potential dangers that may pose a physical or psychological threat, especially if we have not heeded our intuition in our waking life. These dreams prompt you to implement changes in your life before you get hurt.

Archetypal. An archetypal dream deals with a much bigger issue than simply a personal one. It deals with patterns of behaviour or belief systems that are universally shared. (See chapters 7 and 8.)

Numinous. These 'big dreams' bring you in contact with the divine. They are transformative dreams that usually involve spiritual phenomena such as spirit guides. (See Chapter 11.)

Shamanic. Dreams that involve elements of initiation, ritual, healing and guidance for the benefit of the dreamer and others (tribal) are manifested in distinct shamanic ways passed down from Indigenous cultures and traditions. (See chapters 10 and 11.)

Healing. A healing dream is one that heals your physical body, your emotional state and your relationships with others. It can offer you clues as to what illness you may have, even before medical diagnosis.

Para-psychological. Many dreams that cannot be explained logically fit into this dream type, such as telepathic dreams, dream sharing, afterlife, past lives, future or parallel lives.

Lucid/astral travel/out-of-body experience (OBE). Lucid dreaming is 'knowing' or being aware that you are dreaming while you are dreaming. In some cases, you can control the events and outcome of the dream. Astral travel and OBE is being able to dream yourself out of your body and travel in the astral realm, often meeting other dreamers in these places. (See Chapter 10.)

What Dreams Tell You About Your Health

There are a number of symbols in your dreams that indicate illness or potential health problems. Having a mind-body connection means that all parts of our body and all of the emotional responses we have share a common language and communicate with each other. When dreaming of any of these symbols, accidents or parts of the body, interpret them as being a message from your subconscious mind and take the images seriously. Illness can be detected by your body first, which then informs your psyche.

Symbol: House	Possible meaning
Broken or blocked pipes	circulatory problems
Frozen or cold temperature	locked energy flow
Garbage	need to clean out/release, digestive problems
Renovation	healing needed, overhaul, change in diet
Burglary	open to infection, vulnerable
Flooding	excess, water retention, overwhelmed
Infestation	infection
Fire	fever, viral or bacterial infection, heartburn

Dreaming of illness or accident: Have a health check and take precautions in dreams of accidents. The dreams are usually symbolic of your emotional state, but there are cases of precognitive dreams or that your subconscious has picked up early warnings of symptoms or potential dangers.

Symbol: Illness	Possible meaning
Allergies	be more tolerant of those around you
Cancer	something is eating away at you, part of your life is not being lived
Diarrhoea	allow yourself to be nurtured
Epilepsy	out of balance with life
Fever	anger, burning up with resentment
Infection	need to get rid of negative emotions, purify
Pneumonia	overwhelmed with emotions, inner turmoil
Rash	self-critical, unable to express yourself
Breathing problems/asthma	trying to please others, focus on what inspires you
Tumour	feeling unlovable, self-neglect
Vomiting	you can't stomach something, need to speak out and let go of old stuff

Symbol: Accidents	Possible meaning
Burns	anger, soothe it with the balm of forgiveness
Cuts	emotional wounds
Run over or crushed	overwhelmed by stress or someone in your life, something is crushing your vision/spirit
Fall	lack of control, trust in yourself and the universe
Loss of limb	feeling disconnected or disempowered, time to take stock of a situation

Remembering Your Dreams

1. Take a sincere interest in your dreams. If you are interested in your dreams, there is a very high probability that you will remember them.

2. Set a clear intention throughout the day to remember a significant dream. You might want to re-read some of your previous dreams to start connecting to the subconscious imagery or alternatively meditate on a question you'd like answered. You may wish to write the question on paper and place it under your pillow.

3. The way you wake up is very important so that you don't forget your dreams. Within five minutes of waking, fifty per cent of your dream is forgotten. Within ten minutes, ninety per cent is gone. Set a soft alarm to wake you up fifteen to twenty minutes earlier than usual, when you are still in the REM dream state. Better still, avoid using an alarm clock and train your body to wake you instead.

4. When you wake, keep your eyes closed and remain completely still, focusing on the memory of the dream. Recall all the images, emotions and scenes from your dream and jot them quickly in your dream journal.

5. Alcohol, caffeine, recreational drugs and medication diminish the ability to remember dreams, as does vitamin and mineral deficiency, particularly in the vitamin B group. Certain foods affect our dreams and therefore it's best to avoid heavy or spicy foods before bedtime when our bodies have not had time to digest. Interestingly, people who are giving up smoking have longer and more intense dreams – mostly about smoking – as a result of tobacco withdrawal.

CHAPTER 2

When Dreams are a Problem

REST ASSURED THAT your dreams will never give you more than you can handle. All that is bubbling away within your subconscious will only come up to the conscious when it is ready. There will be times when our emotional world needs release and recurring dreams and nightmares are a result of deep feelings and thoughts that we are conscious of. They bring to our attention those things we have repressed, that we perceive to be threatening, overwhelming or devastating at some point in our past. Carl Jung believed that it is our shadow (rejected parts and qualities we do not like about ourselves) that usually appears as frightening nightmares in our dreams if we don't acknowledge them in our conscious state.

> 'The unconscious always tries to produce an impossible situation in order to force the individual to bring out his very best. Otherwise one stops short of one's best, one is not complete, one does not realise oneself. What is needed is an impossible situation where one has to renounce one's own will and one's own wit and do nothing but wait and trust to the impersonal power of growth and development.'
> **– Carl Jung (on nightmares)**

The point of the nightmare is a sign that you are now ready to deal with these emotions and unacceptable parts of your personality for the sake of your mental, physical and spiritual health. Believe it or not, your nightmare is there to help you. Nightmares are just dreams with the volume turned up loud, desperately trying to grab your attention about aspects of your life and self that are ready to be dealt with and healed.

Night terrors

Night terrors happen in the cycle before REM sleep and usually have no visuals, although dreamers wake up screaming. The more typical nightmares are detailed and in colour. It is believed that up to twenty per cent of people have nightmares once a week.

As unpleasant as they may be at the time, nightmares are an essential part of dreaming, as they are the manifestation of stress, anxiety and fears from our daily lives that we may not be conscious of. Vivid images are required for us to pay attention and remember our dream scenes and therefore should not be taken literally. It is more productive to focus on the emotion and metaphors in the nightmares.

Types of Recurring Dreams and Nightmares

There are many types of recurring dreams and nightmares that cause us fear, frustration, terror and sometimes physical pain. Some common negative dream scenarios include *falling, being chased or attacked, being killed or killing someone, seeing someone you love die or in danger, being late or unprepared for a presentation or an exam, stuck in slow motion, unable to move or scream, suffocation, sinister presence* to name a few.

If we don't deal with issues highlighted in our nightmares, by blocking, ignoring or denying them, they may haunt us in other ways, manifesting as illnesses, accidents, conflicts in relationships and other personal difficulties. Nightmares are there to remind us of some urgent business to be resolved.

Resolving Nightmares

There are a number of methods you can use that will assist you in working with your nightmares so that you no longer dread them, but learn to harness the energy they offer. Insights from recurring dreams and nightmares can give you great confidence in expressing your feelings instead of avoiding or running away from situations that are unpleasant in real life.

Some of the most useful techniques include dream re-scripting (changing the outcome of the dream once you learn to go back (dream re-entry) into the dream); and lucid dreaming (being awake in your dream and changing the events, such as asking the pursuer what they want or turning a potential weapon into a harmless object).

How to Re-script a Dream

1. Select a recent nightmare or upsetting dream and re-write the ending.

2. Choose an ending that will make you feel empowered and confident in a new scenario, instead of how you actually felt in the dream.

3. Before going to sleep, sit in a comfortable position and relax your body and mind for a few minutes. Once you feel calm, visualise or recall the dream you've selected to re-script. Go through it as if it were a movie and when things turn scary or unpleasant, replace the old ending with the new, empowering one you've created. Imagine this as vividly as you can. Hold the image in your mind.

4. Tune in to your body and check how this feels. Do you feel confident? Free? Empowered? Imagine these feelings even if you don't actually feel this way yet.

5. Embrace the power of suggestion. Tell yourself that not only are these new thought patterns reaching into your waking life, but also that you will have a new dream that includes a more positive and empowering ending.

It's not always possible to dethrone the tyrants in our dreams that cause us terrifying nightmares. There may be other causes at play such as serious illness, post-operative recovery, medication, drugs, trauma and post-traumatic stress.

Two of my clients had very similar dreams that I traced back to a common probable cause. Both women had recurring nightmares that their child was encased or trapped in a glass container and they were unable to get them out. What caused the terror for both mothers was the fact that the child was visibly distressed. They could see them through the glass, but they were powerless to rescue them as breaking the glass would mean possibly causing the child serious injury.

It seemed that these recurring dreams were brought about when there was a change in the child's routine – day care, kindergarten, school. In effect, when the child was out of range from parental supervision. However, as the child grew up, the recurring dreams continued to haunt the dreamers.

When we traced back the traumatic experiences they had as children, both dreamers said that they had witnessed their younger sibling's death. They subconsciously still felt a sense of powerlessness that they could do nothing to help the situation. This post-traumatic stress revisits the dreamers whenever there are new events in their lives over which they have little control. Both dreamers agreed that this nightmare experience was the most frightening of any other dream, including those that included their own death.

Nightmares with a symbolic or metaphoric meaning are quite different to post-traumatic stress dreams, as they are less intense. This dreamer felt the impact of her nightmare quite dramatically and she made radical changes to her life immediately after.

> 'I had a recurring dream of a white coffin in my kitchen. My mother (who is alive) was lying in it, but my favourite flowers, yellow roses, were strewn all around the coffin.'
> **Karen**

When we discussed the dream imagery and the association she made with the white coffin and her mother, the dreamer understood the message.

> 'The white coffin reminded me of my mother's white kitchen tiles – the ones she was pushed onto by my violent father. The coffin represents my future. It's a clear message that if I don't get out of my present situation with domestic violence, I too will end up in a coffin. The yellow roses made sure that the dream knew it was referring to my future.'

CHAPTER 3

Dreams and Gender

How Men and Women Dream

According to dream research, men and women dream differently. Women have greater dream recall in general. This may be due to the relationship between high oestrogen levels and the ability to remember dreams. Women also have more nightmares than men. Perhaps this is due to the fact that women are more likely to share this information and have better dream recall.

Women dream of people they know, male and female, and mostly in a familiar setting indoors.

Men's dreams take place outdoors, with mostly male characters who are unfamiliar to them. These male characters are usually aggressive, unfriendly or hostile.

Researchers suggest that the reason for these differences is that they reflect traditional real-life experiences. For men, they see the workplace as a hostile place where they compete with other men they don't know. Women are generally more social and co-operative, and build relationships with both genders in the workplace and socially. Despite women moving into the more competitive areas of the workforce that were once traditionally dominated by men, both men and women are wired to believe that men derive a greater sense of self-esteem from success at work (being the provider) and women's confidence comes from maintaining successful relationships.

Pregnancy and menopause

Pregnant women dream more, tend to have better dream recall and experience more vivid dreams than usual. This may be due to the increased levels of progesterone, which many women claim gives them odd or disturbing dreams. Apart from the hormone changes, pregnant women are also going through a very emotional time and therefore their dreams reflect their anxieties.

Oestrogen also has an overall effect on dream recall – it's been reported that women dream more at certain times during their menstrual cycle.

Similarly with menopause, the physical, mental and emotional changes inevitably affect sleep patterns and dreaming. Hot flushes and discomfort are some of the symptoms of menopause and cause insomnia and strange dreams. Pregnancy and menopause are times of great transition – in one there is the birth and addition to the family, in the other it's the empty nest and finding a new role that makes some women feel valued for something other than their sexuality.

Both pregnant women and menopausal women wake more in the middle of their REM cycles and this is a possible reason why they remember their dreams. Generally, menopause causes women to have fewer dreams.

Common dreams for pregnant women

- having a deformed baby
- forgetting to take care of the child
- fish, swimming, drowning, standing in the ocean
- giving birth to animal babies that grow in size as the pregnancy progresses
- giving birth to an alien
- cheating partner
- re-appearing ex-lovers

It is normal for pregnant women to experience anxiety dreams as it reflects their conscious anxieties about the impending birth, change in their body appearance, feeling self-conscious about losing their feminine shape and the pressure of being a good parent. Other emotions associated with this major life change include insecurity, vulnerability, ambivalence towards the new role as a parent and feeling the weight of responsibility for a helpless new baby.

Common anxiety dreams include dreaming the baby is born prematurely or that it is or becomes something other than a baby, such as a furry animal. Women often dream that they can 'see' the baby either through a transparency in their stomach or because part of it emerges. Dreams about ex-lovers or about partner infidelity are also common – both arising from an anxiety about change in body appearance.

The dreams just prior to birth mirror real-life emotions about the expectancy of the event and the responsibility of new motherhood. They may include dreams about impending travel or anxious dreams where the baby is born but something is wrong and only care taken in the dream fixes the problem.

Common dreams for menopausal women

- giving birth
- fire
- losing a baby
- losing the car/possessions
- losing teeth
- finding new rooms in the house

Women's emotions are running high during the 'change' of life and strange dreams are a part of this new phase. Anxiety dreams such as losing a baby, car or teeth are related to feeling vulnerable, older, less attractive and not knowing where things are any more (losing car/baby/possessions).

Fire is possibly related to the discomfort of hot flushes or perhaps it's more emotional – the end of the childbearing years and the beginning of a new and less intense stage. It could be said that it's a metaphor: the phoenix rising out of the ashes (burning of the old self) to reinvent one's life in order to give birth to the new self.

When a menopausal woman finds a new room in the house, it is a positive dream to suggest that she has found a new part of herself – one that was put on hold and has now been rediscovered, such as starting that new university course, doing a charity run, travelling overseas, taking up life drawing and more. It's the opportunity to find a new identity out of the old, rather like 'up-cycling' (a new version or use of the original). This dream is common in women who have sacrificed their passions, ideal career and interests for parental responsibilities.

CHAPTER 4

Sex and Romance

SEX DREAMS ARE not exclusively related to real sex. Sex in dreams is more about relationships and intimacy – starting with the relationship you have with yourself and others around you. It can sometimes be a symbol of your wish to be integrated as a whole person – both the masculine energies and the feminine energies coming together as one (see Chapter 7 The Anima and Animus). It can also be interpreted as getting close emotionally and intimately; that is, a longing for a deeper communication on a more intimate level that connects you to someone else. Essentially, consider your sex dream the wakeup call you need to get to know yourself better and those you have a relationship with. Both men and women have sexual dreams but they differ in content. Men are reported to have more sexually explicit dreams than women, usually with unknown and attractive partners who initiate the sex. Women are more likely to dream about sex with celebrities, their ex-partners, and current partners, featuring more kissing and sexual fantasies about other dream characters. This reinforces the view that women are often more comfortable with their emotions than men.

Freud and sex

Freud believed that most dreams were about wish fulfilment, especially around sexuality, the most well-known being 'penis envy' in women. His narrow outlook, which claimed that the main function of dreams was to act out what was missing in your life, has been disputed and mostly rejected by modern professionals working in the psychology field. A wish-fulfilment dream is about showing you the potential that is within you to achieve. Dreaming of sex has both physical and emotional inter-pretations. For men, a wet dream is a biological function that involuntarily releases semen while they are asleep, sometimes triggered by a sex dream.

For women, they can also experience sexual stimulation and pleasure in their dreams – our bodies crave a physical release. There is research on hormonal and physical changes, and the higher levels of oestrogen that produce more sex dreams. It is believed that during REM sleep, males experience erections and females experience increased vaginal bloodflow, regardless of the content of the dream.

Sex with Other People

Often sex dreams are about how people perceive us and we perceive them. What those people represent in our dreams and how we feel about the experience in our dream will be the telling point as to how we view our relationship with ourselves and with others. Some sex dreams can simply be wish-fulfilment – you lust for that person in real life but can't have them.

More complex sex dreams reflect our personal desires and fears. The dream has to visually convey a strong message so the dreamer doesn't miss it – and it does this through imagery that can be immediately identified. This can be confusing and distressing for the dreamer if the sex dream contains violence, incest or other taboos. The aim of the dream is to get your full attention.

Your boss

Sex with a more powerful or older male/female may be a way for your subconscious mind to make you aware of your own potential. Do you need to share your skills more so that you can be recognised for your abilities as a leader? Note the qualities in your boss, not your real-life feelings towards him/her, and ask yourself if you want to integrate those qualities into your working life. If you dream of having sex with a co-worker, it may simply be pointing out that you have a good working relationship.

Your friend

Dreaming of sex with a friend with whom you have a healthy platonic relationship indicates that there are things you have in common that you want to develop further with that person.

A celebrity

The dream may be a wish fulfilment and a fantasy, but more often than not it means you want to be fully recognised in your own right, or long to be part of a social scene.

Your ex

Having sex with your ex is generally not about having those feelings for him or her in real life (except in some instances where you've been the one 'dumped', and where there may be residual wishful thinking). Your subconscious is doing a few things here – warning you of repeating old habits from your failed relationship or recapturing the best of those past experiences with the view to integrating them into your present relationship. Perhaps you may want that romantic phase that is no longer in your relationship with your partner, as you have moved on to a deeper stage. This is a common pre-wedding dream, as there is an expectation of changes in roles and commitment and what that may involve. Discuss with your partner what you need from your relationship. If it's a recurring dream, it suggests your psyche is healing old wounds and trauma and is trying to assimilate new experiences.

A stranger

Having sex with a stranger in dreams can show up as a man or woman with a mask or no face. Sex with the mysterious intruder can be both a disturbing experience and a gift, as it allows you to experiment with passion in which you learn about what physically pleases you. Your subconscious may be telling you to reveal more of your passionate self, or you are in the process of working out what you want in a partner.

Multiple partners

Having sex with multiple partners at one time indicates that you haven't found exactly what pleases you and you're searching for it outside of yourself. Has your relationship become too routine or lacking in passion? Has your life in general become this way too?

Someone of the same gender

If you have been struggling with the issue of homosexuality or bisexuality, dreaming of these sexual encounters is prompting you to accept that part of yourself. In other words, you wish to come to terms with the possibility that you indeed favour one gender over the other or both. Generally, if you don't have these conflicting feelings in real life, your dream is essentially about balancing the feminine and masculine aspects of yourself in all areas of your life. Are you a 'ball breaker' or a 'metrosexual'?

Can you be either or both? These stereotypes and labels are often buried in our subconscious mind and at pivotal times in our lives are released through our dreams. Similarly, if you dream of cross-dressing or that you are transsexual, you may need to acknowledge, confront or express your masculine/feminine side and what your personal associations are regarding these roles in your everyday life.

Your family member (incest)

If you've experienced incest in the past or in the present, and you associate this with trauma and guilt, dreams re-living this experience need to be taken seriously and a psychologist consulted. As a rule, though, dreaming of sex with a family member is not about wish fulfilment or memory suppression. It is more about qualities and traits the family member has that you admire or recognise in yourself. It may be that you have met someone who has these qualities and your dream is making a connection to that family member. On a negative side, we hear phrases about families that contain the word 'incestuous', meaning that they are close knit and they provide all emotional, physical and financial needs within that family without the need for anyone outside of the family circle. It's worthwhile asking if your family love is too close and stifling. Is it causing you concern or confusion? Do you feel a sense of duty but at the same time wish to pull away? In essence, do you need more emotional freedom and psychological boundaries from your family?

Confronting Sex Dreams

Infidelity

In some instances, dreaming of your partner having an affair with someone else may be mirroring some real-life suspicions. However, this is less likely than the dream giving you insight into the intensity of what it would feel like to be emotionally abandoned, or your partner paying more attention to an interest or their job than you. It highlights your insecurities and feelings that you are being taken for granted or perhaps not measuring up to the expectations of others. Often in our conscious lives we harbour these fears of abandonment as we struggle with our appearance, our lack of confidence and times of major change – pregnancy, wedding, job loss, weight gain, illness and more.

If you dream that you are 'cheating' on your spouse or partner, it may suggest some guilt that you are spending more time on another 'love' – this could be an interest, family, work – other than on your partner. It could also indicate a need to express yourself sexually or creatively in a new way but you don't quite know how to tackle your new desires with your partner.

Rape

To dream of being raped is common for those who were actually raped in their waking life – it is known as a post-traumatic event. Two of my clients have relived sexual violence in their dreams after having escaped from the real-life ordeal. If this is the case, then you need to get professional help to deal with this trauma. Many women also feel the 'fear' of being raped, especially after media reports bring it to their attention. Monitor if you have had rape dreams during intensive media coverage on the topic of rape.

For most people, rape in a dream is about the dreamer feeling violated or powerless and their boundaries totally overstepped. Are you feeling emotionally vulnerable, violated or exposed? Do you need to reset your personal boundaries? Are people taking advantage of you or is someone/something being forced upon you?

Dreaming of being 'taken' rather than forcibly raped could indicate your need to be passive and not have to take control of a situation or in a relationship.

If you were the rapist in the dream, consider why you feel the need to impose yourself or your beliefs on someone else and your need for control. As rape in waking life is considered to be more about violence than sex, think about what is making you feel angry and/or aggressive.

Sadism/masochism/bondage

Dreaming of being in a bondage scene as a dominant or a submissive suggests that you are struggling with balancing your feminine and masculine roles. Ask yourself if these parts of you are perfectly aligned. Duality is about having aspects of yourself that encompass your good and bad, nurturing and assertive sides. Dreaming of being in bondage indicates that you may be feeling repressed emotionally in real life or perhaps are being held back, not able to express yourself freely. Are you experiencing a sense of powerlessness in real life or do you wish for someone else to take responsibility for your emotional needs?

To dream you are in a dominant role suggests a need for power and control in your waking life.

Dreaming of masochism may be indicating your need to 'feel' emotions at a more extreme level. In a religious context, those who were the penitents often flagellated themselves – inflicting pain for their perceived 'sins', faults or wrongdoings. Check that you are not punishing yourself by suffering for your past mistakes.

Impotence/castration/vasectomy

This is a frightening dream for men and can feel very real. At a simplistic level, these dream images suggest a fear of losing power or not being able to measure up to expectations or perform – whether that is sexually or in other areas of your life. A vasectomy can represent some self-image issues or that there is some self-doubt in your real life around your masculine role. At a deeper level it can indicate a loss of creativity. The word 'create' is associated with 'life force' and in the dream this is highlighted as being in jeopardy.

Undress

Dreaming that you are undressing indicates your need to reveal your true feelings. It is often a dream suggesting that you accept yourself as you are and be open to your feelings about your sexual needs and desires.

Images of Animals Linked to Sex and Desire

Sex dreams often incorporate animals or animal-like behaviour. The animals listed below are not exclusively associated with sex, and depending on the emotions felt during the dream and on waking up they can illustrate general qualities often attributed to them. So, if snakes are scary for you in real life they are likely to appear in dreams as frightening, causing the dreamer distress. On the other hand, if the snake appears exotic and enticing, this may be suggesting these qualities are significant to you. These are some of the most common animals featured in sex dreams.

Snakes (male phallic symbol; sexual desire)

Dreaming of a writhing, sensual snake – often a python – can suggest sensual pleasure, depending on the context of the dream. If the snake is feared, then it will not have this connotation. A dream image of a woman holding a snake is associated with a woman holding a man's penis. It is common for a penis to be called a 'one-eyed trouser snake'. If you are a woman and have this dream it may suggest that you would like to touch a man sexually or you have just had this experience and it has lingered in your subconscious. Men having this dream may either be concerned about performance anxiety or have some conflict with their own sexual feelings.

Horses (male phallic symbol; sexual libido and stamina)

Horses are common images in erotic, sexual dreams. Their symbol of power and movement is the ideal metaphor for sexual activity and, in many instances, the male. A stallion suggests an image of sexual power, physical vitality and stamina, including their physical attribute for having a large phallus. Dreaming of a horse can therefore suggest a desire for a healthy libido and a need for movement or stimulation in waking life.

Cats (women and self pleasure)

Dreaming of cats is associated with women (as the slang word for a woman's genitals). The obvious image of a slinky feline in any dream is that of self-satisfaction – the cat-that-got-the-cream feeling. It's particularly apt for enjoyment of sex.

Birds (women and sexual freedom)

Flying is associated with sexual freedom and ecstasy, and so birds are symbols for this emotional satisfaction. A bird is also a slang word for women (chick) and 'dirty bird' is slang for a promiscuous woman.

Dream Landscapes and Places Linked to Sex and Desire

Often geography and setting play a big role in sex dreams. They are a clue to how you are responding to circumstances and relationships in your real life. The more comfortable and familiar the landscape, the more it suggests a sense of being at ease in your intimate life. Surreal and hostile landscapes, however, indicate an almost detached or objective view, which can make the dreamer feel vulnerable. Here are some common settings for sex dreams.

Desert (loneliness, solitude)

A desert or barren landscape that contains an oppressive bleakness suggests a lack of fulfilment or loneliness in your waking-life relationship. Often the dreamer longs to find signs of life, but is mostly searching for it in the dream. The sense of waiting suggests that the dreamer is wishing for fulfilment – a filling-up of the sexual arousal or emotions from their partner. You could be going through a dry period of emotional connectedness, or your love/sex life has 'dried up'. This dream image can occur during a recent break-up or at the very beginning of a new romantic affair when the sexual landscape is still a blank canvas.

Sea/waves/ocean (emotions, needs and desires associated with sexuality and satisfaction)

Seascapes are a symbol of strong emotions and passions. Thundering waves or churning water suggest turmoil in your intimate relationships. Violent seascapes are frightening and can represent feeling overwhelmed by sexual demands or even your own strong sexual feelings that you can't control. Calmer waters indicate that your sensual needs are met. Pleasurable floating sensations in calm waters is a good indication of satisfaction.

Forest (sexual confusion or repression, as forests can be tangled, dark and impenetrable)

Dreaming of a forest can indicate sexual confusion or repression. Tangled and dark forests are where we can reach deeper and more intimate parts of ourselves and our feelings that have been covered up by 'foliage' or camouflaged. Is there an anxiety you are experiencing in your intimate relationship? Are you burying your sexual feelings and frustrations? What desires are not being met?

Having sex in a public place or outdoors suggests public exposure – are you concerned that people will know your intimate details? A bush or forest are associated with pubic hair and so may suggest the hidden sexual pleasure beneath.

Buildings

Castles or forts are generally associated with phallic imagery, and the 'high' that accompanies it i.e. taking your sexual pleasure to another level. The office, on the other hand, suggests work-related frustrations, ambitions and longings. Bedrooms reflect your intimate life as it is in reality.

Actions

Common actions such as flying are associated with sexual release after an orgasm. Eating food or drinking suggests nourishment, appetite, feeding and lush fruits – a common symbol of genitalia. Playing sport indicates games, physical exertion and sweat – all commonly associated with the act of sex.

Orgasm

To dream that you are having an orgasm is a symbol of an exciting end to something you've worked hard at to achieve. What have you completed recently in your waking life? Similarly, the orgasm may represent your need to relieve your sexual tensions and therefore it's a natural physiological release.

Sex Dreams Case Studies

In my work with dreams, I've found that a number of my clients were embarrassed to discuss their sex dreams because they were either confused, disgusted or aroused by their content and this was a matter of concern to them.

> 'I've been having a recurring dream where I have a romantic relationship with someone. That person always changes in each dream but the intense romance is always the same. At first the dreams were just a feeling. Then the dreams became more vivid and intense. For instance I would suddenly be able to feel the actual touch. Then the kiss. And recently actual intercourse where I even climax!'

Julie

This is a common and normal dream. It's rarely about repressed sexuality, as Freud once believed it was. It's about desire and emotional needs and intimacy that perhaps aren't adequately met in real, waking life. You may need more. Sometimes we don't need it from a partner, but we need it from ourselves. Have you been taking care of your emotional needs? Are you giving more than you are receiving? The dream is telling you that it's important to take care of yourself: be your own lover; find more love/intimacy with those around you (not necessarily sexual).

> *'I have these vivid dreams where my husband cheats on me. They used to be recurring but are less frequent now. The scenario on how, why and with whom are always different but the intense anger and hurt I feel is always the same. And when I wake up, I'm so mad I want to take it out on my husband in real life, despite the fact that my husband has never cheated on me or given me any inkling that he might.'*

Nikki

A dream of a partner or husband cheating is not what it seems. It may be that your husband is spending more time on other interests in waking life and less time with you (your perception of this, perhaps not the truth). It could also be that you fear disappointment and being let down and your husband represents this in your dreams. The good thing is that this is no longer a recurring dream, which means it's no longer an issue and you are now concentrating on fulfilling your own needs more.

> *'I had a disturbing dream of a horse standing quietly in a field. I noticed at the base of its back legs was a huge python. The snake made its way up the horse's legs and up to its rump area. I said to myself – "No. That snake is going to try and consume the whole horse." I watched fascinated and in horror as the snake made its way up to the horse's rump, paying particular attention to the seductive way it made its way up the horse so the horse didn't even notice that it was a snake on its body. Eventually the snake devoured most of the horse without the horse knowing. I woke up feeling distressed.'*

Paolo

Both the snake and the horse are common 'male sexual symbols' – the python (penis) and the stallion (also represents the male genitals – power and vitality/the stud).

You say you had not come out as a gay man at this stage in your life, but were struggling to find the courage to do so. This dream was giving you clues from your subconscious that you preferred a male sexual encounter all along.

The python can symbolise sexual urges. In fact, you say that the snake seductively made its way around the horse. It highlights how much you were unaware of your sexual preference, but the desire (snake) was consuming you.

Ignoring your sexual feelings and hoping that it would all go away was going to devour you and literally eat away at you.

If we are all parts of our dream, think about what it says about you. You are the both the horse and the python too. The horse is the part of you that is full of vitality and independence, and wants to move forward in life but is held back. What parts of you were holding you back? The snake is your sexual desire. Will it consume you or will you be able to express your sexuality and be comfortable about it?

How to Work With Your Sex Dreams

1. Be receptive to the message of your dreams where you are gaining insight into your subconscious. Trust your dreams. Discern if your dream is to do with your sexuality, love, romance or relationships in general.

2. Develop a positive mind-set by avoiding labels and not feeling guilty about the contents of your dream. Look at dreams as metaphors and an opportunity to learn more about your emotional/sexual life so that you can strive to become more emotionally intelligent and sexually fulfilled.

3. Record your dreams, and as you look back over the dream diary you may find a pattern taking shape in your dreams that is reflected in your real relationships. Remember that your subconscious is always a few steps ahead of your conscious thoughts and feelings. Use your intuition and unlock the deeper meaning in your dreams. This process will assist you in becoming more confident in your abilities to understand your emotional and physical needs.

CHAPTER 5

Ten Common Dreams Explored

'Dreams are today's answers to tomorrow's questions.'

– Edgar Cayce

INTERESTINGLY, WE SHARE similar dreams with people of all races in the world that transcend cultural and socio-economic boundaries and contain universal themes. Many of these common dreams arise out of anxiety. Often they occur during changes in your life – transitional or even traumatic events can bring up volatile emotions that have been dormant for a while. It's no surprise, then, that the top dreams we all share are highly emotional and mostly negative.

They provide valuable information from the subconscious as to what is really bothering you in your waking life and many times offer suggestions about how to overcome your fears, anxieties and blockages in order to move forward. Once your conscious mind has a good grip on the issue, you can learn to face it both in your dream world and, most importantly, in your emotional world.

Your subconscious has revealed all that you need to know at this point in order to gather information about your life matters. How you then deal with your life situation is up to you – your conscious, rational 'you'.

When you gain insight into what's going on in your emotional world, you are empowered to do something about it.

Recent events frequently surface in our dreams. Sometimes it's because our minds are trying to process these events, and it takes a while for it to do this. Other times, dreams of past events offer us glimpses of information via symbols about our emotional, physical and psychological states – clues on what we need to learn from our past so that issues can be resolved.

When you have had a vivid dream, ask yourself:

- What was going on in your personal life at this time? Think back from two weeks before the dream up until the day of the dream.
- What significant event took place at this time?
- How did you feel while you were dreaming and how did you feel when you woke up?
- Was this dream a recurring dream or similar to one you have had before?
- Was it associated with an event (e.g. starting a new job)? Perhaps it was an event that was about to take place, like a wedding or birthday.

You are the final authority on your dreams, as they are a reflection of what's going on inside you at a mental, emotional, physical and spiritual level. The context and symbols in your dreams mirror your spiritual, social and cultural belief systems. You will best understand your dreams if you take an active role in discovering your own personal symbols and what emotions they evoke so that you are able to find a meaning, one that truly resonates with you.

The Top 10 Dreams

The study of dreams shows that people all over the world share basic common dreams. Many of these common dreams occur during changes in our lives, so it stands to reason then that we all share highly emotional and anxiety-type dreams. Check to see how many of these dreams you've experienced and how you felt at the time. This should give you a clue about their meaning.

For many people, these dreams keep coming back as a reminder of things not dealt with or as a reflection of something that is going on in their life. For example, if you dream of being chased when you are under stress, then every time you are under stress you will have that dream. So, to end the chase dream, for example, you have to deal with the stressful event in your waking life.

These emotive dreams will offer you information on what is bothering you in your waking life, and ways to overcome your fears. The problem is they appear in symbols – like some crazy encryption that doesn't make sense – which is why the message is either misunderstood or ignored when it reaches your waking (conscious) brain. It's important that you work out the dream symbols so that you will be able to gain insight into what's going on for you in waking life.

1. Being chased or attacked
2. Driving or riding in a car – mostly out of control
3. Exam – poor performance, being late or unprepared
4. Falling/drowning
5. Being lost, trapped or stuck
6. Flying
7. Losing your teeth
8. Being naked in public
9. Death/illness
10. Missing bus/train/plane/boat

1. Being Chased or Attacked

Being chased and/or attacked as a result of the chase is our most common dream. It is an anxiety dream reflecting insecurities or fears we experience in our waking life. It is also a very ancient dream that goes back to our earliest encounters with being chased by wild animals – so it's a familiar emotional response to the 'fight or flight' situation we still have today. We don't have wild beasts chasing us but we do have other modern 'monsters' that pursue us. Our dreams, therefore, are really our natural responses to life's stresses.

On a wider scale, we're running away from the greatest fear we share as humans – death. It's not so much the physical death, which we know is inevitable, but endings – death of a relationship, death of a lifestyle, death of a career. We are programmed to feel that change is just as terrifying as death.

If you dream of being chased, ask yourself: is there something or someone you are running away from in your waking life? Is it someone or something that you are afraid of or are unwilling to face? What needs to change in your life?

If you are chased by monsters or shadows, it could just be you. The monsters chasing you could be parts of yourself – the hidden or shadow self – that you do not want to confront or are afraid of facing in your waking life. They may be emotional monsters such as fear, anxiety, anger, envy or aggression, or parts of yourself that you simply don't like. However, by running away from them you avoid having to face them. These dream 'beasts' won't give up and you'll end up with recurring dreams or nightmares.

Your dream is asking you to stop running away and face these negative, self-destructive qualities or habits so that they can be brought up to your conscious mind and dealt with.

Dreaming of being chased by wild animals asks you to look at your instinctive and aggressive traits – the things these animals represent (see individual animals) and be able to either tame, embrace or face them, depending on the contents of the dream.

The chase dream is about making changes. Changes are good for us in the long run, therefore running away is futile. If you dream you are being chased by characters who are out to get you, it can symbolise running away from the inner voice telling you it's time to grow and change and let go of your old identity or the notion of who you've told yourself you are.

If you dream of being paralysed or trapped, don't worry. It's firstly a natural body response when we are in REM sleep. Our body is paralysed but our brain is at its most active. This is to protect us from becoming violent and agitated in dreams where we are being attacked or threatened.

You may be paralysed, trapped or running in slow motion because the dream is telling you that you have to face a problem or an unresolved issue that you won't be allowed to run away from. Running away is no longer an option in your waking life. It could also be pointing out how you are feeling in real life – trapped and powerless. Think about whether you are feeling overwhelmed by some aspect of your waking life and what demands are being placed on you.

If a woman dreams of being chased by a man, a stranger or shadow and feels threatened with violence or rape, it may firstly reflect real fears. The dream can be treated as a warning: be careful whom you trust and be mindful of your surroundings. Don't put yourself in danger.

On the other hand, it could be part of your 'shadow self' – aspects of yourself you don't wish to own. What don't you like about yourself? Do you need to accept your shadow parts?

Confront what you consider to be the unacceptable aspects of yourself so that you can begin to make significant changes. Allow your dream to seep into your consciousness slowly by making yourself aware of small changes you make daily.

Within this section are some real dream scenarios from my clients who have shared their dreams with me and, through bringing their dreams to light, have clearly benefited from the messages gifted to them from their subconscious. These are transcripts from real dreams as related to me.

The Burglar and Escape Plan Dream

'A recurring chase dream begins with someone either chasing me or has broken into my home. A dozen escape plans always go through my head, and when I call for help I always stumble on the number or it takes too long. Just like in bad horror movies.

'The last dream I had like this, a man was chasing me. I ran through my car park area, which has three gates you have to go through to get to my house entrance in real life. I ran through the first gate then slid under the second so the gate wouldn't open all the way and give the man an easy way to get in. As I was running through the third gate, I looked back and saw that he had almost caught up to me.

'I run into the lift and the door closes just as he gets to it. I stumble for the keys into my unit, lock it and run into one of the bedrooms. When I finally call 000 I can hear the man inside my house and the operator is having a hard time getting my address. I finally get the address across and realise it'll take the police ages to get up to my floor as it's a secure building and no one will be able to buzz them in. I panic as I realise I'll probably be dead by the time the police can get to me.

'The man is about to open the door to the room I'm in and suddenly I wake up with my heart pounding a million beats a minute. In my real life I'm always concerned about our financial situation, even though my partner and I earn a good living. I'd like to go back to Paris, where my family lives, but I can't see us making the move back there any time soon and I'm sad about this.'

Christine

Dream Insight

This is a common anxiety dream we all have. If it's not a burglar, it's an animal or ghost or shadow. The main emotions here are fear/terror/help-lessness. The pursuer can represent a real threat, a real fear or a real person. It can also represent a part of you that is trying to get your attention because you simply are not listening to your intuition in your waking life.

So ask yourself, what are you most afraid of? What triggered the dream? Usually in a recurring dream, you are anxious about a situation and the dream reminds you of that fear/anxiety you experience.

I think security is a big fear for you – given the three gates to get to your front door. Something in your waking life is not making you feel safe. It could be insecurity about money as you mentioned or another threatening situation that is repeating (real or imagined). Something always triggers these recurring chase dreams.

There's an emotional disconnect with you and where you are living as you see it is temporary and so it is not a place you feel safe to be you and make strong personal relationships. The intruder represents part of yourself you don't want to face – could it be the inner critic that is punishing you for leaving your old life and at what cost? You say you are worried about not having enough money – is it because you made such a sacrifice and uprooted your life and not being financially rewarded for the inconvenience?

What is the burglar threatening to show you about yourself?

Your sense of safety can be related to moving to a new country and the fact that you have three gates to reach your entrance confirms to your subconscious mind that safety is in place for a reason – there is a security risk; you are not safe.

Dream Wisdom

When you have a chase dream, list the 'threats' you are facing in real life. Most importantly, think about who the pursuer represents. For example, if it's your boss in the shape of a monster, then it's authority or res-ponsibilities you're running away from.

Are you feeling overwhelmed/vulnerable in your life?

What are you running away from? Is it related to relationship commit-ments, work deadlines or anything that you keep putting off?

To grow and change, you have to get away from what's no longer working for you. That's what your unconscious is telling you, but your conscious self – your ego – doesn't want to let go. It's frightened of change. Hence the chase.

As chase dreams are often recurring dreams, it would be best to try lucid dreaming whenever it occurs – that is, try to take control of your dream. Make yourself stop and face your pursuer and then ask, 'What do you want?' (For more detailed information on lucid dreaming refer to Chapter 10.)

Once you do this you will get an answer, if not in your dreamworld then in your waking world once the conscious has been made aware that there's a question to be answered. You may not be able to manage this the first few times, but with practice you will be able to do it. This method will help you. You will overcome your inner struggle both in your dreams and in life.

2. Driving or Riding in a Car – Mostly Out of Control

Cars are symbols of movement, direction and life changes, and therefore represent parts of our physical body, drive and ambition. As we are more reliant on the car than ever before and most of us drive regularly, it's become part of us (like an outer shell) and often a way to achieve our freedom.

What type of car are you driving? The car model might just be representing you. If it's a fancy sports car it may be suggesting that you have a sense of success in your life or it's something that, for you, defines success.

Generally, a car represents your 'drive' (the engine and accelerator) for success and direction in life (steering wheel). It becomes significant, then, whether you are the driver or the passenger as it's a metaphor for your life – are you in control of where you are going? Are you in the driver's seat or is someone else controlling your life and you are simply the passenger?

If you are a passenger, notice who is driving the car. Why does that person (or what that person represents to you) have control over your life?

Are you losing control of the car in your dream? It may be that your brakes fail, the steering wheel is stuck, you're driving on the wrong side of the road or too close to the edge of the winding road or you crash. All of these scenarios suggest that you are feeling powerless and out of control, emotionally, in your life.

If the road ahead is difficult to see, it may mean that you are unsure about your future. *Uphill climbs* suggest that you have challenges ahead of you as you continue with your direction in life. *Roadblocks* indicate obstacles, and *being on the wrong side of the road* is about lacking focus.

In dreams where *there are intersections and streets*, your subconscious might be pointing to the obvious – do you have an important decision or a number of choices coming up? It may be suggesting that you take time to consider upcoming decisions and not go off track until you've made the best choice for yourself.

Other areas in your life it may relate to are your career (moving from one position to another), status (moving up) and major life changes (moving on).

Greek philosopher Aristotle believed that there was a clear connection between dreams and our health. During sleep, we have more access to information about our health as our conscious mind rests without the noise and distraction of our external world. As the car is a metaphor for *our physical body*, it makes sense that dreams connected to mechanical problems alert us to our health and well-being.

The table below shows some common themes around riding in cars.

Theme	Issue	What to do
No brakes	Out of control, burn out	Get more rest and relaxation
Flat tyres	A problem with movement/ legs, depression (deflated), out of balance	Exercise, walking, fun activities and social events
Running out of fuel	Diet not healthy, running on empty, need rest	Rest and relaxation or take a break in form of holiday. Ask for help
Headlights not working	Lack of awareness, poor vision	Medical check-up for general health and vision
Flat battery/ no ignition	No motivation problems/ depression	Join clubs, make new friends, take up a new activity
Radiator overheating	Too much emotion, high level of anxiety	Change diet, get counselling

Some people have experienced these car dreams as precognitive and the dreams have come true. Subconsciously we may notice that the car is not responding to us when we drive, but cast this aside as it's only a niggling thought. It may be even a slight change in the engine noise or the brakes being a little less responsive.

When we dream our conscious mind transfers our fears, anxieties and observations, and we process these in our dreaming state. If you have a strong dream about your car having mechanical problems, have the car checked out.

Driving Uphill Dream

> '*I was driving uphill and getting worried about the steep climb and narrow road. The car was struggling to accelerate. All around me was forest and tall ferns. They were lush and green but also threatening to swamp me. I found myself in the passenger seat and nobody in the driver's seat. I tried to steer and brake from my position, but could not manage the car. I felt frightened that I would reverse and end up falling off the edge of the steep incline. I have these dreams when I'm confused about what direction to take with my business.*'

> **Julia**

Dream Insight

The uphill drive suggests that you are struggling in your life to follow your direction. It may relate to a career path or a set of goals you've set out to achieve. It's an uphill battle. The forest is a place where we are tested – just like our favourite fairy tale characters that get lost there. It's also coming to terms with our true nature. The fact that the trees felt threatening indicates you are experiencing feeling overshadowed or overwhelmed in real life. Is it a matter of 'can't see the forest for the trees'?

As you move to the passenger's seat, you are losing control of your personal dreams and aspirations. By moving into a passenger role, you've relinquished power. This is even more frightening for you because you have less visibility of where you want to be in life – all you now believe is that it's an uphill struggle and you're not in control.

This dream is mirroring an important issue in your waking life. Your energy needs revitalising and a fresh vision required. It's fine to ask for advice, but don't give away your power to someone else and allow them to control your future. Little wins will give you a shot of self-confidence.

The Car Doors Won't Open Dream

> 'My dream is about driving a car which is always going really fast up a mountain, but always screeches to a halt just before I reach the top, and even when I try to get out and walk, the doors won't open!'

Aaron

Dream Insight

You need to ask yourself if you are feeling heavy, unsupported, out of control or worried about something.

How can you feel freer, lighter?

Do you need to be more grounded?

Dream Wisdom

Driving is your very own personal journey. If the car is not functioning properly or you are anxious driving on a dangerous road, ask what's making you feel uncertain in your waking life.

Who or what is making you lack confidence?

Do you need to slow down (brake) and focus (put on headlights) in your working life?

Perhaps your relationship issues are overwhelming and tipping you over the edge of that cliff face into the sea?

The car dream is about being in control of your own goals, ambition and general life path, and being focused.

Is life too hectic, out of control? How could you slow down, act more calmly and 'enjoy the ride'?

3. Exam – Poor Performance, Being Late or Unprepared

Have you ever experienced a dream where you arrive for an exam in the wrong room, you're late, you can't read the paper or haven't studied and your pen won't work? And you just know you're going to fail?

Ask yourself what it is that you're being tested on in real life. People often face issues that challenge their ability to perform well. Perhaps there are changes in your life that you don't feel qualified to handle.

We all have an innate need to achieve and compete for success. In our working life this can at times be difficult to accomplish and results in us feeling incompetent. If we don't believe we're keeping up our grades with the latest work practices and that we're unable to perform, this will show up as an anxiety dream.

The stress of being late, going to the wrong classroom, your pen not working or your eyesight being blurred are all indicators of your real-life frustrations that are preventing you from achieving your best results.

In this ever-changing world of technology, most of us feel that we are barely keeping up. The moment we master a current technology, a new one comes along and turns us into kindergarten-level learners again. This is why we often dream of being back in school. The higher the level of education in the dream, the more pressure for you to perform in real life.

This dream represents a fear of failure and performance anxiety (including sexual, for some dreamers). In real life you may feel that you are being tested and that you're not really prepared for the challenge.

Back in the Classroom Dream

> *I'm a high school teacher and I can't find my classroom. The timetable is in a place I can't find or reach. I am worried I'm going to be late and not be prepared. I'm not sure what subject I will be teaching and, if I'm late, the students will be out of control. A wave of anxiety washes over me and I feel like I'm the only teacher there who's disorganised. Everyone else has their timetable and knows their classes. I'm too embarrassed to ask for help.*

> *'This is a recurring dream for me and I try to lucid dream so that I can get a different ending. It usually ends with me feeling unprofessional and worried about being incompetent when everyone else obviously knows what to do.'*

Anna

Dream Insight

The emotion in this dream is the same – anxiety, not prepared, feeling you're being tested but not being up to the job, everyone else is a success around you.

When you have this dream, you need to review what's been going on for you at home and work. Have you been feeling decidedly like a plodder while everyone else is a flyer? Are you just one step behind everyone else? How will you ever catch up? Given that you feel so humiliated by your lack of professionalism, it's understandable that you don't ask for help in your dreams. In your real life, it would be a good idea to perhaps get advice or coaching on where you want to be and what you want to achieve in your career. If the work you are currently doing is making you feel like an amateur – perhaps you're being underpaid and undervalued. It may be time for you to reassess your career options.

Dream Wisdom

Are you unprepared for something? Are you in the 'wrong' vocation or relationship and is it likely to fail because of this? What do you really want to achieve for yourself? Or maybe it's time you went back to study or up-skilled.

Look at ways that you can challenge yourself more. The dream may indicate that you are about to embrace new kinds of knowledge that will build your self worth. Think about what it is that you might be learning and why it's important for your personal growth.

Exam dreams will give you motivation to step up and take new opportunities that you previously thought were outside your ability. It's a new phase of learning and experience, each grade level, an indication of where you are able to reach.

4. Falling/Drowning

There is a myth that if you dream of falling and hit the ground in your dream you will die. This is not true. Most people dream of falling and actually hit the ground injured or just sore, but keep dreaming. Occasionally we may be sinking in water and in danger of drowning, but we don't actually drown.

The dream of falling feels so physically real that it is the dream most often talked about. If you've ever woken up with a sudden jolt or felt one just as you've started falling asleep, you're among seventy per cent of people who experience this sensation. It may have felt like a huge muscle spasm or shock sensation.

You know the feeling. You're drifting off to sleep and all of a sudden you feel as if you've plunged into a bottomless pit. Startled by this feeling, you jolt back into consciousness before drifting back to sleep.

This involuntary twitching of the muscles is known as a hypnic jerk (a myoclonic jerk that you have when asleep). It happens in the hypnagogic state of consciousness – just when you are falling asleep – and causes you to wake up suddenly. This reflexive jump occurs because when we fall asleep, our muscles relax and lose their sense of function. Our brains send out alarm signals to reactivate our muscles when they sense the loss of strength and activity. Some people may actually fall from their beds during this type of dream.

Researchers have also attributed a sudden loss of blood pressure to the falling sensation in our dreams.

At a symbolic level, dreams about falling may be a reflection of insecurity, lack of confidence and fear of failure. If you are not feeling supported in real life or don't have solid grounding, this dream will be triggered. Losing your job, being unable to cope with relationships or work demands, losing money or making a mistake – anything in real life that destabilises you – could prompt these dreams.

If you recognise a familiar landscape or place – a balcony or stairwell – that you are falling from in your dream, it may be possible that you've unconsciously registered a potential safety problem when you were awake. Carefully investigate the site when you wake up in case this is a precognitive dream of a potential accident.

Falling Off the Path Dream

> 'I had a dream I was walking along an overgrown path and just fell off the path, which turned out to be close to the edge of a hilltop. I think, as I started to fall, I woke up breathing hard. I felt like I had no control of the situation. I would be walking along and it was like the ground just dropped out from underneath me. I woke straight away, or after a few seconds, with a jolt. What was going on for me at the time was my daughter's marriage breaking up and my son had other personal issues to deal with.'

Michelle

Dream Insight

You were likely to have felt unsupported and overwhelmed. The situation with your family was one you had no control over. What did the overgrown path represent to you? Was it an obstacle that you've encountered before? Are there things that you have not worked through in your own life and now they are preventing you from moving freely?

When the ground drops out from underneath you, consider what you will do in your waking life when stressful events happen unexpectedly.

Breathing Underwater Dream

> 'I was dreaming that a man was standing on a boat deck planning on jumping to kill himself. After he jumped, I decided to jump in and rescue him. As I looked down into the water, he was sinking deeper and deeper. I went down further in an attempt to reach him. The further he went the further I went, until it got to a point when I realised that I had gone too far down and needed urgently to breathe. I had to choose to try to return and risk getting the bends and probably not making it to the top without having to breathe, or to just open my mouth and breathe in a load of water.

'I chose to have faith in the process and took a big lungful of water, only to discover that I wasn't dying. I could breathe water and still get enough oxygen to survive. I said goodbye to my friend and enjoyed my time under the water like a dolphin, returning to the surface only when I wanted to. I will never forget how good it felt to be able to breathe in the water. It was a very memorable experience and very empowering.'

Sarah

Dream Insight

This is the best outcome for this classic type of dream. Therapists suggest this method of lucid dreaming for people who dream of drowning. Breathing underwater helps the dreamer to overcome emotional obstacles in their lives; it's like saying, 'Hey, I can do the impossible' to the subconscious mind. The conscious mind picks up on this powerful message and heals the dreamer.

At first you felt brave enough to dive in the water, until you realised you had gone too deeply – this is a reflection of your waking-life patterns. Do you plunge head first into a project that you're excited about and then figure out it's a lot more work than you realised and that you are 'in over your head'? The part where you discovered you could breathe should give you the confidence to know that you can handle emotional situations well and manage complex projects.

Dream Wisdom

If you have a falling dream scene, think about whether you are feeling insecure about some aspect of your life. Who's there to support you when things are tough? Are you feeling overwhelmed and want to give up (fall and hit the ground)?

Look at your real-life stress situation. Are you feeling that life is becoming too difficult? Are you unsupported? What's it going to take for you not to give up?

In the meantime, while you are sorting out your real-life issues and still having trouble sleeping because of recurring falling dreams, sleep with a pillow or cushion pressed against your feet. The sensory stimulation on your feet will help your body to feel secure and stable.

5. Being Lost, Trapped or Stuck

When you dream of being lost in a large city, multi-level car park, the forest or in a high-rise building, it's usually a time when you are experiencing a new chapter in your life and you're not sure how you will react or cope with it. You don't feel that you know your way around (literally) and it makes you anxious. You're having a real-life conflict in deciding how to react to a situation in your life.

Dreaming of mazes or labyrinths suggests confusion over choices you have to make.

Being trapped, not able to move, buried alive or locked in a cage, feeling powerless to scream or unable to breathe are universal nightmares. It's a clear message from your subconscious that reflects our real-life emotional state of being trapped or stuck – unable to make the right choice and feeling powerless to action changes that will free you.

Feeling trapped or paralysed also mirrors what occurs to the large muscles of the body during normal REM sleep, when they're paralysed to prevent the body from acting out the dreams.

Sometimes in our lives we are compelled to follow other people's rules or comply with their demands. However, subconsciously, we want to rebel and dance to our own tune. This conflict within us often brings up emotions that manifest as dreams where we are trapped. Often, they are a reflection of our current frustrations. Do you feel trapped in a relationship or a dead-end job? Are you stuck in a certain pattern of behaviour? Are you addicted to substances or habits that are holding you hostage and preventing you from leading a fulfilling life?

If you have feelings of being trapped in your dreams, then you need to ask yourself what it is about your life that is causing you to feel that way. What's stopping you from making the right choices for you?

The Car Towing a Truck Dream

> 'I see a car towing a truck with a large chain. It was a struggle for the car – a form of torture to have to pull the heavy truck. It was straining hard and the tyres were slipping. The car reminded me of a slave, chained and made to do back-breaking work. It felt as if the car had no choice. It was trapped in a totally unproductive process that made no progress.'

Steve

Dream Insight

What was happening in your working and personal life? Were you having health issues? The word 'back breaking' and the chains indicates some strong messages. Is your back in good condition? In what ways do you feel restricted and unable to move in your life?

Dream Wisdom

How can you get 'unstuck' and find a solution that will free you?

If you're locked in or imprisoned, do you feel that your freedom is compromised or limited? Think about what's going to help you move forward.

Your real-life stress indicates you are having conflicting thoughts on how to handle a situation that's making you feel stuck. What will help you make some progress?

Identify where you feel trapped in real life and how you might explore new courses of action.

6. Flying

Flying is a positive dream about freedom and escapism. It's a dream that invigorates and enthrals, a wish fulfilment and an exhilarating experience that many of us want to recapture in our waking lives. The excitement of flying is associated with something that has recently made you feel free, confident and successful. It happens more often to children, as they are able to access the joyous feeling of freedom without the restrictions that adults have.

Often during a flying dream you'll feel as if you've always known how to fly. It is effortless. Another benefit, apart from the soaring sensation, is that you're unhindered as you fly over mountains, familiar places, through the air. There is nothing that weighs you down and you have the freedom to fly without fear.

One dreamer described it this way:

> *'I don't exactly fly, but if I push my hands down against the air
> – sort of like you do when you tread water – I find I can soar
> up around the roof of a room, or to the top of the trees. I always
> feel triumphant and pleased with myself in these dreams.'*
> **Liz**

Many report their flying experiences as 'fabulous' and 'exhilarating'. Often, flying dreams involve lucid dreaming, in which the dreamer is fully aware that they are dreaming and they are able to influence where they fly (see Chapter 10 for more information about lucid dreaming).

If the lucid flying dream goes off smoothly without obstacles or fear, then it will leave you feeling empowered and ecstatic when you wake. This type of dream indicates that you're feeling good about a situation and that you will overcome barriers that threaten you from reaching your goals. You are certainly 'on top of your game' and 'on top of the world'.

There are, however, flying dreams that include some setbacks and obstacles. Understanding what these obstacles represent can help you work out any real-life issues you are struggling to overcome and the things that might be holding you back from achieving your heart's desire.

Having trouble taking off means someone or something is holding you back, keeping you from moving forward to the next step in your life. It could even be you!

If you're having to avoid obstacles in your flight path, think about what your real-life obstacles are. What's making you feel that you have limited control over your life? What's getting in the way of your goals?

Afraid of flying too high? It may suggest you fear the changes success can bring, that you will simply get burnt if you fly too high. Remember the story of Icarus, who flew too close to the sun? The wax on his wings melted and he fell into the sea and drowned. The message from this myth is not to dare to aim too high or there will be dire consequences. Icarus didn't listen to his father, Daedalus, who had warned him of the danger. Is it any wonder we sometimes fear success even more than failure?

When you are flying upwards, you may be in the process of spiritual growth and striving to achieve a higher level of consciousness. Perhaps you are delving more deeply into your spiritual development.

Falling when flying indicates that you are losing confidence in your abilities in your waking life. You initially had that positive feeling of soaring and now you are about to crash or come down to reality or what you are normally used to being.

If it's a lucid dream, you will be able to change it by doing something like throwing out your arms to take control of your flying direction once again. But if you are a passenger in a plane, you are relying on other people and an aircraft (technology) to get you to your future destination, which results in a sense of powerlessness (refer back to the 'car' dreams and being a passenger). What happens in your dream will indicate how you are feeling emotionally in your everyday life.

Flying may also be a symbol of sexual release. Once tension is released the dreamer has the sensation of freedom, much the same way as you'd feel if you were flying.

Flying and Gliding Dream

> 'I've had experiences from childhood where I "dream" I'm flying. It's more a gliding and it's an incredible feeling. I have an intention in my mind and lean forward and off I go. It's just my body. No plane. As a child it was always in the outdoors.'

Georgie

Dream Insight

Dreaming of flying is more common in children than in adults as they are spreading their wings, so to speak, and exploring life without limits. From your description it sounds as if you had a lucid dream. (See Children's dreams on flying in Chapter 6.)

Running Before Take-off Dream

> 'I have recurrent dreams where I know if I start running between power posts and jump, I'll rise higher and higher until I'm in the clouds. I do sometimes land between jumps, but cover huge distances as I go higher and higher for longer and longer. I can also use it in dreams where I feel threatened. I just get to a street and start running and jumping and off I go.'

Rebecca

Dream Insight

This is an example of lucid dreaming, as you've learnt how to do it in your dreams from your conscious mind. You are aware you are jumping and flying when you are threatened. It means you will rise 'above' all obstacles, negativity and self-doubt. Your psyche is healthy and when it realises it's under threat of being held back, it will fly to freedom so that you can succeed with whatever you need to do in waking life. If you keep practising lucid dreaming, it will help you overcome whatever obstacles life throws at you.

Dream Wisdom

Are you longing to escape from limitations or pressures at home or work? What new horizons do you want to explore and what passions do you want to follow?

If you feel any fear in this type of dream, it would be useful to repeat an affirmation to help you navigate your flight dream such as: 'I can control my flight and go where I choose.' This message will seep through to your subconscious mind and enable you to control your dream so that you can be empowered as you face your fear.

7. Losing Your Teeth

Do you dream that your teeth begin to fall out when you open your mouth, or that you discover broken, decayed or missing teeth? There are many possible interpretations about loss of teeth as so many people have this recurring and disturbing dream.

At a practical level, this dream reflects anxiety about appearance and how others perceive us. Teeth are a symbol of youth and strength. Bad teeth or lack of teeth are a sure sign of ageing. Are you afraid of being found unattractive? It's common for menopausal women to have this dream. This important stage of life brings with it feelings of insecurity about ageing, loss of beauty and vitality.

The dream can also indicate a general loss of power in real life. Perhaps it's due to ageing or life circumstances. It's no coincidence that our most vulnerable are the toothless – babies and older people (with dentures). It is also interesting that the very young and very old are either unable to voice their opinion or their views are not taken seriously.

Teeth in a dream are symbols of social expression and verbal communication. Losing teeth suggests difficulty in being able to communicate a personal issue or be understood. Consider whether you are lacking confidence in a social environment, such as speaking up in conversations or discussions, doing presentations or reports at work or when meeting new people.

Dreaming that your teeth are crumbling or falling out until your gums are toothless and bare evokes a sense of helplessness and a long time of compromise. Are you getting what you want out of life?

Losing teeth may also be an omen that the dreamer is losing their life force and is beginning to be ineffective in their current role. Examine your home, work and social roles, and evaluate whether you've outgrown them. Perhaps they are now draining your energy and vitality. Is it time to let go of the old and begin something new?

A child's fear of losing their teeth can be soothed by compensation from the tooth fairy and the promise of a new tooth to replace the old. As adults, those basic fears of losing parts of ourselves – other than those that regenerate such as hair and nails – create anxiety as we are aware that losing teeth is permanent and comes with ageing.

As mammals, teeth are essential to our survival – to eat – and can therefore be a sign of aggression as part of our natural instinct to survive. Think of the phrase 'getting your teeth into something' – are you floundering in life? Are you making wise choices?

Losing teeth in a dream may mean the dreamer is starting a new phase of life or a physical death, depending on the personal association.

Death and Losing Teeth Dream

> *'I knew when I dreamed of any of my teeth falling out, someone died. Upper teeth were adults that died and my bottom teeth, it was someone younger that died. Each time it came to pass.'*

Lisa

Dream Insight

Your intuition associates teeth with death and so your psyche has retained this information and is able to give you a precognitive dream. In the past you had experienced dreaming of losing your teeth, coinciding with the death of someone known to you. This then became a personal symbol of losing teeth, meaning losing someone to death.

Teeth Fit Back in Dream

> '*I dreamt my teeth fell out and I was totally humiliated. Then I discovered that I could put them back in the gum, one at a time.*'

Fiona

Dream Insight

The first part of your dream highlights your anxiety. It may have to do with expressing your fear of being powerless or lacking in confidence to express your real feelings.

The second part of the dream is empowering. It suggests that by speaking your mind, despite feeling embarrassed (loss of teeth), you've gained your confidence again (teeth back in place).

Dream Wisdom

Ask yourself: are you speaking your truth or keeping peace so as not to lose your job or risk a relationship fall out? And if so, what is the cost of not speaking out?

Maybe you just need to get a grip and let go of what no longer works. Are you feeling unsure of yourself and your choices?

Make sure you're getting your message across. If not, you may need to be more assertive and value your own viewpoints.

8. Being Naked in Public

In your dream, did you bare all in the classroom in front of your peers? Perhaps you paraded around in your natural state at the office or in a job interview? It may have taken place at a public event or simply been completely exposed in plain view of people generally.

Being naked or partially naked in public is a common scenario that highlights your feelings of exposure and vulnerability in some areas of your life. It often includes elements of embarrassment or shame, depending on the context of the dream and the reaction of the other people in the dream.

Public nudity dreams are often about 'being on show' and 'keeping up a façade'. They are associated with a sense of unfamiliar exposure that is due to a change in circumstances – a new job, a promotion, a new romance or other public attention. You are on display, and with this comes a certain amount of judgement. You feel unprepared and off guard. Your mind conjures up the naked symbol because no clothes fit you right at the moment. You are like a naked, newborn baby.

If nobody notices your nakedness, it may be that you are over-thinking your situation – exaggerating your emotional turmoil when in fact it's not a big deal to everyone else. The dream is reassuring you that you're not as imperfect or awkward as you think and the situation is not so bad.

Naked at work. Naked at work dreams may represent unpreparedness. Are you being scrutinised by your boss or colleagues? If you are giving a presentation naked, you might feel the pressure of completing a project or delivery of it that could significantly impact on the future of your job.

Naked at school. If you're showing up naked at school it may be that you don't feel good enough compared to your peers. You may be the target of a bully or are constantly judged and excluded from social groups. Our school years are notorious for bringing self-esteem issues and fear of rejection based on our looks and personalities to the fore. If others are jeering or laughing at you, it often reflects your real-life issues with being uncomfortable in your own skin. By now you should be loving who you are, warts and all.

Real-life insecurities tend to manifest in our dreams of nakedness. All you can think about are your imperfections and awkwardness. Note down when this dream occurs and what's going on in your waking life that's making you feel vulnerable.

Without clothes to cover up your insecurities about your natural personality traits, you feel that they are exposed for everyone to see – and judge. You may be in a new relationship where you are not sure whether to reveal your true feelings in case you'll be ridiculed or rejected by your new lover.

Feeling comfortable or proud with being naked in your dreams shows that you have a very positive image of yourself. You are enjoying your openness in the way you deal with people and you are at ease with your physical nature. You enjoy your body, and are honest about your needs. This is the ideal outcome of a naked dream but one that is not experienced by the majority of dreamers.

Half-naked Dream

> 'I sometimes have the naked dreams, but I find myself out
> and about in my dream and realise that my bottom half is
> naked. Never topless, but always bottomless.'

Tina

Dream Insight

The naked dreams in public and being bottomless is about feeling
vulnerable, exposed and embarrassed. You're out on a limb and out of
your comfort zone. You're worried about what people will think if they
know the real you. What was happening at the time of the dream? How
did people in the dream react to you? What was the setting? This will
give you clues about where in your life you are feeling vulnerable.

Naked or in Pyjamas Dream

> 'I used to have naked dreams all the time during my school
> years. Right through primary and high school I used to dream
> either that I went to school naked or in my pyjamas, and only
> realised once I got there! I always just hoped no one else would
> notice, and as well as I can remember no one did. The dreams
> disappeared after I left school.'

Simon

Dream Insight

We have these dreams in our younger years when we are developing our
social identity and we are trying to make an impression. We're always
comparing ourselves to our peers, trying to fit in, being part of a group,
not wanting to stand out in class for being different so that we will not
get bullied or feel humiliated by not knowing the answer. When we
dream we are naked, we may be feeling unprepared, insecure about our
abilities and appearance and worried that the other kids won't like us if
they knew our real nature.

The fact that your dreams stopped after high school suggests that you
grew out of issues with self-esteem and vulnerability as your confidence
increased.

Dreams of being inappropriately dressed, such as wearing pyjamas to school or being the only person wearing the wrong clothes or shoes for the occasion or not wearing shoes at all, is equally embarrassing to the dreamer as the naked dream. These dreams also express the same concern with social roles, acceptance by peers and conformity.

Our conscious world reminds us of our social embarrassment with metaphors such as 'caught naked' or 'caught with your pants down'.

Sometimes you're inappropriately dressed or partially dressed in the dream. Do you fit in with your current lifestyle or are you pretending to? If this dream occurs when you are making a commitment, such as marriage or signing an important business contract, consider whether the dream is alerting you to be transparent. People will see through you if you're not genuine and you'll be exposed.

Dream Wisdom

Have you revealed too much of yourself in some way?

Do you believe that people can see right through you?

Do you feel that you're under scrutiny and your colleagues/boss might be judging you?

In what areas of your life are you lacking in confidence and skills? Or what is it that is causing you to be embarrassed?

9. Death/Illness

Dreaming of death rarely means an actual, physical death. It's in fact a positive dream, despite the dreamer being disturbed by the images. Dreaming of a death represents a new beginning and life transitions.

If someone or something dies in a dream, it means that there is potential for new growth and that changes are taking place around you. It can also mean that you feel that part of yourself (that you see represented by another person in your dream) is dead or dying. It may also mean that you wish the actual person would leave or that you fear losing them.

If you dream that you die, this is an opportunity to make some changes in your waking life that can directly affect you. Think about how you accept new personal growth opportunities and find ways to embrace change.

Dream expert Patricia Garfield believes that when you dream about an accidental death of any person, that person's death symbolises something in you that is no longer functioning. Look at your happiness scale and see whether it needs adjusting. It will be an indicator of things best left in the past and help you to move on.

Killing in a dream action sequence holds clues to what you are really trying to 'kill off' in your waking life. It may simply be old negative patterns, bad habits, negative thoughts, addictions, or other personality traits that no longer serve you, and the dream alerts you to those things in order to assist you to make changes.

Seeing your own funeral in a dream suggests that a major inner change has taken place and, with it, greater self-awareness. New discoveries about yourself are being made, while the old is no longer there to hold you back from moving forward with your life.

If you know someone is terminally ill, it's not uncommon to dream of their death or for them to come to you in your dreams. (See Chapter 9.)

Being Ill

Sometimes we dream of being ill when we actually aren't feeling well. It's your body's warning system alerting you to disease and infection present in your body. Take it literally and get yourself checked out for medical symptoms. Other times it's a warning that you may become emotionally hurt. When we dream of others being injured or sick, it can mean that they may not be fully aware that they've got some health or emotional issues to deal with.

It is normal for people to dream of death when they are feeling ill. Anxiety and fear for their health shows up in the worst possible scenario of impending death. Or this dream can relate to a state of emotion indicating that you are hurt or are afraid of becoming hurt by someone.

A Plane Crash Dream

'A few months ago I had a dream that was really disturbing. I dreamt my husband died in a plane crash. In the dream I was there and was holding a plane ticket. My husband is doing a lot of interstate travel (fly in fly out) for work.'

Melissa

Dream Insight

Your physical separation may suggest that you feel disconnected from your partner when he's not home. Perhaps this dream is telling you to make a greater effort to reconnect. It may be that you're on a high (plane symbol) when he's home and then you come down 'crashing' when he's gone again.

It is possible that you are consciously worried about his frequent flying trips and your anxiety is increasing your chance of dreaming it. When we worry about the worst thing that can happen, it is likely that we subconsciously create that very event in our dreams. You may consciously also want to 'end' the travel that is disrupting your family routine.

Dad Dying Early Dream

> *'I had a very vivid dream of my dad being dead about five years before he died. I woke up weeping. I almost felt as if I was doing a rehearsal, if that makes sense, although at that time he wasn't ill. Old, but not ill.'*

Cheryl

Dream Insight

It sounds as if something triggered your fears about your dad getting old and dying. Sometimes it's news of someone else dying or media reports. It may be that you were just rehearsing. Our psyche prepares us for bad things that happen in life. That's why when bad stuff happens to us we say it's our 'worst nightmare'.

When our relationships with our loved ones are changing we often think of them dying because qualities of that person are 'passing away' and new ones are being formed.

Dream Wisdom

If someone dies in your dream, look at what that person represents to you. Is it time to let go of that person or establish a new relationship with them? Does the person represent parts of yourself that are not working for you? Are you ready to let go of those parts of yourself?

Is it time to let go of the old and embrace the new?

What parts of you need changing?

In what ways do you feel disconnected from others and yourself?

How are you developing a 'new you' and what are you doing about letting go of the 'old ways' of doing things?

10. Missing Bus/Train/Plane/Boat

This is one of the most frustrating dreams. You put so much effort into getting to your destination only to miss that train or plane by a fraction of a second.

Ask yourself: what do you feel you're missing out on in your life? What's within your reach but you always just miss out? This dream highlights our fear of not being organised or well prepared to reach an important decision or achieve our goals.

It reflects our real-life anxiety of being out of control and therefore not being ready to take advantage of an opportunity, or missing it by a narrow margin. The saying 'you've missed the boat' when we refer to failing to grab an opportunity is one we hear frequently in our waking life.

Other frustrating mishaps include lacking appropriate travel paperwork, the mode of transport going the wrong way or doors that won't unlock.

A variation of this theme is arriving too late for a performance in which you are supposed to participate, and finding that the play, musical production, sport competition or other event has already begun and you are unable to be involved.

If you've got on the wrong bus or train, consider how this might reflect your real-life anxiety about what direction you're heading in at work or your personal life. Could the dream be asking you to take a scenic route and explore options? If you felt excited or curious about where you were going, then it is likely that deep down you might want to 'get lost' in the moment or find alternative routes to reach your goals. It might be time to get out of your comfort zone. Conversely, if you felt super anxious, then you are experiencing a period of feeling displaced and not belonging in your social or work space.

Plane Dreams

> *'I'm rushing to catch the plane but just as I reach the boarding gate the plane takes off without me.*

'I have recurring "plane" dreams. I'm hurrying to try and catch the plane, but lose it and my luggage, too. There's the one dream of sitting on a plane but never taking off, my luggage opening up and going everywhere. Something's always stopping me from getting to my destination.'

Adam

Dream Insight

It's normal to dream of missing a plane if you are travelling regularly, especially if it's for work. The consequences of missing a plane, missing the meeting and messing up the schedule for everyone else fills us with dread and anxiety. It's not unusual that dreaming of missing your plane reflects your everyday concern. On a bigger scale, if you're always trying to take off but obstacles get in the way of reaching your destination, you need to ask yourself in what way does this mirror how you feel about your work in your waking life?

Dream Wisdom

Notice where you are going in your dream and why you are going there. What makes you feel that you are too late and are missing out on an opportunity?

What are you currently trying to accomplish in your waking life?

Is there something missing for you to get what you want at work?

In what ways do you feel unprepared or unequipped in real life to achieve your goals, and how can you change this?

Transport is about connection and transitions – think about how you can be more connected to your own aspirations and inner longings and to others who can help you get there.

CHAPTER 6

Children's Dreams and Nightmares

'I dream my painting and I paint my dream.'

– Vincent van Gough

CHILDREN'S DREAMS ARE less complex than those of an adult's but the emotions experienced while dreaming are the same. Children are prolific and vivid dreamers, as their imagination is limitless.

Your child's dreamworld is a reflection of their developing personalities and their fears/anxieties.

Never underestimate the emotional intensity and importance of your child's dream. Most importantly, never dismiss a child's dream by saying, 'It's only a dream.'

The Senoi, a primitive tribe that lived in the mountains of Malaysia, were advocates of sharing dreams. They believed that dreams were essential to the well-being of their society. Each morning the family would discuss what had taken place in their dreams the night before. They would then share this with the tribe and the family's dreams interpreted and synthesised. Children were encouraged to share their dreams and remember them, and were taught how to conduct themselves in the dreams. Most importantly, children were taught to finish their dreams no matter how frightening they were. If they were being chased, they would confront any danger in the dream. If they were too frightened to do this, they could call a dream helper or friend to assist in the dream. If a child was falling, he or she would be encouraged to fly or land softly and safely. The Senoi children learnt faith in themselves and life in general due to the empowering influence of working constructively with their dreams and the use of positive imagination.

Dreams were seen as an important journey of discovery with endless possibilities, and essential to the tribe's well-being. Interestingly, the Senoi tribe was free of crime, anxiety and mental illness, and had very little physical illness. Anthropologists suggest that this ideal outcome was partly attributed to the dream work, where the people could get rid of their fears through dreams and promote harmony within their tribe.

Why do children dream?

- It helps your child to sort out the events of the day. So much processing needs to happen as they try to make sense of their rapid growth – mentally, emotionally, physically and socially.
- It gets a child prepared for a new experience or coming event. A dream may act out how an event such as a new sibling, a new house or even a family holiday can be reassuring. Death of a family member or pet can prepare the child (sort of like a rehearsal) for this event happening.
- Problem solving takes place in our dreams. Children often sleep on an issue, no matter how simple it may seem to us, and come up with a resolution after a dream.
- It creates fantasy, escapism and creativity. Children get to live out their imaginative lives through fantasy dreams and unrestricted imagination.

Nightmares

Nightmares are more often remembered than dreams because of their emotional intensity. It's generally believed that toddlers do not dream about themselves until around the age of three or four. Nightmares begin around this age because children begin to understand that bad things can happen to them and others around them. Most children therefore experience nightmares from three to six years old – much more than adults – until the age of seven or eight.

A nightmare is often the result of having to process something they experienced as being negative the previous day.

Most nightmares are a normal part of coping with changes in our lives, which usually involve some element of stress. Children will respond to events such as a new school, moving to a new neighbourhood, living through a divorce or remarriage, the birth of a new sibling or a death in the family by having nightmares in which they will try to process the new information.

The bad dreams will settle down once they recover and cope with these stress factors.

For the parent, listening to your child's description of their nightmare is valuable, as it is a measure of the emotional challenges they are experiencing and the level at which it is affecting their waking lives.

Recurring nightmares are a warning of a child's lingering inner conflict. They are repeating dream patterns that are triggered by events that have similar emotional feelings, and these recurring images and dream sequencing can last well until old age.

For example, after being pushed in the swimming pool and swallowing a lot of water, six-year-old Amy felt she would never get enough oxygen to breathe again. Her close call with drowning left her emotionally vulnerable and she began to have dreams of drowning whenever she experienced stress – when her father went away on business trips, when her baby brother was born, when she lost her favourite things. Her drowning dreams had become the emotional response to the stresses she encountered in her life.

From a child's perspective reality and imagination are often confused, and so in a child's mind when they see images or scenes in movies or video games or hear potentially scary stories, they experience a delayed terror that is then manifested in the nightmare. An image or scene lingers for a long time in a child's mind and they don't have the tools to be able to release or shake it off. It is very important to make it clear to them that movies or stories are 'not real'. Viewing of real-life events, such as news items showing vivid shots of killings, bombings and other disturbing events, need to be carefully screened or avoided, as children will often replay these images or scenes during their sleep time and potentially have nightmares as emotions around death, abandonment and safety are a key factor for their emotional stability.

Taking a child to a funeral must be done with extreme sensitivity and family discussion is needed around what is to be expected.

Below is a list of common fears that may trigger a nightmare or anxiety dream:

• Absence or loss of a parent. This is the number one fear for children as their survival depends on being taken care of by an adult.

• Abuse or violence, sometimes including custody disputes. If a child's security is in danger they experience great stress.

- Bullying and other social difficulties at school, including having a learning problem or friendship break-up. As school takes up most of their waking time, it is essential that children feel protected and supported. When this is missing due to bullying, friendship issues, learning problems, school inefficiency or lack of action on important matters, the child will likely have nightmares.

- Major changes such as a new school, new sibling, death of a pet or loved one, moving house, parent's change in working hours, new teacher. Changes affect everyone, but children more so because they have no yardstick to measure what changes might mean for them as they have not had that experience before. They are not equipped emotionally or socially to deal with these changes and therefore their fears and survival instincts are released though their dreams and nightmares.

- After watching scary images from film, TV, internet. As previously mentioned, images linger well after the event and remain in the child's memory so that they create anxiety and fear at sleep time. Reality and fiction are blurred.

- During the Halloween period. These days masks and costumes are becoming much more grotesque and real; many are based on characters from horror movies. Young children are especially influenced by these horrific images, especially when they appear at their front door. Older children will understand the concept, but some may still experience some fear.

- From traditional stories, such as fairy tales and some biblical events. Some of the most violent and frightening scenes have been from myths, fairy tales and even the Bible, so it is wise to edit some of the more disturbing stories.

What to do.

1. Reassure them. You don't need to explain your child's nightmares. Assure them that all is fine and give them a hug to show them that you take the experience seriously.

2. Diary and drawing. Encourage your child to create a drawing of the dream (a monster, witches or dinosaur). Make it a special time – use

dress-ups, costumes, storytime in the same way you would a fairy tale. This helps your child share their dream in safety, being in the role of the narrator instead of being 'inside' the story as the victim. Play acting is familiar to children, so this is the perfect way to dispel their fears and help them cope with going to sleep without the issue of a potential nightmare.

3. Re-write the ending. Talk to your child about re-imagining the dream so that the child can be empowered to change the outcome of the dream. Terrifying dream monsters can be tamed or banished; they can be drawn with funny characteristics – bows on dragon ears, lollipops coming out of a monstrous mouth. With some magic tools such as fairy dust, invisibility cloaks, spells and other 'magical forces', the dream ending can be totally restructured to give your child increased confidence and minimise their fears. Treat it like a fairy tale with a new and happy ending.

4. Create magic tools to make the new ending more realistic. The child may wish to create these magic tools in real life – teddy might be 'super ted' in dreams and a new outfit can make all the difference, or you could try a magic wand in the tradition of Harry Potter. The Japanese have small sculptures of a mystical animal called the Baku (dream eater). The child can call out for the Baku in their dream and the creature will eat the nightmare right away.

My own childhood nightmare

As a child I was afraid of witches, so one way to trick them was to have them think that I was a witch too – that I was one of 'them'. I used our straw garden broom – the one that looks like a real witch's broom – as my magical tool. It leaned outside against my window in plain view of any potential witch visitor. This helped me get through a difficult emotional period in my childhood when I felt like an outsider and different to the other kids at school. Eventually, I integrated this dream story into my waking life and began to form good friendships.

Common Children's Dreams and Nightmares

Monsters

> *Monsters represent the adults in a child's real world and/or the child's major, significant fears.*

A variety of monsters, including witches, dinosaurs, ghosts, vampires, and goblins that are chasing, attacking or hiding, invade children's dreams often. The common theme is that they terrorise the child in some way. It can be that the monster is under the bed or lives under the house or on the front porch or it's chasing the child in a threatening manner.

Generally, these monster types represent an adult the child encounters in real life. It could be the parent, who can get cross and yell at the child, sometimes when the child does not expect to be reprimanded so harshly. Remember, a child's perspective is very different to an adult's, as they don't have the rationale to understand why their parent is nurturing their every need one minute and showing frustration the next by raising their voice or handling the child a little less gently than when calm or not sleep deprived.

This parental behaviour can translate into monster dreams for the young mind. An annoyed teacher or grumpy neighbour are also likely to be represented in dreams as monsters.

When your child tells you of their monster dream, don't dismiss it as 'just a dream' or say 'it's not real'. Instead, ask questions such as what the monster looked like, how he smelled or the noise he made. Then encourage the child to draw it. You may wish to help colour in with the child's permission. Then it's a good time to 'make fun' of the monster and find ways to 'bring him down'. It can be silly, like tying its shoelaces together so it falls down. This is how the child can change the ending of the dream.

Think back to people in your child's life who can appear to have 'monster-like' qualities and work out ways in which you can present them in a more 'humanised' way.

Ability to Fly or Do Magic

Represents a child's wish to 'fix' a situation in real life where they feel it's out of their hands to solve.

This fantasy dream of having special magical powers to rescue, perform heroic deeds or fly into other realms or galaxies to 'right' a wrong gives your child the opportunity to experience success by using the power of their imagination, ability to feel empathy and courage and use cunning and problem-solving techniques. This occurs in their subconscious mind, of course, and when brought up to the conscious mind by talking about the dream with the parent it becomes an ideal process to raise any issues.

When the child outwits the villain as they fly away or create magic, it shows them that they have the intelligence and imagination to face their difficulties. Children who want to escape (fly) from the pressures (villain) they are facing in their family life often have this dream.

Think about what is making your child feel insecure. How can you help your child to gain more self-confidence? Consider ways you can encourage your child to be strong and independent.

Falling

Like adults, this dream occurs when a child is feeling unsupported, insecure, out of control and off balance.

The falling dream comes at a time when there is an element of disorder or instability in a child's waking life. Dreams of falling off a cliff or roof, into an abyss, a pit or into water or down a hole like *Alice in Wonderland*, a water slide or into space can frighten young dreamers.

Your child may be feeling that their ordered world is slipping into chaos. Perhaps small things are now mounting up and they cannot handle the stress.

If the nightmares continue, check for a medical reason. Falling dreams are also a symptom of ear infections following bad colds due to the inner ear being out of equilibrium.

If you don't know what's making your child feel unsupported, ask them questions such as: 'What seems scary to you right now?', 'How can we make you feel better?' or 'What can we do to help you?'

Being Exposed in Public

> *This dream reflects the child's vulnerability and sense of identity.*

The fear of being exposed is as real to children as it is to adults. The dream revolves around the dreamer being in public half-dressed or undressed, or trying to use the toilet that is not flushing or in an open area in full view. It usually occurs when the child moves to a new environment where expectations are higher or where they will feel exposed to ridicule or judgement. It could be when starting school, moving school or starting a new grade. It may also mean performing in a school play or a new sports team. Basically, it's an anxiety dream about the potential of causing embarrassment and having attention being brought to them in their waking life.

It can confuse parents when this anxiety is not true to real life and the child has actually succeeded in making new friends and adapting. However, it's the fear of what *might* happen, not what is actually happening, that concerns the young dreamer.

Ask your child if they are feeling nervous/silly/embarrassed about something coming up and let them know that it's okay to have these feelings.

Threatening Animals and Insects

> *Wild animals that become threatening or enraged and give chase are often a representation of fears in a real-life situation. Insects are a symbol of agitation and irritation. In nightmares they grow to much larger proportions and the child will feel suffocated and terrified by their presence.*

The animals that are chasing or being threatening indicate that a situation in a child's waking life, involving a particular person, is troubling them. Take note of the animals and the dream scene. Common dream scenarios include being chased/attacked by a wild animal or insects such as bees or giant spiders; being trapped in a cage with a wild animal; an animal escaping from the zoo; an animal hiding under the bed.

Try to analyse the frightening situation going on in your child's psyche. It may not look like it's anything for your child to be worried about, but the fear is being stored in their subconscious ready to emerge during their sleep as a nightmare. A harmless animal that turns mean and nasty suggests that your child may be struggling with a situation or person who is normally familiar and predictable, and this scenario has taken the child by surprise. It would be a good idea to look at friendship-group dynamics when this dream comes up or an unsettling home environment. Children are often sensitive when it comes to losing a best friend to another child or not fitting into a group. A loss of job or marriage difficulties can also make home-life interactions strained – there may appear to be a normal routine at home, but with an undercurrent of tension at the same time.

Encourage your child to come up with creative ways to change the dream sequence. Bring the positive dream ending into the child's daily life by making changes to the house décor or child's room, planting a new garden, buying goldfish. By incorporating 'new' and positive things into the home life it will affect the predictability of the chase nightmares, distract the child from their present concerns and hopefully promote a feeling of well-being instead.

Water/Tsunami/Drowning

> *Water in dreams is a symbol of emotions and deep feelings.*
> *Tsunamis appear in dreams when there's a very significant*
> *emotional issue present in real life.*

Floods and tsunamis overwhelm the dreamer and are emotionally challenging dreams. They suggest your child is being swamped by a serious emotional issue and is trying very hard to survive or escape from its powerful force.

Other common water themes include drowning; being unable to swim to the surface; swimming in deep water with dangerous creatures below; or sailing a boat.

A positive water dream is when a child dreams of finding themselves underwater, and just as they are struggling to hold their breath they find that they can breathe. This dream is common in children who are experiencing a vulnerable and emotional time in their waking life. It shows them that they can survive (breathing underwater) even in new and sometimes isolating situations (water).

Suggesting creative methods of surviving a drowning incident, such as special artificial lungs, or silly ones like a special fish strapped to your mouth, can give your child the confidence to lucid dream and make the nightmare less frightening. You could even bring these ideas to life through a craft project or design them in a drawing to help your child visualise a means to escape when they next experience their water dream.

Getting Lost/Eaten/Kidnapped

> *These terrifying situations mirror the child's emotional state as they go through rites of passage, such as separation anxiety when they are spending more time away from their parents, visiting new locations that are noisy and congested and daily routines being interrupted.*

It is a common belief that reading fairy tales helps children work through their deepest fears; however, very young children don't often have the ability to distinguish between reality and fiction. It's important for parents to read age-appropriate stories, especially before bedtime. Even less threatening ones such as *Goldilocks,* who nearly gets eaten by bears, or *Cinderella*, who is emotionally and physically abused, give voice to a child's fears and vulnerability.

We can blame these favourite fairy tales for a child's fear of being eaten, whether in a dream or in real life. *Hansel and Gretel, Jack and the Beanstalk, Little Red Riding Hood, Snow White* and many more involve some form of cannibalism. Young children don't really want to hear adults say, 'You're so cute, I could eat you up!' It can literally give them nightmares.

Getting lost is a common anxiety feeling among children of all ages – the younger children fear big, unfamiliar places such as malls, airports and car parks and where it's generally busy and crowded. Once they have experienced losing sight of Mummy and Daddy, their fears will catch up with them in dreams that will usually result in a nightmare.

Children being kidnapped and going missing is another favourite theme in fairy tales such as *Rapunzel*. The media is also to blame for their continued news coverage of missing children and abductions. Apart from these obvious images, children dream of being kidnapped when their routines are changed and so feel that their time is being 'snatched' away by having a new baby in the family or working out schedules in a newly divorced family.

Older children tend to have this nightmare when they are feeling sensitive about having to take on added responsibility and one day having to leave the safety of the nest to be out on their own.

Coping with night terrors

Night terrors are not to be confused with nightmares, which happen without the dreamer becoming active within the dream. Night terrors appear suddenly from the deep, non-dreaming sleep phase, which occurs when the brain switches between NREM (non rapid eye movement) sleep, or non-dreaming sleep, to REM (rapid eye movement) sleep, or dreaming sleep phase. When this process does not function properly, it is known as a sleep transmission disorder and it is this that causes night terrors. The brain at this time blurs reality and dreaming.

When a child experiences a night terror, they will suddenly sit up, talk or scream in a confused or agitated manner and often experience some kind of emotional terror. The sense of panic and fear can last for up to twenty minutes and can be distressing for parents, who find that they are unable to settle or comfort their child. The child will eventually fall back to sleep and in the morning will usually not remember this experience.

Once the child is calm, put them back to bed, leave a dim night light on and stay until they are asleep.

Adolescent Nightmares
Murder/Dead Body

> *Witnessing a murder or seeing a dead body is a typical adolescent nightmare that indicates a rite of passage as they leave or 'murder' their childhood to create a new identity as a teenager.*

It may possibly be related to watching more violent or horror movies, or perhaps playing violent video games, that adolescents often dream of finding a murdered body, being murdered/murdering someone or burying a body.

However, this is not the whole explanation as to why these dreams are so prevalent during adolescence and end abruptly in their twenties. Several years ago, when I was employed as a high-school teacher, I would hear of these disturbing dreams that were deeply distressing for my students. They had common themes such as experiencing fear that they'd murdered someone and the body would be discovered or that they had witnessed a murder and now they were to be the next victim.

What I observed was that these young teens were at a stage in their lives where they were undergoing physical changes – developing from the body of a child to that of a young man or woman. All of a sudden there were not only expectations about appearance, grooming, attractiveness and new responsibilities, but their new identity also brought up society's expectations for their future. 'What do you want to do when you grow up?' was now a reality – the selection process as to what career would be chosen could no longer be delayed or seen through the wishful eyes of a child. 'I want to be famous' was not an option – choosing suitable subjects and potential tertiary courses was now their reality for the future.

The teen years are therefore a time when the child steps up to the plate – a time when they begin to glimpse the world of adulthood and when childhood dreams no longer seem achievable or practical.

The murder theme relates to having to 'kill off' the previous identity of the child in order to enter the new phase of adolescence. The buried body and fear of its discovery represent the old parts that need to be buried so that the new can emerge – especially if the 'geeky' kid wants to become a sports jock or the shy child wants to transform into a social butterfly. The physical transition from the old primary school into the new high school also allows this dream to come up more easily during sleep.

This is a time for parents to be intuitive and understanding as their adolescent child experiences enormous physical and emotional changes. As with any transformation, this is a challenging time. The hormone changes affect moods, confidence and attitude. Many parents will grieve for their child's lost identity too, as they must also enter a confronting new phase of adolescence with their child. It's important to remain calm and supportive of your adolescent if they experience the murder nightmares.

Death of a Parent

> *Following the murder theme, dreaming of a parent dying is another common teen dream. The transition from childhood into adolescence is a very unsettling time as young people feel they have to establish a new relationship with their parents and 'murder' the childish one they've had previously.*

New rules, the struggle for freedom and identity, privileges and responsibilities, rivalry and all the things that come with the teen years propel the subconscious to dream of the death of the old, comfortable child-parent relationship.

Generally, dreaming of death is a symbol of the end of something and the changes that will follow. It represents a rite of passage with opportunities for new beginnings.

It's a good idea to discuss this dream, especially if your teen or adolescent child is distressed by it, and explore and reiterate to your adolescent that these issues of death are part of the process of letting go of the old and a new beginning that awaits them.

Children's Dream Case Studies

The Kidnapper

> 'My ten-year-old son dreamt that he was approached by an unkempt, "homeless" type of man, accompanied by two teenage girls. We were in a shopping centre, and I had gone to the toilet. He was waiting for me when this man approached him. He grabbed my son, and put him on a table. He was not restrained.
>
> 'The man then went to the toilet, and I came back and found my son. I asked the girls, "What has he done to you?" and they replied, "He kidnapped us when we were shopping. He said he is going to hurt us once he's done something to your son."
>
> 'The man came back and had a white tube containing red stuff.

'He put some of this red stuff on his nose, then my son woke up.

'Should I be concerned about this dream? My son has been bullied at school for not having any friends of his own gender, as he plays only with girls. He's artistic and imaginative and the total opposite to his brother, who plays a lot of sport.'

Emma

Dream Insight

This dream sounds like it's related to events surrounding fears in your son's daily life. There are three dream themes that children experience – those that are reality based, fantasy ones and nightmares.

What's been happening recently in your son's life that in the dream he was feeling disempowered? As he's had the bullying issue at school, this dream may be triggered by the feeling of being 'kidnapped' from his natural state of being.

The teenage girls and you represent the feminine side, and it is this part of him that feels safe but he is being made to let go of because now, at ten years old, he needs to 'man' up. Someone or something is making him feel this pressure. It could be a new school situation or teacher, and general peer-group pressure to conform.

The red that the man is smearing on himself is the whole 'man' thing – the masculine, primitive energy of smearing the blood of an animal that was hunted. Again, it sounds to me like a rite of passage – from childhood to pre-adolescence. I think your son is a little fearful of leaving his boyhood/childhood behind and having to accept the coming of adolescence where there are more 'male' defined roles and responsibility. Perhaps, too, he is feeling like he has to be 'man' of the house if his dad is not around often.

The themes and symbols in his dream are vivid and real, reflecting what he's experiencing in his waking life such as kidnapping (helplessness and being forced to do something), the going to the toilet (release) and the homeless man (metaphor for mystery of entering the new stage of manhood).

Overall, I see it as an anxiety dream of losing childhood and finding a new identity as he's entering puberty.

Dream Wisdom

Bullying and feeling ostracised for being different is a scene played out in every schoolyard. Anxiety dreams are a result of the child's real-life fear. Finding positive role models is a good way for children to be inspired by, and not restricted to those who are considered 'blokey'. Encouraging social interactions with children their own age and trying new activities where they are praised for their efforts will help them to cope better.

The Witch

> 'As a child, I used to dream of a witch cackling in my brother's bedroom off our kitchen. Recurring. Lucid. So much so I still remember it and am equally horrified and fascinated by witches. They were so dark.'

Meg

Dream Insight

Witches feature commonly in children's dreams. Think of all those fairy tales with bad witches in them – our imagination was filled with them. They were dark, frightening and unpredictable. Thanks to the Brothers Grimm and our parents, we got the message that witches are synonymous with fear and anxiety. So when we got scared in real life, we dreamt of witches. When adults in real life acted a bit scary (to a child this can be anything such as a frown, loud voice, scolding) then in the dreamworld, the witches would represent these adults.

This recurring dream must have come at a time when the adults around you were threatening and you, as a result, felt unsafe. As adults looking back at our childhood dreams, we need to ask ourselves what was going on during that period in our lives to bring up some frightening images in our dreams.

If you can remember your recurring childhood dreams, work out the approximate date or year and see what critical events were taking place at the time that were making you feel more vulnerable than usual. This may explain the vivid and scary dreams.

Dream Wisdom

Comfort your child if they've had a bad dream about witches or other forms of monsters. Share the dream and come up with interesting ways to give the dream a new ending. This will be a great way to help the child to learn lucid dreaming and feel a sense of control both in the dream and in real life.

Consider what's happening in your child's life or new people that may be making them feel unsafe or afraid.

Haircut

> 'My ten-year-old, who has medium-length hair, dreamt the other night that someone cut her hair and made it into a bob. I asked her how she felt about it, and she said she was okay with it. It wasn't scary.'

Lucy

Dream Insight

At ten years old, it's a time when children make a transition into pre-pubescence or pre-adolescence. In other words, they are leaving their childhood behind to embrace the next stage of growth and initiation. There could be lots of anxiety in the next few years until they are more comfortable moving into this uncertain stage when their bodies are undergoing obvious physical changes.

Cutting hair symbolises losing the old childlike self and coming into the new, more mature adolescent self. The dreamer is obviously not worried about having to give up her childish ways (long hair) and growing up (bob).

Dream Wisdom

Ask your child: 'What do you like best about being older?' and 'What things worry you about going up a year level?' Talk about what new activities, interests and fashion items appeal to them or that they would like to try. Discuss with your child ways that they can start to become more grown up and the responsibilities that come with this new stage in their life.

Snakes

'I used to dream of snakes slithering around the floor of my bedroom in the night. I was in a bunk bed, and in the dream I was too terrified to get up and go to the toilet. I'd wake up and the bed would be wet. So vivid. Still feel the pit in my belly. I was around eight years old.'

Pete

Dream Insight

The snake dream is a common fear dream for children. Snakes that quietly slither around you without you being aware of their danger is an old primitive dream we may well share and experience at times when we feel vulnerable and in need of being on 'fight or flight' watch. At eight years old we are more aware of the dangers around us and that we are not always safe – from people, peers, situations, the world; they all seem dangerous or untrustworthy to us. The slithering snakes in this dream represent those fears.

Dream Wisdom

Take your child to a zoo or a sanctuary where they can see snakes in their natural environment. You may find a good documentary, but be wary of anything that may exacerbate your child's fear (such as a python swallowing a goat). Talk through why people should be wary of snakes but not be overly afraid that they will come and attack as they are usually more likely to be afraid of people. This may show the child that they can overcome their fear by rationalising it – in much the same way as they rationalise their fear of the snake.

Sharing Dreams

'When I was a kid, a friend and I had identical dreams, with each other in it. We got together the next day and recreated the exact steps of the dream in and around the old woodshed and we were convinced that we had the same dream. We were worried it was real since it involved aliens and us running away from them through the woodshed and being separated in a stand of totara and cabbage trees. Is that possible?'

Bridget

Dream Insight

This is called 'dream sharing' or 'dream meetings'. When you are close to someone, like a friend or even in a family, people share the same dreams or meet in each other's dreams. The alien is a fantasy theme dream where the dreamer is fighting or escaping from strange creatures. Children often dream of aliens, as they also represent their imaginative spirit and a welcome escape from reality.

It's important to note if the child is feeling frightened in the dream, as this may suggest an underlying fear of changing surroundings or losing what is familiar to them such as a home or family.

Dream Wisdom

Encourage your child to talk with you about their dream first thing in the morning. Discuss what it might mean. If it's a scary dream, suggest alternative endings that are funny or heroic. Ask: what made the dream so scary? Were you worried that you were in the same dream as your friend? Did it feel weird but kind of fun, too? How about we talk to (friend) and see what he/she remembers and then maybe make up a little play or write a song about it? (Anything creative that can be extracted from the dream and potentially turned into a positive experience is very useful.)

Keeping a Child's Dream Diary

The idea of keeping a dream diary is to keep a record of a child's dreams to excite their imagination and to lessen the impact of nightmares.

If your child is too young to write down their dream, write it down for them. You may wish to help them illustrate the dream in a dream diary.

A blank diary or thick exercise book is perfect, but it needs to be sturdy enough to use regularly to record their feelings, visions, fears and adventures after every dream as a future reference.

The dream entry should include:

• actions (what happens in the dream)
• location and theme (where things happen in the dream)
• characters, people, objects (who appears in the dream)
• colours, shapes (how things appear)
• emotions and atmosphere (what makes the dream memorable)

Once your child has written down and drawn their dream in the diary, revisit the dream by changing the ending or any aspect of the dream that they did not like.

If it's a monster dream, ask:

- How will you trick the monster?
- How can you get away from the tiger/robbers/dinosaur/zombies?
- Will you grow wings to fly above the scary scene?
- What does your safety place look like?
- How can you make yourself stronger?

Then ask your child to write a new version of the dream sequence and draw a picture of it. This process will empower the child in the dream state and promote lucid dreaming where they will learn how to control dreams and emotions. It will lead to a new confidence in their waking life and make them less likely to have nightmares or recurring anxiety dreams.

Imagine this scenario.

Your four year old has been having nightmares of being chased by scary monsters. After the dream re-entry, your child turns around to face the monster and asks the question, 'Why are you chasing me?' The monster replies, 'I was scared of the monster chasing me' or, 'I wasn't chasing you, I was chasing the butterflies in front of you. Come on, help me catch them!'

Think of your child's sense of relief and the renewed confidence they will experience in this one dream episode.

Family Dream Stories

Begin a new tradition. Have the family share their dreams in the morning. Each family member is asked to tell their dream and how they felt after waking up from the dream. After listening patiently to the dream, the dreamer waits for the rest of the family to contribute to the dream from the point of view of 'If this were my dream . . .'

Your child will take away only the insights that resonate with them. This method respects the dreamer and the dream as it does not make anyone an expert on another person's dreams, but rather offers different perspectives from people the child loves and respects.

We can't deny that we have some animal qualities in the way we live as communities: packs, herds, hives, loners (hermits). When we observe both humans and animals we can see common factors that we can make sense of in dream associations.

Birds. Birds are often associated with freedom, as we tell children to be as free as a bird that flies high in the air. It suggests your child is using their imagination and wants to move on to the next interesting activity.

If the child fears the bird dream, as we have seen in horror movies when the birds attack people, you will need to find out what is going on in waking life. Has the child witnessed birds attacking other birds or magpies swooping in order to scare away people from their nest?

Cats. In stories and family movies, cats are portrayed as cool, clever, aloof and villainous. They can be seen as affectionate but also spiteful (catty behaviour). If your child has a positive dream of cats, it indicates a good understanding of boundaries – giving people their space – and therefore respect for others, as often cats don't like being patted or held unless they want to be. If cats scratch or hurt the child in the dream, it may be time to investigate if all is well with friendship groups.

Dogs. A dog barking often frightens young children because they are taught that is a warning i.e. the dog protecting the house from an intruder, so if the dream has a barking/growling/biting dog, perhaps your child needs to listen to a warning or pay attention to something in their waking life. Alternatively, it can reflect their real-life fears of dogs. It can take a number of times to reassure a child that dogs sometimes bark just to get attention.

Farm animals
Farm animals are generally associated with the countryside and their usefulness. City children are introduced to sheep, pigs, goats, cows, chickens, ducks and rabbits at petting zoos in shopping centres or suburban fairs. Depending on what the child is told about these animals or their experiences with them is how the dream meaning will unfold.

Sheep are known for their willingness to follow others and not lead.

Pigs are dirty and fat.

Goats eat anything and climb anywhere.

Chickens are cowards.

Ducks can swim well.

Rabbits are quick, but timid (non-confrontational).

Cows are productive and nurturing.

The presence of one or more of these types of animals could represent certain characteristics in themselves or in real people in the child's life.

If a harmless creature turns menacing, be aware that your child may be struggling with a real-life parallel to the dream. Perhaps a normal situation sometimes changes in a surprising way and it's difficult for the child to adjust; it can be something like their best friend doesn't play fair or home life is not consistent.

Foxes

There are countless stories of the cunning, sly fox stealing chickens or being hunted by hounds and escaping. They represent the trickster. Perhaps your child is afraid of being 'tricked' or wants to explore their inner trickster and get up to more mischief.

Horses

Horses are common in children's dreams, as a galloping horse or riding a horse represents your child's wish for adventure and freedom. It's a good idea to talk to your child about new activities that they would like to try and encourage them to take a leap of faith. Children will learn how to take calculated risks and make adventure part of their lives by experiencing this dream in a positive way.

Insects, bugs and spiders

Insects and bugs in dreams represent irritation and a feeling of being suffocated when they present in swarms. See if you can discuss with your child what is annoying them and why they are feeling stifled. Spiders can be interpreted in many ways, depending on if the child is frightened of them. If this is the case, the dream is a representation of fear. If the busy spider is weaving its web happily in the dream, it highlights your child's love of creativity and that they are industrious in their approach to tasks. Overall, it's a good sign if there is no fear involved.

Rats, mice and bats

These animals are characterised as sneaky and cunning as they are quiet and nocturnal. A 'dirty, scheming rat', 'quiet as a mouse' or 'blind as a bat' are common sayings and reflect our attitude to these animals. Additionally, Batman movies and cartoons have helped to raise the bat profile to a more positive and heroic one. The popularity of vampire movies featuring malicious, blood-sucking bats have added to their prominence in children's nightmares.

Look at your child's social life and see whether your child or someone in their social circle is displaying any of the above human characteristics attributed to these animals.

Reptiles and amphibians

Crocodiles. They are the most primitive creatures and are closest to resembling a dinosaur. Through a child's eyes, a dinosaur is also very similar to a dragon. These associations are terrifying, and when an unfriendly crocodile appears in a child's dream it brings up the fears of hidden dangers that are lurking all about. In *Peter Pan*, Captain Hook is missing a hand thanks to a crocodile snapping it off.

There is a big fear your child is experiencing. Make sure you are aware of their vulnerability and not feeling safe, and be reassuring.

Snakes. Slithering quietly, they dangerously appear in nightmares. The child feels they are in a 'fight or flight' situation and are vulnerable to potentially being killed. Most children experience the snake dream in a time when they are not feeling safe with people, peers, and the everyday world. The snakes, therefore, represent these fears.

Frogs, toads and lizards. They are symbols of change and transformation, and lizards are adaptable creatures. Children are likely to dream of these creatures when there are changes going on.

Sea creatures

Water represents our emotional lives and our spirit. Dreaming of creatures that live in seas, rivers and lakes indicates the need for self-expression. For a child, water is usually associated with play and free expression.

Dolphins and whales. Swimming with dolphins and whales means the dreamer is wanting to explore deeper waters – in other words, the child is ready to be more independent and do things on their own. Dolphins have associations with intelligence and guidance; whales are large and calming figures. In Native American tradition they are known as the 'record keepers' that carry our collective memory.

Sharks. Like crocodiles and snakes, sharks bring up fears about feeling unsafe. What's making your child feel threatened? Fears are also heightened when the news reports shark attacks and people being killed. Monitor or discuss these incidents to minimise nightmares.

Wild animals

In the movie *The Wizard of Oz* Dorothy was aware of the dangers of meeting up with lions and tigers and bears. *Lions* and *tigers* are symbols of courage and power, while *bears* indicate brute force and protection. The teddy bear is a small version of a large wild bear, so a child feels its protection and nurturing nature and uses it as a comforting friend to assist them when they are going to sleep.

Since wild animals represent our instinct and our real personality, they can show you some aspects of your child that need to be curbed, recognised or encouraged. They can also highlight your child's fears that are a result of something going on in their everyday life.

Elephants are associated with a good memory and large size.

Monkeys are mischievous and playful.

Other wild or exotic animals such as panthers, gorillas, hippos, kangaroos, wombats, llamas, camels and more can come up in dreams after a trip to the zoo, or after reading or watching a show about animals or with animals as the characters in the show. What's interesting is the reason why that particular animal showed up in the dream and how it acted towards the child.

Wolves. The stories of Little Red Riding Hood or The Three Little Pigs are possibly the first introduction children have to wolves, unless they are living in places where there are wolves in the wild. We have been told that wolves need to be feared as they are dangerous and come in 'disguise' – a wolf in sheep's clothing and, as we know, the wolf dressed up as Grandma.

Big bad wolf

The recent blockbuster movies on werewolves have also done wolves a disservice, as they are portrayed as bloodthirsty shape shifters. When a child dreams of a wolf it's most likely to be a nightmare. In younger children a wolf could represent a person they are afraid of or don't trust. The best way to help a child through this nightmare is to explain the true nature of wolves and reassure them that these wild animals enjoy their own environment and will not descend on suburbia.

Buildings/structures

Houses and buildings represent the dreamer's sense of self; the rooms and features of these structures represent different parts of ourselves. Allow your child to describe the house and rooms in their dream – if they are in disarray or in chaos, this will indicate how they are feeling about themselves or their current situation.

A castle or a fortress. This indicates that the child feels under attack and therefore needs protection. Does your child need more freedom or is their personality a little insular and defensive?

Cellars and jails are symbols of hidden fears, as the room is dark and away from the family group. Perhaps your child has been sent to a time-out room when they've been naughty or it could have occurred at school. Now the scene in the dream is much more heightened and emotions such as guilt, shame and abandonment are more intense.

Churches or temples. They are places of safety and contemplation and are especially relevant if the child has had an experience of a faith or tradition. It may be that your child is seeking reassurance that they are part of a community.

School, playground and shops. They are usually a representation of what's going on in a child's daily life. Ask your child how he/she feels in the dreams. This will indicate what emotional issues are going on for them.

Walls, fences and gates. They represent obstacles and boundaries. What is causing your child to feel hindered and frustrated? Do they need restraint? Are they having problems communicating freely with others?

Emotional dreams

Fighting in a dream could either reflect what your child may be experiencing in real life or some personal conflict within themselves. Look at peer groups and their influence on your child's actions and social conscience.

Just like adults, children dream of being frozen in fear and unable to move. It is usually an anxiety dream or nightmare where they are powerless to move or act. It comes at a time in their lives when they feel that they have no control over what happens to loved ones or the world around them. Sensitive children often respond negatively to and are greatly affected by vivid descriptions on the news about disasters, accidents or animal cruelty in particular.

Literally frozen

There is also a physical reason for the dream of feeling frozen and it's to do with waking up from REM sleep. When we are in REM sleep, our muscles are relaxed and not prepared for movement. If we wake up suddenly from REM sleep, there may be a time lapse between movement and regaining consciousness.

Toilet dreams

Dreams that include urinating and looking for a toilet need to be taken literally with younger children. Bedwetting is a major problem for some children and should be treated accordingly. Often, a dream about urinating can warn of the need to use the toilet and the dream itself can induce bedwetting. The need to urinate is a symbol of wanting a release. Does your child need to let go of something? Perhaps they are ready to become more independent but are afraid of letting go of past childhood ways. Looking for a toilet in a dream indicates that your child is looking for a private place to release their emotions.

Landscapes

Lakes, rivers, ocean or creeks. These are images our dreaming mind associates with our emotions. A calm body of water is indicative of a feeling that all is smooth sailing. Contained areas of water suggest that your child generally feels safe at an emotional level and has a confident frame of mind, unless the river is running too fast or the lake is very large, which can symbolise that they feel out of control and in turmoil.

Sea and ocean waves. The sea can be turbulent, therefore, if your child dreams of a stormy sea or murky waters it suggests they are experiencing emotional turmoil or unrest. If there is drowning, it indicates a feeling of being overwhelmed emotionally in real life. It would be advisable to talk with your child and find strategies to help them cope with these feelings.

Forests. Forests are dark places often depicted in fairy tales as a place where children can get lost and where strange creatures lurk. In a child's dreams a forest is a confusing place where they are surrounded by tall trees blocking them from moving forward and this becomes an obstacle that must be overcome. This is a reflection of a child's mental and emotional state. It's important that your child shares their forest dream so that the parent or adult can help them make sense of it and give reassurance.

Mountains. They symbolise goals that need to be reached or an obstacle that needs to be overcome. Check if your child is anxious about performing well at school or sports.

Caves. If a child dreams about caves, it represents their inner personality or unconscious. It's about their talents and potential being hidden instead of bringing them out for all to see. Children need encouragement to come out of their 'shell' or 'cave' so that they can bask in the glow of their success.

Natural elements

Fire. Fire plays a dual role in dreams. It can represent emotions that are consuming or out of control, or the emotional warmth and security the child normally feels in the home.

Rain. A flood is an overwhelming emotion; perhaps it's time to wash away the old and make a new start. Dreams about storms that batter the child may indicate the child is feeling stressed and needs to release emotions in a safe way.

Snow or ice. This means your child needs more emotional warmth in their lives. Perhaps they can't deal with certain situations and feel frozen. If the dream occurs around Christmas or you've had a holiday at the snow and the feelings associated with the dream are happy, the interpretation needs to be adapted to the more obvious meanings.

People/characters

All kinds of people feature in children's dreams and they can either be emotionally disturbing for the dreamer or rewarding, depending on whether it's a pleasant dream or a nightmare situation. Family matters are very important to a child and conflict with parents and siblings in real life often play out in dreams.

Parents. A scowling parent in a dream can make a child feel intimidated and criticised. A shadowy parent can indicate that the child feels emotionally abandoned. Relatives in dreams represent support or a wish for more support in a child's waking life.

A stranger. Somebody who frightens a child in dreams can symbolise a real person your child is afraid of or it can be a general fear. For example, fear of the dark, fear of meeting new people, fear of doctors or dentists, fear of certain noises, of other children, of certain teachers, of scary movies, of getting lost, of spiders or dogs, of crowds – these are all general fears.

Celebrities. Seeing celebrities in a dream suggests your child's fantasy of being popular or famous and regarding the particular celebrity as their role model. Familiarise yourself with these stars, as you can guide your child through the world of celebrity and teach them about what's real and what's sensationalised. Young people often believe that what they see on TV is real life.

Authority figures: doctors, teachers, royalty, police and other leaders or officials. These people have different meanings depending on the dream context. Ask your child if the figure's role is encouraging, scolding, protective or aggressive. This will give you an indication of the way your child interacts with these figures in real life and why.

Angels and fairies. Angels and fairies actively play a part in a child's imaginative life as children embrace that which cannot be explained rationally. A child will feel protected when dreaming of angels and fairies in a magic realm. In a crisis, children have dreamt of angels and this has helped them cope. Generally, angels and fairies remind us of our spiritual lives.

Toys. They are often seen as real to young children, each toy with its own personality and name. It's no surprise, then, that toys can become real in dreams. Allow the child to tell you what role the toy plays in the dream. This will give you insight to what the child is experiencing with friends in their daily life.

Transport

Children spend a lot of time in various modes of transport – cars, trains, buses – and it's no surprise that they dream a great deal about these vehicles. Generally, transport is a symbol of moving forward and making huge advancements. Children's personalities and stages of growth change at a rapid pace, so the transport symbols represent how they are dealing with their emotions as they move forward – if they feel the vehicle is moving too fast then perhaps they don't feel ready to move to the next stage of their development.

The family car. Dreaming of the family car indicates the child feels contentment; however, if there are negative feelings about being in a passenger in the family car, it suggests they are feeling trapped and powerless.

Boats are about emotional journeys, and *trains* and stations in dreams indicate the need for movement and change. Missing a train or bus is a common anxiety dream, meaning that the dreamer isn't well prepared but feels the need to move on.

Trucks carry heavy loads and so, in dreams, this highlights the feeling of carrying a heavy emotional load or workload (school work, perhaps?) or of being out of control.

Dreaming of planes is a child's way of wanting to spread their wings and experience freedom or simply escape from chores or problems. Discuss what things your child wants to break free of.

Rocket and spaceship. These dreams are usually fantasy dreams and a desire for adventure.

PART 2

Intuition

YOUR NEXT STEP is to enter the labyrinthine world of dreams and use your intuition for understanding the dream images.

The metaphor of the thread as a 'life line' and connection is an ancient one, continuing in the ancient Greek myth of Ariadne, Theseus and the Minotaur.

Legend has it that the Minotaur, which was half-bull, half-man, lived in a labyrinth on the island of Crete. Every year, or nine years depending on the version, the monster demanded a sacrifice and seven young men and women were sent into the labyrinth to their death. The hero, Theseus, decided he would kill the beast and found his way to Crete to pose as one of the volunteers. By the hand of fate he met Ariadne, the daughter of King Minos, who fell in love with him and agreed to help him.

Ariadne gave Theseus a spool of thread as he entered the labyrinth and held on to the other end. In the darkness of the labyrinth, Theseus slew the Minotaur and followed the thread back to where Ariadne was waiting for him. The dark underground labyrinth represents our unconscious minds waiting for a glimpse of activity in order to awaken from its inertia and come up through the subconscious into consciousness. The lifeline that Ariadne gives Theseus can be seen as a symbol of our dream threads, which connect us to our deepest intuition as represented by the Minotaur, which is half-animal.

The thread allows the hero to return safely. In the same way, it is safe for us to go deep within ourselves and journey back with the knowledge that we have learnt something more about ourselves. The trick is in having faith in the thread, and that when you are feeling lost in the dark it can guide you to some unknown part of you and back out to the light again.

'Fil d'Ariane' or 'Ariadne's thread' is what French cave divers call the guideline that they lay when cave diving so they can find their way back out no matter what the conditions – where there is no light, silty dark water or just endless chambers that resemble one another.

Dreams are also threads that lead somewhere. Part of you is holding that thread so you can complete the dreaming process safely.

This second part of the book focuses on our intuition. You can glimpse your intuition from your dream world and treasure the magic it brings to your waking life. Armed with this intuition you can gain entry further in the underworld, deep in the unconscious, in the labyrinth where Theseus killed the Minotaur and return safely as you follow the thread out.

CHAPTER 7

The Collective Unconscious and Archetypes

'Until you make the unconscious conscious, it will direct your life and you will call it fate.'
– C.G. Jung

CARL GUSTAV JUNG described the 'collective unconscious' as the part of our unconscious mind that holds ancestral memories, knowledge and experiences we share as a species. The collective unconscious is therefore the product of the repeated experiences of humanity.

Archetypes are universal themes, experiences, images, patterns and symbols that reside within us all. In other words, they represent models of universal behaviours or personality traits. They emerge in symbolic form in dreams, mythology, fairytales and fables, religions, art and literature. Look no further than the most recent blockbuster movie, bestselling novel or latest video game to see the power of archetypes we share with everyone in the world.

Themes include the classic good versus evil (*James Bond*); the hero's journey to save himself and those he loves (*Harry Potter*); courage beyond duty (*The Hunger Games*); and redemption and forgiveness (*Les Miserables*). Why do we love these perennial themes that recycle on our screens and theatres? Jung would say that it's because we share these archetypal patterns at a collective and unconscious level.

In our dreams, archetypes can be triggered or activated when we are experiencing significant transitional periods in our lives such as illness, leaving home, beginning or ending a relationship, changing jobs, divorce. You know an archetypal dream when you have one, as they evoke deep emotions and are more vivid and more easily remembered than ordinary or everyday dreams. You'll feel that you've learnt something important about yourself that will have a real impact on how you live your life.

They are what Jung called 'big dreams', where they feel more real and intense than real life – and have a clear message to the psyche.

Jung identified our most common archetypes; there are many more that appear in our dreams. I have selected some of my favourite archetypes that have helped me to work with themes in my dreams, and that may also assist you with your own mythic journey through life.

The Self

Dream images: a sense of yourself being in the dream – as a narrator, a director of the scene, a victim, a player, the abuser or an objective observer. The self can appear as a circle, a square or four squares in a circle, a mandala, or even a child, as these images represent perfection, completeness and wholeness. This is something the self is searching for.

The Self is the product of integrating one's personality (known as individuation). Jung represented the Self as a circle, a square or a mandala. A mandala ('secret circle' in Sanskrit) is a drawing that is used in meditation because it helps you to focus on the centre. It represents the union of our unconscious and the conscious. When all parts of ourselves, the various aspects of our personality, are integrated we create the Self. By working with our dreams (unconscious) and responding to them as we make appropriate changes (conscious), we honour the role of the unconscious where those parts of us that are lost, rejected or ignored can be retrieved.

Once we bring them into consciousness, we listen to our bodies and learn to appreciate the intelligence of our emotions. This, in turn, may lead us to make important contributions on many levels. We become examples to others who need to understand the importance of self-awareness.

How to work with your Self dreams

You may see yourself possessing certain traits from these archetypes below. Work out how to best integrate them – good and bad personality traits – in order to reach a harmonious state within yourself.

Questions to ask if you dream of the Self

• Who are you in your dreams? Are you seeing yourself in the first person, where the action revolves around you, or in the third person, the observer in the dream?

• How do you integrate parts of yourself so you can achieve your full potential and live a fully creative life?

The Persona

Dream images: any image the psyche conjures to show the public image. Negative images may include a scarecrow, a tramp, a desolate landscape, a beggar or an outcast. If you are naked, you are without a Persona and that's not a bad thing. It may indicate that you are confident in being the you that you want to be.

The Persona is how we present ourselves to the world. Persona comes from the Latin word for 'mask' and represents our public image. When you dream of a Persona, it represents the different social masks you wear when you are in different groups and situations. This acts as a type of shield or barrier as protection for your psyche.

It may be you as you see yourself in your waking life or you may be looking at yourself as a third person and being an observer. In some dreams, the self may not resemble you physically or behave the way you would normally. The Persona can appear as a train driver, an exotic dancer, a street beggar or a priest. You simply know it's 'you' in the dream, even though it does not have your appearance.

It's important, therefore, to be aware of all the people in your dreams, as they are all aspects of you: the 'you' that wears many different masks in your public life.

How to work with your Persona dream

The Persona and masks and roles are an insightful way of looking at the relationships we have with ourselves, the world and people around us. If you or others don't recognise the roles you are able to perform, it's difficult to make significant growth in your personal development.

When we are young we choose to develop the good girl/boy instead of the bad girl/boy. Perhaps we get rewarded for a talent we have in fixing things and begin to develop this ability. Treat your Persona dream as a play – is it a drama, comedy, horror, sit-com, mystery? What roles are being played?

Questions to ask if you dream of the Persona

• What types of clothing are your characters wearing in your dreams and for what occasion?

• What are the dream characters doing?

• If you are in the dream, what is your role?

The Shadow

> Dream images: *character of the same sex as the dreamer; a sinister or threatening figure often with darker hair or darker skin than the dreamer; a hostile animal – a monster, a dragon, a snake, a demon or 'wild'-looking creature. In fairy tales examples of the Shadow are a beast (like in Beauty and the Beast) and an ogre (like in Jack and the Beanstalk).*

The Shadow can appear as a dark, frightening, shadowy human figure (the bully, murderer, stalker) that lurks behind you hiding, veiled in shadows. Or it may not have a shape at all. It may surprise you that the figure is someone you know in real life – someone of your gender who has qualities you don't like, or your boss, your relative or close friend.

Jung defined the Shadow as 'the thing a person has no wish to be'. He regarded the Shadow as the instinctual side of ourselves, and that the Shadow contained elements that were unacceptable to us (due to conditioning) but not necessarily bad or dark. In fact, the Shadow may contain the entirety of our repressed potential – the 'golden Shadow' of our personality.

Poet Robert Bly describes the Shadow as 'the long black bag we drag behind us' in which we put all of our unacceptable qualities – everything we've forgotten, denied, rejected or not yet realised.

Our conscious mind rejects this part of our personality that contains those things that we fear in ourselves, such as anger, aggression or even grief – any qualities that are unappealing. What happens when we deny this element of our own psyche is that we project it on to others in real life and never learn to face our 'demons' or complexes. Except in our dreams, of course, where the unconscious mind has the opportunity to bring out our shadow side.

If the Shadow is not integrated into your conscious mind, it will simply secretly control you outside of your awareness. If you ignore those aspects of your undesirable self or negative emotions, you'll experience feelings of shame, anxiety, fear and depression in waking life. Nightmares and recurring anxiety dreams are another way for the Shadow to reach you. It makes sense, then, at a metaphoric level, that once you can acknowledge your Shadow it will result in the death of the 'old' you.

How to work with your Shadow dreams

Repression is an inherent feature of the Shadow. Understand that the Shadow represents those things we reject, disown or devalue and will remain hidden in your subconscious, where they increase in strength and power. Dreams and nightmares are a way of releasing it. Human beings are a paradox – we are made up of opposites, and when working with our Shadow side images considered confronting, violent and shocking will show up as the reflective side of our nature.

Questions to ask if you dream of the Shadow

- What makes you feel angry and scared?

- What are you forced to confront about yourself that you don't want to see? Are there habits that you hate or are out of control?

- What negative personality traits don't you want to own? How do you suppress them? The public Persona or front you've put up for everyone to see is hiding your 'other' self that is not acceptable to you or you don't want to admit you have. Is it because it would make you feel imperfect? Flawed? Not good enough? Not up to others' expectations?

- What vital parts of yourself are you rejecting?
- What are the recurrent patterns of the Shadow dream?
- Can you find new strategies to shift these patterns and recognise the emotional trigger in your waking life?

The Anima and Animus

Dream images (Anima): character of the opposite sex; sister; cow, cat, tiger, cave and ship, the seductive nymph, damsel in distress, goddess, witch or dancing girl.

Dream images (Animus): character of the opposite sex, brother, wise man, sorcerer, king, athlete, muscular man, criminal, eagle, bull, lion, tower, knight or warrior.

We are made up of both masculine and feminine energies; however, most women equate themselves with just the feminine and men with the masculine on the conscious 'ego' level – our outside self. To balance this, we carry the opposite energy subconsciously at an inner level. That is, women carry inner male energies and qualities called the Animus, and men carry the inner female equivalent, the Anima. Both of these words come from the Latin word meaning soul or spirit.

The Animus' positive qualities (women's inner male energy):

- assertive
- passionate
- protective
- supportive
- action-oriented
- ambitious

The Anima's positive qualities (men's inner female energy):

- creative (giving birth)
- receptive

- intuitive
- nurturing
- compassionate
- empathetic

Yin and yang

The ancient Chinese book of wisdom, the *I Ching*, recognises the opposing masculine and feminine energies and calls them the yang (the creative masculine) and the yin (the receptive feminine).

Yang (active masculine): light, directed, focused, logical, action-oriented, independent, static.

Yin (receptive feminine): dark, diffuse, intuitive, receptive, emotional, ambiguous, fluid.

The basic difference between the two is considered that one is 'doing' and the other is 'being'.

Neither the traditional feminine nor the masculine qualities should be discarded or disowned because together they bring balance in our lives. They need each other for wholeness and must contain a piece of one another's understanding.

The balance is vital – too much yin and we remain too long in our inner world and feeling life, where we experience little action and fail to fulfil our potential. We need the yang's focus for targeted goals. Too much yang, in which we are focused and ambitious and we become domineering and controlling, requires the yin's inclusive nature to remain in touch with our intuition.

In other words, men must come to terms with their emotions and vulnerability as they develop their capacity for relationships, while women need to become more action-oriented to enable them to gain independence and courage. Our inner relationship is mirrored in our outer relationships.

These dream images appear at times when there is an opportunity to integrate the feminine and masculine qualities within yourself. They serve as a reminder that you must learn to acknowledge or express your masculine side (be more assertive) or feminine side (be more emotional). If you are experiencing relationship issues, the Anima/Animus is likely to appear in your dreams.

'Anima' means soul with a female form. It is pure romantic love. In mythology it is expressed as a siren, a mermaid, a wood nymph, or any form that was said to infatuate young men. In ancient times, the Anima came either as a goddess or a witch – that is, aspects of the female that were out of men's control.

Anima may appear as an exotic dancing girl or a weathered old hag – the shape generally reflects either the condition or the needs of our psyche. In dreams, the Anima and Animus can be exaggerated – just so you don't miss them.

Violence and danger in a woman's dream can be associated with her Animus. If rightly identified and worked through, the Animus can provide a woman with confidence in her abilities to take care of herself.

The aim for us all is to embrace and utilise both our male and female qualities to create a harmonious balance in our relationships.

Inner marriage

When the opposites of the outer and inner life become joined in marriage, it's a match made in heaven – a marriage of opposites. This combination of the Anima and Animus is known as the 'syzygy' – or the divine couple. The syzygy represents completion, unification and wholeness – the inner union and integration of our psyche.

With her loving, intuitive direction and support, she helps him gain strength and manifest his goals using his planning and logic. He learns to trust her intuitive abilities and supports her through his ability to focus and remain strong. When we combine these aspects of our nature, it's a win-win for everyone.

If we dream of kissing, having sex or marriage in a dream, it could suggest this desire for our inner marriage – an integration of our Anima and Animus qualities. This longing is representative of our need for wholeness.

Kathleen Noble, in *The Sound of a Silver Horn,* describes wholeness as: '… independent without being alienated; courageous without being contemptuous of the weak; powerful without dominating or exploiting others; rational without suppressing or abandoning feeling and intuition; autonomous within interconnected, independent and equal relationships; nurturing without denying or sacrificing her own needs; and androgynous without compromising the best attributes of femaleness but affirming the wholeness inherent in all.'

How to work with your Anima/Animus dreams

The Anima and Animus can influence a person in either a positive or negative manner. If a man is under the influence of the positive Anima he will show tenderness, patience, consideration and compassion. The negative Anima manifests as vanity, moodiness, bitchiness and sensitivity to hurt feelings.

A woman with a positive Animus shows assertiveness, control, thoughtful rationality and compassionate strength. The negative Animus reveals itself through strong opinions, ruthlessness, destructive forces and always having the last word – the 'my way or the highway' attitude.

Study your dreams and notice what qualities your male and female characters portray and what emotions they evoke in you. The best way to work with this dream is to confront and accept the unacceptable aspects of yourself so that you can begin to make significant changes. Be aware of the relationships between your male and female figures – is the male the aggressor and attacking a female or is the female the victim, running away or hiding?

Allow your dream to seep into your consciousness slowly by making yourself aware of small changes you make daily to integrate both masculine and feminine traits in your waking life.

Questions to ask if you dream of the Anima/Animus

- What is the current balance of the masculine and feminine energies in your life and what needs further development?
- Will adopting masculine traits compromise your femininity?
- Will adopting feminine traits compromise your masculinity?
- What do you need to do to achieve an inner marriage?
- What needs are not being met in your relationship?

CHAPTER 8

Major Archetypal Characters in Dreams

THERE ARE COUNTLESS character archetypes, but the following are the most common, recurring archetypal images we share in the land of dreams. They are not static – they are composites and overlap in different dream scenes.

The Divine Child

Dream images: a child, baby, elf, young animal and jewels.

The Divine Child represents your inner child – your true self – and is a symbol of your innocence and vulnerabilities. It also symbolises your full potential, as it embodies a metaphor for hope and promise for new beginnings. It means you are open to all possibilities. The most famous Divine Child we can use as an archetypal symbol is the child Jesus, who personifies the promise of Paradise regained. It gives us hope that new beginnings will lead us to our personal paradise or achieve our full potential.

The archetypal image of the Divine Child comes to us in dreams of a baby or young child. It evokes in us a longing for innocence, a rebirth, a new beginning that will lead to our salvation. It may be that you've been laid off work after twenty years or your marriage unexpectedly comes to an end and you have no choice but to begin again. With a sense of helplessness and vulnerability, you go back to the time when you started the job or just got married. Then you begin all over again, fresh with the hope of having a second chance.

The Divine Child can also appear as an elf, animals or even jewels. It represents those childlike forces in our lives. When part of our consciousness is too one-sided the Divine Child may appear in our dreams, helping us find our creativity and achieve our potential.

How to work with your Divine Child dreams

Generally, dreaming of a baby is about a new career, a new project – a new phase in your life. This is the time you need to nurture your inner child and make sure it's protected and given care. Keep your baby away from the inner critic and those around you who feel they need to point out the potential pitfalls and give you negative feedback.

You need commitment to the responsibility it requires for that 'baby', that new plan or part of you, to grow. More than that, the Divine Child archetype represents a promise that you can transform and redeem yourself, therefore making the child a symbol of a renewed sense of hope.

When the Divine Child appears in our dreams, he/she offers us possibility for transformation at a time when our human resources or knowledge are limited and when our conscious efforts are not enough, reassuring us that faith is possible in times of despair and hopelessness.

The dream with the Divine Child reassures you that all is possible and you are gifted with direction and purpose.

Questions to ask if you dream of the Divine Child

- In what ways do you feel vulnerable and new?
- What new beginnings are you concerned about starting?
- Are you feeling overwhelmed with responsibility and care?
- How can you nurture yourself as you grow into the person you want to become?

The Great Mother

Dream images: a goddess, female figure, nurse, other female figure associated with fertility, a priestess, Mary Mother of God, the Church, country, the earth, the woods, the sea, a garden, a whale, a ploughed field, a spring or well, trees, cooking utensils, a cave, a witch or negative female role model from mythology.

A mother figure *can* appear in your dreams as your own mother, grandmother or other nurturing figure, and normally provides you with advice and reassurance. However, the archetype of the *Great Mother* is more than simply a reflection of our relationship with our own mother. Motherhood on our planet is as old as life. We are born into this world ready to want our mother, to look out for her and connect with her, so this archetype holds all these evolutionary patterns of behaviour and experiences.

The archetype of the Great Mother appears in dreams as one who nurtures, helps and protects. She encompasses all of the positive qualities we associate with good mothers (nurturing, nourishing, loving) and also all of the negative qualities we associate with bad mothers (smothering, neglect, manipulation). We can attribute these qualities to Mother Earth, who can be both loving with her gentle ocean breeze and destructive with a cyclone or earthquake.

Pilgrims flock to the shrines and temples that honour the feminine goddesses, including Mother Mary, as people feel the mystery of the Great Mother in those healing and holy places. P.W. Martin describes the mother in these terms: 'She is the maiden. She is the earth mother. She is the queen of the underworld. She is the goddess of war, the goddess of nature, the goddess of love, the goddess of marriage, the mountain goddess, the goddess of the chase, the goddess of herds, goddess of agriculture, goddess of fecundity, goddess of the moon.'

So whatever image of the Great Mother we meet, it is only a synthesis of something much more powerful and active than the role she is given. It is up to us to figure out how to access and work with the various mother images that come to us in our dreams.

The Great Mother's shadow side may show up as a witch or old bag lady, in which case they can be associated with seduction, dominance and even death. At the same time as a mother is a nurturer and giver of life, she can also keep her children helpless and dependent on her through oppression so that they won't grow up and move away from her.

The positive aspect of the archetype is motherly love and warmth – qualities that are well celebrated in art, song and literature. It is our mother who gives us our first identity in the world. Yet mothering can also have a negative side – when it's not used in a way that will release us – and we become totally dependent. She has become an archetype of fate – good and bad. Jung considered the Great Mother the most important archetype because she represented life and death.

How to work with Great Mother dreams

We are told to not hang on to our mother's apron strings once we become self-sufficient, and that we need to live our own lives. The umbilical cord needs to be well and truly severed and the apron strings cut by the time we move out of our parental home.

But our inner child protests. We want our archetypal parents to be 'God' for us – in that they should love us unconditionally, be nurturing and never ever leave us for the rest of our lives. It's unrealistic and we know this at a conscious level. But our wounded or abandoned inner child wants to know where it can regain this unconditional love and devotion. It's this search that stops us despairing when life deals a bad hand.

It's the thread we hang on to for dear life – the umbilical cord that once sustained us at the source – our mother, the original creator of us and of every human. These unrealistic expectations are what cause us to meet with the ideal Great Mother archetype in our dreams, who shows herself in many guises that our mortal mother does not have a hope of living up to.

Working with the Great Mother archetype dream is possibly the most significant and challenging as it projects our deepest fears, insecurities and sense of loss and abandonment. After all, she is the most powerful primary archetype we have in our lives and her role is perfectly described as 'the hand that rocks the cradle rules the world'.

The Hand that Rocks the Cradle

Blessings on the hand of women!
Angels guard its strength and grace,
In the palace, cottage, hovel,
Oh, no matter where the place;
Would that never storms assailed it,
Rainbows ever gently curled;
For the hand that rocks the cradle
Is the hand that rules the world.

– William Ross Wallace, poet

Questions to ask if you dream of the Great Mother archetype

- Do you need to be your own inner nurturer? In what way do you feel this?
- What aspects of your mothering need to be examined?
- Are you over-mothering and/or smothering your children?
- Did you miss out on being mothered the way you would have wished?
- If you could interview the Great Mother archetype, what would you ask?

The Wise Old Man/Woman

Dream images: king, magician, prophet or guru, guide, doctor, father, strong male figure, judge, grandfather, priest, teacher, any authority figure, crone, witch, guide, grandmother, strong female figure, older priestess, fairy godmother or healer.

The Wise Old Man is a symbol of a primal source of growth and energy – it can either heal or destroy, support or discourage, endorse or oppose, attract or repel depending on the dream. This archetype may appear as a magician, doctor, professor, priest, teacher, father or any other authority figure, and by its very presence or guidance convey the sense we are within grasp of our higher consciousnesses.

The Wise Old Man is the helper in your dreams who serves by offering guidance, advice and words of wisdom. He appears when you need to be pointed in the right direction. This archetype represents knowledge, insight, wisdom, morality, guidance, advice and other qualities that are attributed to authority figures.

However, like the wizard or the shaman, his personality is not fully divine and can lead us away from our higher calling – in other words, he can convince you to take a stand or move in a certain direction. On the other hand, he can lead you towards your ambitions, aspirations and hopes.

In mythical stories, the hero is commonly guided by the Wise Old Man. In *Star Wars* he is played by Obi Wan Kenobi and, later, Yoda. They both teach Luke about the force and, as Luke matures, they die and become a part of him. The hero then grows to become the Wise Old Man. In *Lord of the Rings*, Gandalf is the ultimate wizard and guide, as is Merlin to legendary King Arthur.

The Wise Old Woman makes her appearance as the archetype of feminine experience – all that she has learnt from being a maiden, a mother and a crone. She embodies the sum total of the lived experience of all women. Because she's lived through so many of life's stages, she can walk us through love, hope, fear, sorrow and all those emotions that come with each rite of passage.

What's more important about the Wise Old Woman is that she's learnt the secrets of life and death, and is often portrayed as the gatekeeper between the worlds. She appears in myths and dreams as grandmother, witch or crone and sometimes as fairy godmother. She is often seen as a healer, working in tune with nature, and a guide to those ready to leave or enter this world.

How to work with your Wise Old Man/Woman dreams

When the Wise Old Man/Woman comes into your dreams, pay attention to their advice. They've been there and seen it all. Their guidance is invaluable because of their life experience. If you dream of your grandfather or grandmother you may be experiencing a genealogical dream, where you will gain information about your family's history. What is left unsaid through generations comes up in our dream state and offers to shed light on what has been kept hidden in the past.

How you feel when you are in the presence of this archetype will give you clues as to what you need to implement in your waking life for closure, progress, direction, peace and anything that you seek in your waking life from those you consider mentors or counsellors.

Old Wise Man Dream

A client came to me with a dream:

> 'I dreamt I was a young boy visiting an old man who lived near the sea. The old man could not speak and was very frail. When I sat next to the old man and closed my eyes, I went into another world – one of medieval adventure. There, as I faced the evil Red Knight on his black steed, the old man came and spoke to me and gave me the secret of how to joust the Red Knight and win. Only, he was no longer the mute old man, he was a stately wise knight who knew the art of battle and was prepared to teach me how to fight my opponent and win.'
>
> **Vince**

This dream came at a time when you were feeling overwhelmed with work responsibilities and pressure – you felt dragged down and could no longer fight the fatigue, the battle. Inside you felt like the little boy lost. The Wise Old Man had transformed himself into a wise mentor – someone who had been in battle and had earned his knighthood. The dream showed you that he had to access his inner wise knight to fight the battle and beat his opponent, and that giving up was not an option.

Questions to ask if you dream of the Wise Old Man/ Woman

- What advice do you need?
- Will you take advice regardless of whether it's encouraging or arduous?
- If you had a mentor, how would you use them?
- If you knew the mysteries of life and death, how would that change the way you lived your life today?

The Trickster

Dream images: fool, magician, clown, jester, joker, villain, destroyer, coyote or fox.

The Trickster, as the name implies, plays jokes on you to keep you from taking yourself too seriously. He may appear in your dream when you have overextended yourself or misjudged a situation, or you could find him in your dream when you are uncertain about a decision you need to make. The Trickster often makes you feel uncomfortable or embarrassed, sometimes mocking you or exposing you to your vulnerabilities. He may take on subtle forms, sometimes even changing shape. He's known as a shape shifter and your dreams may contain confusing scenes of the roles he plays. Know that it is his intention.

The Trickster's role is to obstruct the hero's progress and to generally make trouble. In Norse mythology, many of the gods' adventures originate in some trick played on them by the half-god Loki. He is a symbol of transformation – an untamed and surprising energy.

As an agent of change, the Trickster makes things happen. His transformative quality when he appears as clown or jester makes us see those parts of ourselves we ridicule or that are a source of embarrassment.

In native American mythology the Trickster is sometimes represented by the coyote, and in character symbolises charm, deception, illusion, inquisitiveness and cunning. Just like a coyote or a fox, the Trickster is an outlaw, a rebel who also shows us those parts of ourselves that can't or won't be tamed.

Represented in the tarot cards as the Fool, a young man begins his journey and almost steps off the cliff as he looks up towards the sky. The Fool is numbered 0, the number of unlimited potential. It is a card of new beginnings, new journeys, uncharted territories and innocence. The archetype of the Fool indicates that anything can happen and the opportunities are just waiting to be taken advantage of. He's a free spirit and represents spontaneity and creativity longing for self-expression.

The negative characteristics of the Fool or Trickster archetype are foolishness, risk-taking and recklessness. Court jesters at times took things too far and created major political friction and disunity in royal courts. We're all aware that a practical joke gone wrong also has serious consequences. The Shadow archetype, the Joker in the Batman movies and comics, is a perfect example of the dark side of this archetypal energy.

How to work with Your Trickster Dreams

The Trickster/Fool offers light relief from tension. He's not controlled by societal boundaries and can step outside approval and conditioning, therefore he has freedom to express himself.

He manifests in our dreams when we should be serious and sensible and do the right thing, despite the fact that, even when we know we shouldn't, we would rather have fun and break a few rules. Laughter clears negative energies and gives us a sense of release that makes us feel both exposed and free.

It's risky to encourage the Trickster archetype, though, because you just know that when there is an oppression of energy around you it makes you feel you want to misbehave, which will inevitably be met with disapproval by the 'sensible' people around you or even by your own inner critic that keeps you in check.

The Trickster invites you to show your vulnerability – be free to act as silly as you want to be so that those parts of you that are under control and dominated can be liberated. Give up the seriousness. Surrendering may be a relief. However, if you are going to encourage the Trickster/ Fool into your waking life, make sure you've got the Wise Old Man around to check on him and not allow him to roam too far.

Questions to ask yourself if you dream of the Trickster/ Fool

- What lesson do you need to learn if you consider yourself a fool?
- Are rules working for you?
- Do you feel naïve and unsure as you begin your journey to self-growth?
- Would you like to take a few more risks and not take yourself too seriously? What's stopping you from doing this?

Some archetypes that appear in your dreams will come from ancient myths, legends and fairy tales, and reading these tales can be an important part of exploring those dreams that are 'mythic' in structure.

The Damsel in Distress/Princess

Dream images: a young woman, beautiful, needing rescue, qualities of innocence, vulnerability and purity.

A Damsel in Distress refers to a young woman who is beautiful, vulnerable and in need of rescue by a brave knight or prince and, once rescued, she will be thoroughly taken care of in style and comfort.

This traditional archetype promotes the view that women are weak, and teaches them to be helpless and in need of rescuing. It encourages the woman to expect to have someone who will fight her battles for her while she remains loyal and forever beautiful inside her lavish castle. The stereotype is still alive and well for many women who expect to marry a man who will give them a castle and take care of them. And men are encouraged and raised to expect to do just this.

The archetype resonates with both males and females even though it's considered a sexist view of both genders. We have a number of women today who could never be described as helpless, and yet the archetype still survives. And it inevitably results in disappointment for the women who do not fit into this mould.

For the Damsel, to learn to go it alone, fight her own battles, become empowered and be the hero of her own myth is the path to becoming self-aware and evolving into a queen.

Fairytales that glorify damsels in distress, such as Snow White, Sleeping Beauty, Rapunzel and Cinderella to name a few, continue to spread and promote this quality as being desirable in girls even today. Daddy's Little Princess is also a modern archetype of the Damsel in Distress, who represents purity, innocence and naïveté. It implies an adoring father who brings up his daughter surrounded by beauty and abundance. On the other hand, she can play the game of being manipulative to get what she wants without having to work for it herself, relying on her charms rather than her ability.

The Princess and the Damsel are both taught to be helpless and yearn for the knight in shining armour or the prince to sweep them off their feet. The implication of this is that without a knight or prince they are powerless.

How to work with your Damsel in Distress dreams

In reviewing your relationship to this archetype, return to your fantasies as a young girl and note what your expectations were in looking for a mate. Most significantly, take note of whether you were influenced by the stereotype of the Damsel and if this has changed for you with maturity and experience.

Questions to ask yourself if you dream of the Damsel in Distress

- In what situations do you think or behave like a Damsel?
- Are you hoping to be rescued from your current situation (either by a man or a sudden change of fortune)?
- If have experienced a broken relationship, are you able to recognise patterns of the Damsel in Distress/knight model?
- If you are you the knight in shining armour, are you sabotaging a potential relationship with a woman who has a healthy level of self-esteem and does not need or want rescuing?

The Hero/Heroine

> *Dream images: how we view ourselves in dreams with qualities such as being a defender, a rescuer, a champion, warrior or knight.*

The Hero/Heroine represents us, the ego (our conscious self), and is often engaged in fighting the Shadow, which may come in the form of dragons and other monsters. The Hero is often naïve and reluctant to begin with until he finds his purpose and is called to act. Luke Skywalker, in the *Star Wars* films, is the perfect example of such a hero.

When we dream of heroic acts we've performed in our dreams it shows how the Hero, our ego, has chosen to begin his own journey of self-exploration, which is expected to end in individuation – the process of reconciling the conscious/unconscious aspects of our psyche.

As a character, the Hero fulfils the necessary task or quest and restores harmony or justice to a community. He is the classical rescuer, the knight in shining armour, the valiant prince or ancient warrior hero who rescues the Damsel in Distress.

As part of his individuation, he rescues the maiden in order to reawaken and connect with his Anima. When he slays the dragon he's facing his Shadow self, which he needs to control and overpower before integrating that animalistic part of himself.

When the Hero conquers impending death or returns from a victorious battle it gives us hope for such things as life after death, release from suffering, peace and justice.

Think of modern comic book heroes – Superman, Wonder Woman, Batman, Captain Marvel and countless other characters we see on our television screens – who continue to perpetuate the Hero myth.

The Hero's journey/quest

The Hero's journey or quest requires the hero to encounter obstacles, hardships, villains, temptations and most of all danger. Joseph Campbell's work *The Hero With a Thousand Faces* describes the Hero's journey as our personal mythic journey in life. The Hero must successfully pass through several stages in his quest to accomplish something for the greater good.

> *'A hero ventures forth from the world of common day into a region of supernatural wonder: fabulous forces are there encountered and a decisive victory is won. The hero comes back from this mysterious adventure with the power to bestow boons on his fellow man.'*
>
> **– Joseph Campbell**

The three main stages of the Hero's journey are:

- separation
- initiation
- return

Briefly, the Hero's journey structure involves leaving the known world and being cut off from your roots; then you begin your adventure, and this is when you discover your deepest self. Through encounters and battles with obstacles and fears during the quest you will gain an understanding and acceptance of your heroic qualities. You then return to your old world, and bring back the prize or the victory to share with your community for the greater good.

This process is essential for our spiritual growth and development and it happens many times over in our lives. We step up and become our own heroes through adversity, by using our courage and relying on our intelligence so that we may come home, back to the Self, having grown in self-awareness.

One of the ways that we can connect with the mythic landscape of our psyche, be it a personal myth or the collective myth, is through our dreams.

Writing our story using myths and fairy tales

We've been exposed to fairy tales since we were young and therefore recognise archetypal figures that match those in our lives, even though they are a magnified version – our stepmother becomes the 'wicked' step-mother in Cinderella; the bully in the schoolyard morphs into the ogre from Jack and the Beanstalk.

Hidden within these stories are universal themes and archetypal patterns. We all have favourite fairy tales that tell us something important about ourselves and our view of the world. We love these fairy tales because they tell the story of our lives with all its complexities, and serve to reveal our heroic feats. They give us a glimpse into the collective unconscious and, if used wisely, can show us the way through obstacles and difficulties. Metaphorically, once we enter the forest we must find our own way; there is no map, and when we leave the forest we are no longer the same person who entered it.

What makes the strange and fascinating fairy tale plots and characters so appealing is that they are exaggerated versions of ourselves. The exaggeration and distortion is necessary for us to gain a greater sense of who we are and who we want/don't want to be. By magnifying the characters and narrative in fairy tales, we are less likely to miss the messages they present.

The process of writing down our life story in myth or fairy tale structure has a symbolic significance. It allows us to enter the archetypal patterns we are so familiar with and gives us the opportunity to use the power of story to gain greater clarity upon seeing our reflection in the mirror.

As a child, Mia used to dream of scenes from fairy tales where she was imprisoned in a castle like Rapunzel, held against her will like Beauty in *Beauty and the Beast*, and made to work hard like Cinderella.

> 'I would replay these scenes in waking life after my dreams and feel very much like a victim. I was being bullied at school since moving from another school, so I had the victim mentality well and truly implanted in my consciousness. For some reason, I decided to change these dream scenes in my waking state. I would replay the original and make some changes where I reinvented the story and added clever ways in which I could free myself from unpleasant situations.
>
> 'My dreams mirrored my new and improved version of my victim scenes. The Wise Old man appeared and pointed out where I could find the key out of the castle. The fox (Trickster) showed me how I could do tricks and disappear, and I found my twin brother (Animus), who threw me a rope to escape from the giant's dungeon.
>
> 'I now understand these archetypal symbols are all those qualities I have in me: Wise Old Man – my inner wisdom; fox – cunning and wit; twin brother (Animus) – my focus/action. It became clear that I could save myself and be my own Hero in my story.'

Mia

How to work with your Hero/Heroine dreams

Write your own myth – your life story from the perspective of being a character from a fairy tale, legend or myth. Notice the archetypal mythic structure and themes and who you most identify with. Some themes are:

- Little Red Riding Hood – danger/survival
- Cinderella – sibling rivalry/neglect
- Hansel and Gretel and Snow White – abandonment/abuse/survival

This exercise may filter through your dream world and possibly open the door to symbols and archetypal images that may assist you in understanding your life journey and explore ways in which you can become empowered to be your own hero.

Questions to ask yourself if you dream of the Hero/ Heroine

- Do you feel like you're your own hero?
- What must you do to become heroic in your own life circumstances?
- What qualities do you need to enable you to begin your journey that leads to greater self-awareness and growth?
- What stage of the Hero's journey are you at?

Overview of Archetypal Dreams and How to Use Them

Archetypal dreams are also referred to as 'mythic dreams' or 'big dreams' as we know they mostly occur at significant times or transitional periods in our lives. They are often vivid and intense, and you get the feeling that you've learnt something vital about your life and yourself. Jung believed that archetypal dreams carried healing energy, allowing us to change on an inner level – at our deepest core – which bypasses our logical mind. As the language of the subconscious mind is in symbols, when we are able to communicate to our unconscious using archetypal images, it enables us to make powerful changes in our waking lives.

When working with symbols and archetypes in dreams, Jung suggested we need to follow these guidelines:

1. The interpretation of a particular dream needs to be supported by the meaning of other dreams you've had previously with similar themes.

2. The dream has to have meaning for the dreamer.

3. The dream needs to have an effect on the dreamer and lead to results.

Archetypal or big dreams can give us a sense of empowerment by taking us beyond the everyday imagery our dreams usually present. If you believe that every archetype is an aspect of ourselves, then treat these dreams as gifts from your higher self. It demands effort to work through these breakthrough dreams, and the rewards may not be obvious immediately, but it's well worth it in the end.

CHAPTER 9

Death, Grief and Loss Dreams

'Grief does not change you… It reveals you.'
— **John Green**

GRIEF IS A transformative experience. The experience of grieving is some-times described as being disassembled and put back together again, but the end result is not quite the same. Some describe it as a sudden identity vacuum that comes with the loss of a loved one. Having dreams during grieving is an important part of the process of identity loss and confusion. If both parents die, for example, one is technically an orphan and is therefore no longer identified as having parents or being the child of those parents. The same applies to parents who've lost their children and who are no longer classified as parents. Married men or women become known as widowers and widows on official forms following the death of their spouse. Their identity and that one aspect of self, therefore, has changed dramatically.

In dreams, we internalise the people we've lost and loved by under-standing the role they played in our lives. Hence, we dream of a deceased grandmother when there's an issue in our life about family traditions or wise counselling is needed. A lost parent can come in our dreams when we need to take care of ourselves and self-parent. Their function of 'parenting' comes through our dream to give us that important message.

Visitation Dreams

Many recently bereaved people experience vivid and deeply meaningful dreams that feature the presence of the deceased. When we experience the death of a loved one, we are initially in the grieving stage and visitation dreams serve to connect us to their memory. The dreamer generally knows in the dream she or he is interacting with a person who has died. The deceased come into our dreams to inspire, guide, warn and advise and to remind us and tell us that they love us.

At a traditional Chinese funeral, a red thread is given to each attendee to be tied on their finger. It can be interpreted as honouring the dead person who they had a connection or shared part of their fate with by remembering them as being significant in their lives, knowing that the red thread may not be visible any more but it will never break.

As a death-dream experience, the red thread, the original umbilical cord that gave life, helps our loved ones find their way back to the source – the cosmos, God, the Great Mother – whatever that is for each of us. The well-known medium Edgar Cayce explained our connection to our deceased loved ones by saying the 'thread of love stretches beyond the grave'.

Types of Death Themes

Death themes in dreams can be classified into three types.

1. *Someone being killed or dying, the dreamer seeing their own death or being at their own funeral*

We may have these dreams when there are huge internal changes going on, and something needs to die or end so that the new self can emerge. It's basically the death of the old – patterns, beliefs, lifestyle, ideas, relationships, job – so that there can be a new beginning.

It is a symbolic death of something that needs to be released, discarded, cut away for there to be potential for a new self to be born or new opportunities to come into your life.

2. *Dreams prior to the dreamer's own death, or if you know someone is dying*

This dream visits us when we need help with our fears to move on from denial of our impending death to final acceptance. Some of the images that are common in these pre-death dreams are: reuniting with loved ones who are deceased, clocks that no longer work, candles lit or at low flame, sailing and other metaphorical and vivid images that have a luminous quality.

When Alex's mother was in a coma, he had this dream:

> *'In the dream, my mother is confused that their outside enter-*
> *tainment area with the decking, table, chairs and barbecue is*
> *no longer there. Instead it's been replaced with vibrant green*
> *grass. She can't understand why this has happened and is*
> *genuinely sad at the loss.'*
>
> **Alex**

In this dream scene, both the dreamer and the person in the dream (mother) were preparing for major changes. She passed away two weeks after her son's dream. When I asked him what the entertainment area represented to him he told me that it was the family hub, where everyone came together and socialised. The vibrantly green grass had Alex's attention because it was unnaturally green in colour – something that was yet to happen – a hologram, perhaps, of what was to come. A green field may have been an ancient symbol of life after death – the mythical Elysian Fields or Elysium, a beautiful meadow located in the Underworld as the home of the dead who were judged worthy.

The grass can also be understood as the carpet above the earth – that which covers our graves or ashes.

3. Visitation dream: dreaming about someone who has passed on

The parting vision or goodbye dreams are different from other dreams. Although they are partly a product of our grief in which we need to have some temporary release from the pain of loss, these dreams are messages from the departed sending us assurance and love.

Dream expert Gillian Holloway explains the basic structure of the goodbye and visitation dream that distinguishes it from other dreams:

• Realistic setting – usually in the dreamer's bedroom.

• Lacks a dreamlike plot. There is simply a message and no other action.

- Sensation of visitation and convincing elements. The dreamer felt that the dream experience was more real than any other dream and that there was no doubt it was the deceased.
- Impact on the dreamer. The visitation brought the dreamer comfort and clarity about decisions that had to be made.

The purpose of a visitation dream is to work through the grieving process at a subconscious level, releasing trauma, grief and overwhelming emotion that has not been externally expressed in waking life.

The focus of this chapter is on understanding the patterns of dreams that come to us during our grieving process, how they help us recover from the loss and come to terms with emotions that are yet to surface. When someone close to us dies, we begin a process of grieving that has its own time line – it can range from months to years. For some, it will always be there. Some people find ways to process their losses that are very helpful, and dream work can be particularly useful in bereavement. Without these outlets, some people experience prolonged grieving processes.

According to therapist Alan B. Siegel, 'Suffering a loss can become a transformative experience that leads to a deeper experience of meaning and purpose and a positive resolution of our relationship with the person who has died.' In our grieving process, dreams give us access to those emotions.

Dreams can provide us with insight and guidance during the most vulnerable times in our lives when our loved ones appear to us in dream visitations.

The five stages of grief

Just as there are stages of mourning in our waking lives, so there are stages of grieving the death of our loved ones in dreams. Elisabeth Kübler-Ross, in her pioneering book *On Death and Dying*, lists five stages of grief we mostly experience when facing our mortality or the death of a loved one.

They are: denial, anger, bargaining, depression and acceptance. These phases are guidelines, as we don't all go through them and they are not static or linear – they overlap and we move back and forth with these emotions.

Common Types of Grief and Loss Dreams

According to one dream study on death and visitation (University of North Carolina dream collection, Barrett, 1992), it was found that there were common types of grief and loss in visitation dreams.

Stage 1: *A few days or months after a person dies*

At this stage, the dreamer is amazed or distressed to see the deceased alive. There is a certain amount of denial of death during the actual grieving process going on at a conscious level. The dreamer's emotions are quite intense and vary from being a positive visitation to an upsetting episode upon realising that the person is actually dead.

Stage 2: *Several months after a person dies*

Dreams that arrive after several months involve the deceased person giving the dreamer advice, ranging from personal to trivial to very important. Usually the deceased appears at a time when the dreamer is under stress or making significant life choices.

Stage 3: *Several months to many years after a person dies*

This category fits under the 'resolution' dream theme, where the loved one explains the circumstances of their death and assures the dreamer that everything has worked out as it was meant to. It's usually a positive dream and brings relief to the dreamer – especially closure if there's been a feeling of guilt in waking life, such as final goodbyes if they did not happen in real life and if the person died of old age or illness. In this phase, the deceased are normally well and younger than their actual age when they passed away. The deceased may appear as an angel or ghost or from another realm, and there is a positive focus on their past relationship with the dreamer.

Stage 4: *Many years after the person has died*

It's less common, but this stage of dream grieving comes to the dreamer as a discussion about the nature of their own death with the deceased. It tends to occur if the deceased is a distant relative or someone not emotionally close to the dreamer. It may be that the dreamer is concerned about their own mortality, and by 'discussing' it rather philosophically or in a detached way with someone who has died it will help to ease their own anxieties of facing death.

Common Patterns in Visitation Dreams

Studies have been carried out on the effects and impact that visitation dreams have on the bereaved and their process of mourning. For most people, it is a positive experience in helping them cope better with their grief. Patricia Garfield, author of *The Dream Messenger: How Dreams of the Departed Bring Healing Gifts*, has studied over a thousand dreams about the dead. In her findings she discovered a pattern and that, similar to near-death experiences, visitation dreams have a number of elements in common. Not every dream about the dead contains all of these nine elements, but most dreams about the dead have several of them. They are:

1. the announcement
2. the arrival
3. the appearance, age, condition and clothing of the dream messenger
4. the attendants
5. the message
6. the gift
7. the farewell embrace
8. the departure
9. the aftermath.

In my experience with dream work, I've come across a number of clients who have experienced many of these dream elements. There was a great variation and many of the dream elements overlapped or were not relevant; however, I found it very useful to use a structured framework from Garfield's research to map out my personal experiences with my clients' dreams that involved visitations. The dreams in this section have been selected from my case studies of people who have experienced visitation dreams.

Getting ready to see your loved one

In Leah's dream, her deceased grandmother rang her on her mobile phone. Leah was surprised that her grandmother knew her phone number as she had died before she'd bought the mobile phone. In the phone conversation with her grandmother, Leah wanted to know why she'd called so early – at 3 o'clock in the morning – and how she got the number.

By the time she woke up she'd forgotten her grandmother's responses in the dream, other than that they had been reassuring and comforting. When she checked her mobile phone, there was a missed call at 3.01 am from a blocked number.

This is an interesting version of the announcement stage of a grief dream. Perhaps the mobile phone rang first and Leah made an association with her grandmother or the visitation dream coincided with the phone ringing. Some may even say that it was a connection from the spirit world – an ADC (after death connection). Ultimately, the emotional and healing experience of the dreamer is what's important. Leah felt the connection with her grandmother, which made her feel comforted.

In this type of visitation dream, we sense there's a kind of signal predicting an announcement that the deceased is going to show up. It may be a doorbell, knock, telephone, familiar sound or smell, opening door or even a light. This certainly feels like an old-fashioned announcement – like a stage announcement, or the use of fanfare, a bell or the local town crier announcing the arrival of a significant figure. When I discussed this theory with Leah, she agreed that it was a formal way to make an entrance, but perhaps it was done so the dreamer would be prepared, rather than seeing the departed without warning as an apparition. Our psyche does need preparation if we are to be confronted with someone we've lost and had an emotional connection with. The announcement, therefore, is a way to prepare for the dream message from the departed messenger.

The visit

> *My mother loved the beach and I have fond memories of her putting on her swimming cap and goggles and swimming in the ocean. It wasn't such a big surprise to see her visit me in my dreams in a beach setting after her passing – the very same one*

*where we used to go swimming in summer when I was a child
and a teen. She smiled at me, waved and took a swim.'*

Jack

It was comforting for my client Jack to see his mother in a familiar setting,
as it reinforced his memory of her when she was younger and healthy. A
number of people dream of their loved ones in the hospital rooms where
they last saw them or by their bedside at home, sitting at the edge of the
bed. One of my clients dreamt of her mother in the hairdressing salon
where they worked together. It seemed natural that they should meet in
the place they both spent so much time together.

The visitor, however, can also appear in a new setting, as if to make a
statement that they are no longer sharing the same physical space as the
dreamer. It's also common for these encounters to take place in settings
that have to do with transportation, such as train stations, on a bus or
boat and other such places that denote that sense of transition. This
seems to make it easier, at a conscious level, for the dreamer to accept
the reality that the person has 'crossed over', 'departed', 'passed on', 'got
a one-way ticket' and other such euphemisms that convey the message
that they have journeyed on to their death.

Appearance of the deceased

You almost always recognise the image of the dead person in your dream
visitation. Most dreamers tell me that if their loved one was old or ill
when they passed away, in dreams they appear younger and healthy – the
way the dreamer would have remembered them when they were at their
best before their decline. One of my clients told me about this change in
appearance: 'My mum just died a year ago and recently I dreamed of her
being in hospital looking healthy and smiling, instead of how she really
looked when she passed away from cancer.'

If the deceased is very young, however, dreamers often meet them
looking older. Karen dreamt of her stillborn son growing into manhood.
He would visit her in dreams at different stages of his development – as
an infant, a young child, a teenager and a grown man.

She felt a surge of pride and comfort at knowing he was still 'growing'
in the spirit life. 'I loved seeing how he grew and was able to talk and

discuss all sorts of things. He would now be twenty-eight years old and when he came in his last visitation he was giving me advice on investments. My, how he's grown up.'

For Karen, this was a comforting dream. However, it could also be confronting for the dreamer if they have not yet fully dealt with their grieving stages.

Some common characteristics of the dream visitor include:

• They may appear to have aged, or be more ill than when they died.

• They may be young and vibrant. The old usually appear younger and fitter and children may appear older, as if they have grown in their years.

• Their condition is much improved, with no illness or disability that contributed to their passing.

• There is a radiance and luminosity in clothing, and light around them.

There are times, however, when the dream visitor comes in disguise. He or she may appear to be anything or anyone – whether it's a stranger or an animal, but the dreamer almost always 'knows' who it is.

Before her grandmother passed away, she told Angie that she would have an old-fashioned romance and marry someone like her uncle – a decent, honest man who worked hard and was a country boy. Recently Angie dreamt of a wolf dressed in pink. She also dreamt of a pink house that looked a great deal like her grandmother's.

'I'm sure it was my grandmother in my dreams,' she told me. 'She always liked to read me Little Red Riding Hood and take me to the play. I have found the exact house for sale near where I've met someone I'm romantically interested in. I think it's her way of telling me this is the old-fashioned romance and I should settle down.'

There are other clues that are familiar to only the dreamer and the visitor, but even smells (such as perfume) or flowers from the deceased's garden, cigarette smoke or other objects can help to identify the deceased.

Other figures in the visitation dream

Dreamers have expressed their surprise when the deceased does not come alone in visitation dreams. They can be accompanied by other figures (the attendants).

My client Ellen once said to me, 'I've had several dreams of people a couple of days before they died. This occurred after my dad's passing. He was always in the dream with these people, like he was some sort of minder or assistant or even the third party, speaking on their behalf.'

When I asked Ellen how she felt about these dream visitations and the role her father played, she replied, 'It's typical of him. He's continuing to be the protector and guide in the other world. He was the type of person people easily gravitated to for advice and guidance on anything.' This dream was a confirmation for her that her father was 'still himself' and that her connection to him was still available.

Attendants or other figures can include not only other family members who have died, but also shadow characters. It is suggested that this shadowy character that has no definite features could represent death to the dreamer.

If you see other characters in your visitation dream, look at their facial expressions, how old they are, their clothing and other mannerisms. Are they menacing? Elegant? Dark? Ragged? All of these symbols may indicate your feelings around the theme of death and how you are coping with your grief.

Messages

Messages from the dead can be delivered in dreams in various ways, such as in spoken words, telepathically, by phone or letter, via email or through a computer screen. Generally, most messages are given in person. However, phone communication is also very common.

'I dream often that my grandmother rings me and we speak on the phone,' one of my clients informs me. 'But a lot of the time she rings and I'm so happy, but by the time I answer it she's not there.'

In many instances the dreamer may hear a phone ringing, and when they answer it the deceased gives them a short message. Sometimes the messages may not make sense or be clear. In my conversations with people who've had this dream they express a sense of relief in being able to connect with someone they've lost, especially if they'd not had an opportunity to say their final goodbye due to the deceased being in a coma or suffering a sudden death. However, if the communication was not clear, the messenger's voice was distorted or they sounded distant, it added to the dreamer's sense of loss and grief. In some cases, the dreamer consciously made efforts not to dream at all in case the dream turned into a recurring nightmare.

Common statements

It's common to receive a message such as 'I'm suffering' from your loved one, however, it's distressing for the dreamer to hear it. If you have seen your loved one suffering, these words may be a reflection of how you perceived their prolonged illness.

One of the most frustrating visitation dreams is when the visitor insists that they are not really dead, or you see the person who has died but their death is described as a mistake. They may be doing what they normally do in real life, as if they were still alive. Garfield's research indicates that this visitation dream comes in the early stages of grief when the dreamer has not yet accepted the death and it may cause them to be pleasantly surprised or angered to see the dead in this dream.

A woman once wrote to me and said she felt a sense of guilt dreaming about her father being alive in her dreams. She was aware that he was dead and he should not be in her dream sitting at the kitchen table reading the newspaper as if he were still alive. 'I loved seeing him but on one level I knew he should not have been there.'

I suggested that the dream was highlighting something unresolved in the dreamer's relationship to this death. When delving further, she admitted that she lived far away and felt guilty for neglecting her father when he needed her the most. The words 'should have been there' were, in actual fact, referring to her absence before his death, not to him appearing in her dream.

In most visitation dreams the deceased reassures the dreamer that they are fine where they are. The typical dream messages are 'I'm okay', 'Don't worry about me', 'Everything is fine', 'I'm happy', 'I love you'. To prove their point, the majority of time the visitor looks happy and healthy.

Nadia's son died of a serious bacterial disease. He visits her regularly in her dreams, looking as he did before he got sick – fit, young, healthy and energetic. 'He tells me to stop worrying about him; that he's all right. Then he starts to give me advice as to what I should do in various aspects of my life that come up. This dream makes me feel so connected to him. It leaves me feeling positive and he always confirms what in my gut I know I should do.'

Usually when a death has taken place at a distance from the dreamer or a death is sudden, the visitation dream can include physical contact and an affectionate goodbye. To hear a loved one saying 'Goodbye' may give the dreamer a sense of closure and help them with their grieving process. For others, the finality may cause them great distress. It's important to be aware that everyone's response is unique and there is not a right or a wrong way to process grief. Visitation dreams can either assist the bereaved to move on or amplify their sense of loss.

Warnings

I've often had people ask me what it meant when they dreamt of dead people giving them a warning about a potential danger. My answer has consistently been that I take the dream at face value. As a starting point I assume the dream to be true and then follow the advice as best I can.

Some would argue that it's our subconscious mind that has been alerted to the fact that something may not be right or there's a reasonable level of risk. During the day, our conscious minds are too busy to notice the subtle things that fly under the radar and don't scream for our attention, and in our dreams we release these concerns that are then projected as a loved one protecting us. Regardless of how you interpret a warning dream, it's sensible to avert potential risk by heeding it initially, and if it doesn't eventuate into anything serious then look at the symbolic interpretation.

Some have experienced receiving a gift from the deceased in the visitation dream. It may be a special something that only the dreamer understands and appreciates what it represents to them. It can even be in the form of comforting words. Whatever it is for the dreamer, it is generally a positive visitation dream that is usually vividly remembered.

Saying goodbye

'I saw my deceased mother and I was so delighted to see her. I felt her giving me a strong hug – this was a real physical presence. I was sad on waking but also comforted.'

I've had many clients express great happiness when they've experienced a farewell embrace dream such as this one. When you dream of one last hug, kiss or embrace as a farewell, it may be an encounter that gives you joy and comfort. This is the general reaction, however, every dream has a different quality and every dreamer will have an individual response. One may not yet be ready for the final embrace, as the finality may cause further grief.

In Jane's visitation dream, she felt the messenger's sense of urgency to leave quickly. In this dream element, the deceased has to leave immediately after relaying the message.

'I dreamt my departed grandmother was walking with my uncle, who had just died. She was taking him on a paved path and was in a hurry. I quickly caught up and greeted her. Without wasting any time on pleasantries, she said, "The power is in your hands. Whatever you choose to do with your new life is the right choice." Then she quickly left – like she had only a limited time to spend with me. All I could think of was that I could make or break my new relationship and that if I chose to remarry then it was the right choice.'

Interestingly, the abruptness and brevity of the visit reflected Jane's time limitation in her real-life situation – she had to make a choice and there was no more time to waste deliberating the options. The dream message highlighted her course of action.

After the visitation dream

What happens after the visit and after the loved one leaves varies greatly from person to person. The dreamer may experience many emotions from happy and relieved, the emotional pain gone, to euphoric and a great wave of feeling loved. The essence is that the dreamer begins to feel that they can move on with their lives. That's the ideal outcome, but there is no guarantee of this being true for everyone.

Both of the following dreamers in a dream group I guided described their visitation dreams as being a healing experience, which offered them insight and closure.

'About ten years ago my aunt died. She'd been in hospital and we knew she wasn't coming home. Both she and my uncle – who was still living at that point but very ill in hospital – came to me in a vivid dream in really bright colour. They were much younger, forties or so, and they were cuddling up next to each other on a couch. My uncle was wearing tennis

whites and runners and he had thick black wavy hair. My aunt was youthful and pretty. They were smiling broadly and telling me how happy they were. It was a lovely dream.

'Ten minutes after I woke up I got a call from another relative to tell me that my aunt had passed away during the night. I wasn't really surprised and I was so happy she was able to reach me, but what about my uncle who I dreamed was with her? A week later I went to visit him in hospital where he had fallen into a coma. I whispered to him that he should go, that my aunt had shown me how happy she was – how happy they both were – and it was time to join her. He died peacefully the very next day.'

Sharon

And this one from Rachel:

'I had some difficulties surrounding my grandmother's death and funeral, and for many years kept dreaming about her funeral. Different scenarios. The last one, which must've been the resolution dream, I was riding to her funeral on a horse and carriage.'

Rachel

To the dreamer, this final recurring dream became a resolution in that she finally came to terms with the circumstances that surrounded her grandmother's death and funeral – and her own emotions. By attending the funeral in an old-fashioned horse and carriage, she has overcome past events around her grandmother and her death.

Resolving Loss

In dreaming of the death of a grandparent, parent or our first major family death-related loss, our grieving is influenced by what our relationship was with that person and how we've coped with losses generally in the past. With a parent's loss, we lose that sense of security that they will be here to protect us and be our emotional and financial anchor. Eldest children tend to come to terms with their own mortality at this time, as they consider themselves likely to be 'next' in the family to face death, following their parents.

Alan B. Siegel, dream therapist, suggests that to grieve our parents we must 'learn to cherish the memory of what our parents gave us. We must also learn to heal wounds from occasions when they failed us by not giving us the quality of empathy, attention and love that we needed.'

Losing a child is one of the most traumatic and painful experiences – and one that every parent fears the most. In cases of an infant's death or a stillborn, the parents can experience 'searching for my baby' dreams immediately after a baby's death. This recurring dream only stops after there is an acceptance of the loss and that the child will not return.

After the death of any child, whether it's a miscarriage, infant or older child, both parents can experience dreams with themes of guilt and self-reproach. Emotional wounds heal slowly and dreams are a way of 'checking in', like an emotional compass, to see what's going on at a subconscious level and inform us about whether we are healing emotionally in our waking life.

When dreams come

In past eras, mourners would sleep on the grave of their loved ones in the hope that they would dream of them. Some would have a 'relic' that they would keep beside their bed in order to induce a visitation dream. It's best to be open to receive whatever dream comes – even if it's painful or distressing.

Marianne had nightly dreams of her recently dead husband that became too painful to remember. In a visitation dream she told him to stop coming into her dreams. And he did. And so her memory of her dreams stopped as well:

> *'I missed him so much it was agony to see him in my dreams.*
> *My subconscious then blocked off all dreams from my memory,*
> *so I could not experience remembering any dream. And I miss*
> *dreaming. Now that I realise this is what happened I am*
> *going to put into practice ways to be open up to any dream,*
> *however painful it may be.'*

Marianne

Grieving for Our Pets

When our pets pass away, we experience grief in the same way we would for a close friend or family. We form attachments to our companion animals that fill vital emotional needs that aren't met by human relationships. Our pets provide us with companionship and loyalty, and comfort in times of need.

Seeing our deceased pets in dreams is common in times when we are experiencing changes and upheavals in our lives, when our love for our pets is triggered by seeing a similar animal or a very young animal or at any time we are in need of companionship. Most visitation dreams are reassuring and positive. Some may be disturbing if the pet has been accidentally killed and there's an element of guilt on the dreamer's part.

It's important to allow yourself to follow a grieving process just as you would for a friend or family member and give yourself time to resolve your loss.

If you dream of your pet, it can often represent that part of yourself that needs special attention – in other words, what parts of you need unconditional love? Your pet may also be acting as an animal guide to 'show' you what aspects of yourself you have been neglecting or need to embrace. For example, I see my dog as 'happiness on legs' and 'unconditional love'.

Celebrating the Dead

In autumn, leaves fall and we begin to turn inwards, remembering our fallen loved ones with whom we long to be reunited or communicate with. Personally, I have found myself dreaming more of my losses at this time. As there is more darkness and we are sleeping more, we are able to induce dreams perhaps a little more easily.

It's the season when the nights are longer and, according to ancient lore, the walls are thin between the worlds, especially the Underworld – where the departed rest. In the northern hemisphere we have rituals that take place during the season of autumn that commemorate the dead, such as Halloween, All Souls' Day, All Saints' Day, Day of the Dead (Dia de los Muertos), Samhain and other days that celebrate the lives of those we've lost.

Chinese and Vietnamese traditions include a month of honouring the departed with hungry ghosts celebrations.

In celebrations such as Dia de los Muertos and hungry ghosts, food and drink are a way to feed the memory of the dead so that they will not feel neglected and not haunt their earthly family or home.

The hungry ghost festival begins in the seventh month of the Chinese calendar and is celebrated with a parade with decorated lanterns, which are then carried to the water, lit and released. The glowing lanterns and boats are meant to give directions to lost souls and help ghosts find their way to the food offerings. Special food, flowers and candles are offered to ancestors on altars. Other offerings are made to 'feed the ghosts without relatives' that are said to have been released from hell for the month and are free to roam the earth, where they seek food and fun. These ghosts are believed to be ancestors of those who forgot to pay tribute to them after they died, or those who were never given a proper ritual funeral. Other activities include burning incense and burning joss paper, and other fine goods for the visiting spirits of the ancestors. Elaborate meals are served for everyone to share, with empty seats for each of the deceased in the family, treating the deceased as if they are still living.

El Dia de los Muertos (the Day of the Dead) is a Mexican celebration when special foods are prepared and joyful activities held in honour of those who have parted. Streets near cemeteries are filled with decorations, flowers, candy *calaveras* (skeletons and skulls) and parades of dancing and music. Mexicans believe that the spirit of the dead visit their families on 31 October and leave on 2 November and, as during the hungry ghosts festival, families make altars and place offerings to the dead relatives. It is important that a photo of the deceased is placed on the altar along with yellow marigolds, bread baked in shapes of skulls, incense and candles. The point of the celebration is to mock death, as it is an inevitable event.

Funerals, other deaths, anniversaries, birthdays and special occasions are often triggers for dreaming of a deceased loved one. Be prepared for a possible visitation dream. If you receive a dream message ask yourself what your answer would be, for example, 'Be at peace', 'I love you too', and in this way you bring it to consciousness and complete the cycle.

Healing Through Visitation Dreams

There have been many controversies regarding the importance of whether or not these visitations or lucid visions of the dying are real and whether there is indeed life after death. The images may simply have been conjured up by the dreamer to cope with their bereavement or they may be real encounters.

Elisabeth Kübler-Ross calls dreams 'true contacts on a spiritual plane'.

It's not about whether this spiritual connection is real or not, but what's been shared collectively and the ways in which people have been transformed through this dream experience. It's the personal meaning that's most important of all. Generally, visitation dreams can have a healing effect on our lives and offer comfort. For some these dreams take on more of a nightmarish quality, especially those who've experienced the violent or sudden death of a loved one or watched them decline in a painful state. In these cases, there is unfinished business that has left the dreamer feeling unable to have closure, which in turn has left them feeling a sense of hopelessness.

Working with these dreams can help lead a grieving person through their journey toward healing.

Some ways to work with grief dreams

- As you work with your own visitation dreams, check in with your emotions.

- If you struggle to communicate with the deceased, are you expressing unresolved feelings of anger, grief or guilt?

- How has grief affected you – are you in denial, are you suffering depression, anti-social behaviour or becoming addicted to substances for relief?

- You may have memories of past losses you've experienced, such as earlier deaths, and these may surface at this time. Acknowledge your feelings – and if you experience signs of numbness, depression, loneliness and addictive habits make others aware of this and seek help if you need it.

- Share your dreams with people you trust and ask for support if the dream has been upsetting for you. Always seek help if you are feeling overwhelmed with grief.

- Record your dreams. Write and/or sketch your dreams in a journal.

- Work with your emotions that come up in the dream, especially in cases where there has not been closure.

- Don't expect to understand all the dream symbols and messages. It may take some time and patience to work out what it means to you. You are the only expert on your dream.

- If you can't remember a visitation dream but know that you've had one, try sitting quietly at different times during the day – early morning or sunset – and look around in nature for signs to trigger some of the dream. It may be that a stray cat wanders by your letterbox as you collect the mail and the colour or the shape of the cat will jolt a memory of what your loved one did or looked like in your dream.

- Most importantly, grief is a process that demands its own time. Know that the dreams we have during our grieving time allow us to resolve our loss and help give meaning to our suffering. If you allow yourself the chance to feel grief for as long as you need to, you will be guided by it. The gift you receive from grief is that it allows you to become someone it would have been impossible for you to become otherwise. As a result, your loved one will live on in your dreams – and inside your heart.

CHAPTER 10

Spiritual and Para-psychological Dreams

'By healing themselves, each generation heals their ancestors.'
– Mapping the Healing Journey, 2002

OCCASIONALLY WE ARE privileged to receive the sort of dream experience Jung described as a 'big' dream. They are known as numinous dreams – dreams that have a strong spiritual quality and move us beyond our everyday experiences. They propel us into the spiritual realm as they invite us to be in the presence of divinity with the purpose of enlightenment. To make sense of them at a logical level would be to devalue their message – sometimes the inner knowing and sense of connecting to a higher source that the dream sends us is a gift in itself.

The best way to work with these dreams is to gain insights from the spiritual teachings they offer and accept divine guidance for healing and wisdom in your life.

As we each hold the truth within and listen to our intuition speaking directly through our soul, we connect with dreams from a spiritual realm, the very same place through which our ancestors accessed their wisdom.

Classical Greek mythology talks about the process by which souls choose their new lives – in other words, are reincarnated. After initial rites, they must drink from Lethe, the River of Forgetfulness, so that they will forget all the things they've chosen as new souls for their new life that's awaiting them. The belief was that before we reincarnate we have to forget all our previous life/lives so that we can start a new life again as a baby. Once asleep, the souls are carried upwards towards the heavens like shooting stars on their journey to be reborn.

Just like our mythical ancestors, we are made of stardust – which scientists call atoms and molecules. Through our dreams we can find threads or memories of who we used to be at the beginning of time. Our dreams act to wake us up.

The Science of Time

There are a number of people who believe in reincarnation, explained as the process in which we return to the living in a new body over and over until we have learnt our lessons. In between reincarnations we pre-plan the conditions for the next life so that we have the best chance of learning the lessons. Perhaps we get glimpses of this pre-plan through our dreams or during meditation when we are not distracted by our physical body's needs, and therefore can access this unconscious part of ourselves.

Quantum physics explores the nature of reality and time – an electron can be in two places at once, for example – and we are made up of countless electrons. Can we pick up information from our dreams that has no obvious physical source? Science is catching up to non-scientific knowledge from sources such as indigenous and mystic beliefs about the nature of time – that it is not linear or constant and that all time is happening at once.

The great Albert Einstein stated, 'People like us, who believe in Physics, know that the distinction between past, present and future is only a stubbornly persistent illusion.' If this is true then why shouldn't we have memories of the future as well as the past?

Dreams and Waking Up

When your dreams are of a spiritual nature, your altered state within your dreaming can be seen as if you've woken up finally and that your real life is the dream, not the other way round. To 'live your dream', then, takes on a whole new meaning. Those who experience vivid and profound dreams are often more engaged with their life during those dreams.

The concept that this world is actually a dream, and reality is some-where else, is an ancient one. The oldest Hindu scriptures, the Vedas, suggest that we are reincarnated back into this world, which is a dream, and after breaking the cycle of reincarnation ('waking up') from this dreamworld we gain knowledge/completion.

Indigenous people, including shamans, also known as earth-keepers, believe that we are dreaming our world into being. Author and shaman Alberto Villoldo teaches that, 'Shamans live in a world where the Creator is not separate from the Creation, Heaven is not separate from Earth, and Spirit and matter infuse each other. There is no division between the body and the spirit, nor between the visible world of form and the invisible world of energy.'

This concept is especially true of the Dreaming in Australian Aboriginal culture, where time and space exist simultaneously without separation. Stories of their culture – passed down through generations – are interwoven and inseparable with the indigenous land or 'country'.

Villoldo explains the Dreaming tradition as that which 'infuses all matter and energy, connecting every creature, every rock, every star and every ray of light or bit of cosmic dust. The power to dream is the power to participate in creation itself.'

It's important that we understand the spiritual beginnings of dreams and the connection with the Dreaming. It's a way of bridging the two worlds of waking and dreaming – between the multidimensional reality of dreaming and everyday waking reality.

To receive the many gifts that these heightened dream states can bring to us, we have to go back to the beginning to make some sense of it – at least at a soul or subconscious level – in order for us to participate in them willingly and/or fearlessly.

The Dreaming Explained

The Dreaming in Australian Aboriginal culture does not relate directly to 'dreaming' as we know it, but rather to indigenous belief about how all things come into creation. In the Aboriginal culture, the world was created in the Dreamtime. What is referred to as the 'Dreaming' are stories owned by different indigenous groups and their people that explain the creation of life – humans and animals – from the Dreamtime and which feature greatly in their spiritual lives. However, the 'Dreaming' can also be experienced while actually dreaming.

The Dreaming

Indigenous Australian Elizabeth Russell-Arnot explains the term 'Dreaming' simply yet evocatively in its original context:

'Imagine, if you can, that each and every thing that exists is made of the material that came from the stars before the earth was born. The earth was born of that material.

'Now imagine that each and every particle in existence has a component or characteristic that imbues it with the memory of each and every event in its existence.

'Now imagine that each and every particle in existence has their characteristics given to them by the particles of which they are made, which also includes the memories of actions and events, feelings, emotions and natural law.

'Even the rocks had an animate life prior to their existence as an inanimate being, and the memories of great eons of time are locked into their being. This is why they are revered by so many traditional societies. They are visible evidence of such ancient connections to existence and contain memories of incredible events.

'Animate beings also carry the memories of their ancestors and the memories of all ancestral beings right back to the star times, when we were particles of dust, light and gas.

'When we talk about the Dreaming, we talk about our ability to understand and be in touch with the memories of our ancestors that live within the very fabric of our being. The stories of the Dreaming are written on our DNA. Yours and mine and all beings that exist, both animate and inanimate. We are all related. Joined together by the star memories to which so many of us still respond.

'If we are truthful to ourselves and to all things, the pathway to hearing and understanding these memories within ourselves is clear and we are able to hear the voices of our ancestors.

'We can often, when tired or ill, when dreaming or hallucinating, have these ancestral memories revealed to us. We wake feeling as if we have had a real-life experience, bringing with us to the waking world memories which are new and yet very real. Listen to the ancestral voices. They are real and know all things that need to be known.'

Soul Retrieval/Medicine Dreams

The shamans of the Iroquois nations were powerful dreamers and had the capacity to interpret dreams and use them as medicine to bring healing to the dreamer. In the shamanic tradition, dreaming is the link or bridge between matter and spirit. If someone is physically ill, it is because they are experiencing an inner conflict. The shaman would use drumming, chanting and special herbs to allow the sick person to enter an altered state – like we do when we are lucid dreaming – and retrieve parts of the soul the person had forgotten or rejected.

This was a means through which, once remembered, these 'parts' could be reintegrated into the person and used in waking life, resulting in healing. This was the shaman's medicine. Like Jung's Shadow dream work, all parts of ourselves must be integrated for wholeness. This 'forgetting' that we are inextricably linked though our collective unconscious is a theme that goes back to our indigenous ancestors.

How Do You Recognise Spiritual Dreams?

So, how do we recognise spiritual dreams? Often it depends on your own belief system and what spiritual significance the dream has for you. Ancestors, our departed loved ones, totem animals, characters from past lives all come through in numinous dreams as guides. For some, religious figures such as Jesus, Buddha, Mother Mary, angels or other god-like or divine entities may appear in spiritual dreams in times when comfort is needed.

Other dreamers experience a deep spiritual truth about themselves through a sound or a feeling of expansion. Symbols such as a white or golden light, other dimensions, colours or geometric shapes are common.

Whatever way these dreams reveal themselves to you, you will know you've had a spiritual dream because there is an inner knowing that this dream was different. It moved you and had more intensity than a normal dream. Numinous dreams have a quality of moving people to joy or to experiencing a deep sense of compassion and other emotions. That's why it's called a 'big' dream.

The third dimension

It is believed that we live in what is called the third dimension. The astral plane and out-of-body experiences are in the fifth dimension. There are other dimensions within the astral planes and general dimensions outside of that plane, but these are for the highly evolved.

OBEs occur when the non-physical parts of us leave the physical body and the third dimension and go to a different dimension, such as the fifth. This travel is said to take place in dreams, in astral projection, in near-death experiences and at death.

Psychic Dreaming

After the terrorist attacks on the World Trade Center (September 11, 2001), a number of people came forward claiming they'd had vivid dreams of the disaster in advance. Up to days before the 9/11 disaster, there were also significant reports on the internet of precognitive dreams and premonitions of the horrific events that were to occur. Numerous people reported vivid dreams of this disaster with images of planes crashing into buildings, on the ground, city buildings collapsing and on fire, feelings of terror and death. Many dreamers woke up in terror during this nightmare that was to become reality. Why didn't people report it? Nobody knew for sure the actual details of the dream as it related to waking life. The where/why/what/who/how were not specific enough in the dream for it to be a warning for authorities.

One of my clients reported that her five year old kept having nightmares of planes crashing and bursting into flames only weeks prior to the tragedy. After September 11, internet websites and discussion lists were established in order to help people record precognitive dreams and tips on how to 'tune in' to possible disasters.

Research into dreams collected around major natural events or disasters has found that a number of people 'tune in' to a future event in their dreams. Some may dream the actual event, while others dream important elements of it or have a 'feeling' about the outcome of the event.

When a disaster of this magnitude affects so many and collectively people dream of it beforehand, it makes us wonder how we can predict future events. Most people who have precognitive dreams only realise after the event that they had experienced a prophetic dream. The details are often not accurate enough to be able to know exactly how and when the event will happen, although many of these dreamers just 'know' that something terrible is going to happen in the near future.

It is likely that whatever is picked up by the collective dreaming mind is not bound by time, place or space. How is it that globally we participate in this web of consciousness that connects us all through our dreaming?

Famous prophetic dreams

American president Abraham Lincoln dreamt of his own corpse laid out in a room in the White House a few days before his assassination.

I have had only a few precognitive dreams and they've remained with me because of their intensity. Twice I have dreamt of earthquakes, only to discover the next morning that they have actually occurred in certain parts of the world. I have either seen a number such as 4.2 or later made a connection to a tremor scale or I've seen bridges and roads move.

Precognitive Dreams

Dreamers who experience precognitive or warning dreams pay attention to their dreams when they involve tragedy or disaster as they are more vivid and dramatic. What about smaller precognition we call déjà vu? Many people claim to have experienced déjà vu from their dreams 'recognising' people and places from their dreams. According to dream researcher Gillian Holloway, these dreams are 'future snapshots' in which 'the dreaming mind tends to borrow imagery from a day or two into the future as easily as it does from a day or two in your past'.

Studies suggest that we are more likely to experience para-psychological visions and precognition in dreams rather than in waking life. Researchers who have collected and studied dreams around major global events have discovered that many people 'tune in' to a future event in their dreams. Interestingly some people dream of the actual event as it happens, and others recall only the most important part of the dream or simply the prominent emotion.

On 21 October 1966, a landslide of coal came down a mountain in Aberfan, Wales and buried a school, killing 144 people; 116 were children. Just weeks before it happened hundreds of people experienced a premonition about the disaster, both in their conscious life and in their dreams. The dreams were not specific to the location, but there were sensations of choking, children screaming and ominous coal dust clouds.

Is this similar to Jung's idea of the collective unconscious? Is there a global net of consciousness at work? We have yet to know for sure, but something was picked up by the dreaming mind worldwide as a collection of people from all walks of life and cultures dreamt of this disaster now imprinted on our psyche.

Research is still being carried out on how to make these premonitions and precognitive dreams helpful in predicting natural and man-made events.

Dream Sharing

Thousands of people report having an identical dream at the same time as someone close to them. Dream sharing is very common among spouses, siblings, friends, parents and children. They all have an ability to 'tune in' as they are emotionally connected.

Anne from our dream group recalls a synchronised dream that was a combination of a precognitive and sharing dream:

> *'This is the most clear and vivid synchronised dream that I ever encountered. I was sleeping with my approximately 8–10 year-old daughter at the time, in my bed. It was morning time, ready for awakening for the day. I was disturbed in my*

sleep and felt myself roused by the turmoil. I was witnessing a mass cull in an ocean setting in a cove, blood was filling the waters and the sound was so excruciating: fear, threat, pain, death, distrust and chaos.

'My daughter woke me with her crying and calling out, "No, don't, don't kill them!" Our heads were touching (my right temple on her left temple) and she was totally immersed in her dream happening as I realised she was still asleep. When I asked her what she was dreaming of, she told me of her dream with tears in her eyes and streaming down her face.

'She told me of men in boats, rounding up the dolphins in this area as there were too many of them for the locals' liking. She saw them feeding them and drawing them into this closed-off section of the water with nets, near a shoreline where most people couldn't see. She told me as they got the dolphins closer to the shore that they began shooting at them and the waters turned to blood and bubbles as they were trying to escape.

'To my total shock and horror, this was a reality, prophetically played out in our dream states. A week or two later there was a wildlife report about the mass culling of dolphin pods near an island setting in a cove, generally out of sight to the public, however this was filmed and broadcast on national television. We instantly recognised the cove, the boats and the culling when aired – it was revealed that this was an annual event and there was a documentary made of it to bring awareness to the practice.'

Anne

Memorable and highly dramatic dreams with a deep emotional component indicate that you may be experiencing psychic dreaming. Record your dreams and all precognitive dream incidents, and learn to recognise a pattern. If there is some premonition in your dream warning you about your safety or that of your family, always err on the side of caution and take relevant measures to keep yourself safe.

Lucid Dreaming

Lucid dreaming is knowing that you are dreaming while you are dreaming, also known as conscious dreaming. It's being awake and dreaming at the same time. This odd state of awareness is best described as being aware that your body is lying on the bed, aware of the contents of the dream and aware of watching yourself dream. This process moves back and forth and sometimes you get so caught up in the action of the dream that you forget you are dreaming. (See also Chapter 13 – Practical Dream Work.)

The shamans understand the lucid state as it is their doorway into the dreamworlds through which they make their ecstatic journeys, in dreamscapes created and mapped by previous dream travellers.

In lucid dreaming one must value the dream to participate actively in holding the awareness while dreaming. Active lucid dreamers are those who value and pay attention to their dreams over a long period of time, recording each dream and its insight.

With practice, you can usually prime yourself up for lucid dreaming before drifting off to sleep. Remind yourself during waking hours that the dream world is no more a dream than your waking world is. Your subconscious mind will program this in so that you will manage to have lucid dreams and, with practice, astral travel.

An active dreamer, Kirsty, explained how she managed to lucid dream successfully:

> 'I actively ask a specific question before I go to sleep. I program the question or the thought so that I will receive guidance or a message through the dimension of dreaming. I do this through holding the belief that I will receive the message, clarity, guidance I am seeking.
>
> 'I sometimes imagine that I have already been given the dream and assume this as a feeling of peace within my body that I have arrived at a resolution or an understanding.
>
> 'Often because my conscious mind is out of the way I am able to perceive situations and relationships with greater scope and far less judgement through dreaming and this is why I use it as a tool of great value. When I am dreaming I

am holding the awareness that I am now being shown what it is that I asked for.'

Kirsty

Obviously a lucid dream feels much more alive and real than other dreams. This is also the case in astral projection and OBEs (out of body experiences).

'I've had dreams of flying above myself, looking down and then being aware I'm not able to move. My body is locked up. Then I felt my soul drift out of my body up toward the ceiling. I didn't know it was my soul until I turned around while I was drifting up and saw my body lying on the floor below me. It was terrifying that I could not return to my body. A minute later I was able to wiggle my big toe and my soul came crashing back down into my body.'

Kathy

Out-of-body Experiences

Out-of-body contacts (OBCs) and out-of-body experiences (OBEs) happen while you are asleep or in a deep meditative state. For some, they can be extraordinary and phenomenal experiences during which a person leaves their physical body and visits another location on earth. Out-of-body experience is also known as astral projection or astral travel.

If the experience of finding yourself out of your body is new to you your first instinct will be to jump back into your sleeping body, which will cause you to pull out of the dream. In his book *Conscious Dreaming*, Robert Moss tells us:

'When you journey outside the physical body you are using a second body (or dream body) that retains the semblance of physical form. When you use this vehicle to visit people and places on the physical plane, your dream body is your natural body.'

He explains that in this astral dimension you meet other people who are also moving around in their dream bodies – dreamers, dead people and entities that never had a physical form. The dream body will assume the shape and form of your thoughts and so there are many ways to present yourself in the astral world.

CHAPTER 11

Common Spiritual Guides

YOUR GUIDES CAN appear in any form: male, female, animal, creature, non-terrestrial or even a mixture. They appear as teachers, trainers, mentors, loved ones and angels. They may shape shift into any form that has a personal association with the dreamer in order to pass on a message, a warning, a teaching or any information that the dreamer needs to know. In other words, your unconscious mind is the conduit through which a message is received and brought up to your conscious, rational mind.

Some people believe dream guides are a creation of your mind that speaks for your unconscious and acts as a bridge between the two states of consciousness. As archetypes, their role may be the dimension of our higher self or spirit world. Like the Archangel Raphael, their unseen presence guides us through life and does not reveal itself until we've learned to trust it and be led by it. They come as an intermediary between our waking world and the deeper world of our unconscious.

Others believe a spirit guide is an outside entity that enters your dream to teach or guide you for their own motives.

A contemporary view is that dream guides are a projection of your own unconscious, or memories of someone else, especially with dreamers who are skilled in practising lucid dreaming. If you do have an encounter with dream guides, it is possible that they may be able to enlighten you in some way that will help you in your daily life.

In the Tibetan Book of the Dead there are a number of guides who try to get the attention of the deceased and persuade them to follow them in the direction of where they will have a better existence in the afterlife.

In indigenous cultures around the world, shamans have long been able to use techniques of heightened states to journey to spiritual realms where they act as guides and healers. Native American Indians, Australian Aboriginals, Inuit, Latin American shamans and Tibetan monks are some of the most common guides in this category of native guides in dreams.

More than one may appear at a time when we are ready to receive the next lesson for our soul's journey. Depending on the native guide, it is up to you to ask the questions you need answered or simply observe the lesson and write it down on waking.

It is widely believed that we all have a dream guide and some of us have more than one, and they appear off and on as we are ready to receive the next lesson for our soul's/life's journey.

Deceased Spiritual Guides

A deceased person you knew in real life, such as a member of your family or a deceased partner, may appear as a dream guide, not to haunt you but to offer you advice and help. The deceased person has already crossed over and has returned to bring you their gift of wisdom. The departed who have not transitioned and remain as earthbound spirits are the souls in need of guidance themselves, as they have a lower vibrational energy level. (See Chapter 9 – Death, Grief and Loss Dreams.)

Good vibrations

Everything in the universe is made up of energy that vibrates at different levels of frequencies. Even things that look solid are made up of vibrational energy fields at the quantum level. You are also an energy that is composed of different levels of energy – physical, mental, emotional and spiritual – each with its own vibrational frequency. The lower your vibrations, the more you would be experiencing negative emotions, poor health, disempowering thoughts or lack of spiritual awareness. In the spiritual dimension, negative energy is lower vibration because it is darker, denser and heavier, while positive energy is higher vibration because it has more light, is finer and lighter.

If a departed loved one appears to you in dreams as a guide, ask them to help you to awaken your own inner wisdom, which can then assist you to make better decisions in waking life or grant you knowledge that will help you move on.

Whether these departed spirit guides are projections of ourselves, perhaps coming from a genuine desire to communicate with the person again, or whether they are entities from the paranormal/spiritual realm must be decided by you, the dreamer. What's relevant to this type of dream is how you feel after understanding or coming to terms with the message, warning or lesson.

'My departed father came to me in my dream. He was standing on the banks of a large river. In the middle of the river were sharp rocks that made crossing it very dangerous. I was on the other side of the river, ready to swim across. I heard my father's voice say, "Don't cross the Rubicon."

'He created waves with his hands, which splashed me and woke me up.

'I knew immediately what his message was: don't start a feud with your brother.

'My father was a history teacher and so I'd learnt about history from knee high. To cross the Rubicon means to pass the point of no return; that there is no turning back once you're set on course. It refers to Caesar's crossing of the river – which was considered an act of war.

'My brother and I had been feuding over our joint business venture. I was at the point of breaking away and perhaps not ever having anything to do with him again. My father guided me through this difficult time and showed me to steer my course in a different direction before it was too late.'

Joe

Ancestors and Spiritual Guides

Due to the advances in science, especially in the field of genetics, our understanding of the history of mankind is increasing at a rapid pace. We now know that via our DNA each of us carry tiny pieces of those that have gone before us. These tiny ancestral messages contain information that not only makes each of us unique, but they also define where and how our forebears made their place in history.

Especially interesting is the fact that it is the female side of the human species that passes on the mitochondrial DNA to the next generation. In his book *The Seven Daughters of Eve*, Professor Bryan Sykes suggests that we can trace our ancestry through our mothers back to a key group of women in our heritage line.

Perhaps this cellular information also contains particles of other attributes? As we all know, one of the other things common to us all is that we dream. What's interesting is that we may think they're our dreams but, in fact, the dreams could be passed down from generational memory banks.

Animal studies suggest that behaviour can also be affected by events in previous generations that have been passed on through a form of genetic memory. This is known as 'trans-generational epigenetic inheritance' – that the environment can affect an individual's genetics, which can, in turn, be passed on. It is one mechanism by which descendants show imprints of their ancestor. In other words, you may have inherited certain characteristics from an ancestor who had to adapt to a series of physical or psychological responses.

Our inner ancestral 'voices' are what can be expressed in dreams. Sometimes this is confused with past lives dreams. Dreamers who experience an ancestral guide dream claim that it feels very real, as if it's part of them. The reason for this may simply be that the lives of our ancestors come out in inherited DNA dreams.

> *'An ancestor dream guide came to me. In the dream I asked her who she was, and she told me she was of my clan. She showed me where she was from on an ancient map that resembled the Arctic continent. She said it was "before they drew the lines on the land", meaning before countries were defined.*
>
> *'She said she walks with the wolf and told me that together they watch over me. The wolf is traditional medicine for a strong protector and spiritual teacher. Having both my grandmother and the wolf in my dream gave me a reassurance that I was on the right path as a reiki practitioner – and to give up my day job as receptionist.'*
>
> **Sofia**

Does our dreaming mind have access to information about our family background and lineage that we are not consciously aware of? It seems that it is possible.

'I dreamt of a house I'd never seen or been to before. It was exactly the same house I found on the internet a week later. I traced it back to my family history, as my great-grandparents had originally settled there. I kept on researching until I found records of where my grandmother was born.

'It was the same address as the house I'd found on the internet and the very same house – in its original state. It was a beautiful period home from the gold rush era in the country. My grandmother had never spoken about her early childhood, but on researching my family history and contacting relatives, I discovered that her family had lost everything in the Great Depression and suffered great poverty as a result.

'I was looking at starting a bed-and-breakfast business. I ended up buying it and felt "at home" the moment I walked past the front gate. Had this been my dream or had I dreamt through the eyes of my grandmother? Did I now restore her dream of what was taken away from her?

'Soon after I purchased the house I had a dream visitation from my grandmother, who was now looking younger than I'd ever seen her and happy. I always remembered her as being someone who frowned a lot and was short-tempered. She showed me an old plan of the house and, to my surprise, when I followed her instructions, it led me to an underground cellar that had been covered over. In there were original family heirlooms that had been left with the hope that one day they would be claimed. I felt like I had done this for her and for me too. There was finally closure.

'She had come to me to apologise for having passed on what she'd kept hidden, and in that moment I recognised the inherited shame that had passed through my own psyche via the invisible red thread. It explained why I'd never felt "good enough" despite there not being any indication of having failed at anything.'

Karina

Claiming your authentic roots

Parental and generational conflicts that are kept hidden or allowed to become unconscious create an intergenerational wound. It causes the child to feel the conflicts of the ancestors and suffer them as if they were their own.

> *'Nothing influences children more than the silent facts in the background … The child is so much a part of the psychological atmosphere of the parents that secret and unsolved problems between them can influence its health profoundly. The participation mystique … causes the child to feel the conflicts of the parents and to suffer from them as if they were its own. It is hardly ever the open conflict or the manifest difficulty that has such a poisonous effect, but almost always parental problems that have been kept hidden or allowed to become unconscious.'*
>
> **– C.G. Jung**

Interesting cases exist of people who had no conscious knowledge of their ancestors dying in the Holocaust but, once the truth came out, everyone in the family was able to heal and the family lineage be restored. Not only do we heal our intergenerational wounds, but the ancestor is also expanded in consciousness in their spirit world.

Claiming your authentic roots is part of the healing of the psyche. That's why our ancestor dreams are so very important. In indigenous cultures it was expected that the ancestors would keep in touch with the living through dreams. By meeting in the dreamworld, relationships were healed and wisdom was gained.

We are responsible not only for healing our own wounds and traumas, but those of past and future at a personal and collective level. To do this is to become aware of spiritual dreams that whisper words of wisdom in their nightly visitations.

DNA and transplantation

DNA or cellular memory is only now being explored by Western society, as transplantation has revealed the ability of memories to be transferred from donor to recipient. Cellular memory is the concept that the brain is not the only organ that stores memories or personality traits – that memory can be stored in other systems of the body in organs such as the heart and liver.

The instincts, likes and dislikes, tastes and even behaviour of the donor are reported to be transferred to the recipient, as the body's organs 'remember' their original owner's experiences and carry those memories over. There have been a number of studies and books authored by recipients who have experienced dramatic changes after their transplant. Although a change in food preferences is probably the most noted in heart-transplant patients, other common changes have been noted in temperament, language, beliefs, attitudes and tastes in music. Dr Paul Pearsall questioned a number of heart transplant recipients and observed that when the heart transplant recipient woke up from surgery, they would exhibit an unusual change in taste, cravings and other mild personality changes. Many forums and blogs also support this phenomenon of cellular memory and the donor's memory being left within the donated organs.

One of my clients, Meredith, had a cornea transplant and reported some very similar side effects of cellular memory as transplant patients of other organs, but what made it more interesting was the fact that her dreams changed visually – perhaps as a result of her new cornea.

> *The dreams are clearer, sharper, and I see more colour in my dreams. I have less nightmares than before my transplant, possibly because I couldn't see well in real life and in my dreams it was the same. This caused me to be afraid, not knowing where I was going, not being able to see what was ahead of me or around me.*
>
> *'Taste in food also changed dramatically. I never liked Italian food and now I do; I also like odd combinations of food like Vegemite and feta cheese on toast. Dreams of places and people I've never seen before dominate my dreamworld. Generally, I feel more confident.'*

Meredith

Integration of someone else's DNA, complete with their own inherited ancestral memories, can bring about invaluable rewards.

To put it in a collective perspective, all things that are given to us by our ancestors in the form of our instincts, which are really our ancestral memories, come from the Dreaming – before our DNA – from the 'seven sisters of Eve'.

How to work with ancestral dreams

For those of us who don't have strong family ties and ancestry knowledge, we are bound to feel more 'orphaned' from our ancestral DNA. To reintegrate those things lost in our ancestry, begin by working with creating a space in your home where you know the origins of every object – right back to the materials used to make this object. Once we find some kind of connection, it may encourage us to dream of our ancestors.

Past Lives Guides

Dreams connected with our past lives appear to us when we are dealing with life or relationship situations that have a karmic link with the past. The dreams are not dreams at all; rather they are past-life memories assisting us or guiding us through challenging situations in our real life and, in doing so, helping us to release our karmic baggage.

Like all spiritual dreams, a past-life dream is very vivid and the emotions are intense when experiencing that memory presented to you in the dream. The reason is so that we pay attention to them and remember these dreams on waking.

Characters in your dream will look different, come from a different era, culture or race, but you'll know who they represent in your real world. You may even see aspects of yourself – younger or older or of the opposite gender.

The place will feel different with the era that's represented and the dream will have a story-like quality to it. It will normally be a repetitive dream because of its karmic nature. Guides or characters from past lives or your 'old' selves are trying to prevent you from making the same mistakes as you did in your past life, which prevented you from learning your karmic lesson. You may need to cut the negative karmic connection to someone around you and heal your wounds from the past.

Karmic or past-lives dreams are designed to bring unhealed past-life issues to the forefront of our awareness. This is particularly valuable to us if we require healing from the past in order to move forward.

'I was bathing in the river in India with other young women. I was about fourteen years old and very beautiful with long luscious hair and long flowing robes. I was about to be married to a maharajah and be one of his wives who lived in his harem. He only chose the most beautiful women in the kingdom.

'I had been groomed for this role since birth, for which my mother had prepared me. She was very proud of my beauty. I even had a birthmark on my back, which she said was a sign from the goddess that I was special and blessed.

'The maharajah accepted this to be true, but he hated any markings on his wives. He couldn't bear to touch a woman with a birthmark. So he never called for me. The other wives would come and go to him but I was never called. So I cried out, "When will it be my turn?" Many tears later I found myself scrubbing the mark red raw in a desperate and futile attempt to erase it.

'It seemed that I was in the right place with the right people with the right qualities but it was never my turn. Everybody got to do what they wanted – had recognition and approval, but not me.

'In this lifetime I find myself asking the same question. When is it my turn to shine? I'm tired of being at all the right conferences, meeting a cross-section of publishers and my writer colleagues get the contracts while I miss out.

'As a writer, I want to know when I can produce work that will be recognised by my peers and publishers as being of value.

'I felt the dream had a deep message for me that came from another time, another place, another part of myself. I decided it was time to try a new strategy that began with me feeling good about who I was and not focusing on my flaws (birthmarks).'

Robyn

How to work with past lives dreams

Whether our dreams contain a past-life memory or not is not as important as understanding what effect these dreams have on us. They are a direct line into our inner selves and, for the majority of us, they are related to events and issues that are happening or preparing to happen now in our lives.

Dreams surface in our subconscious minds to teach us about a truth that we cannot yet see and help us to make better conscious decisions in our lives. The past-lives encounters serve to enlighten us about how to live a better life this time round.

Human Spirit Guides

It is believed that there are a number of humans who actively help souls cross over to ensure a safe passage in dreams and act as greeters when they reach the spirit world. They are generally seen as the gatekeepers between the worlds.

Josephine is one such human worker whose job it is to complete a spiritual assignment in her non-physical form while she sleeps. This spiritual task can be quite challenging but she is devoted to help the newly deceased cross over the other side and does so on a regular basis.

She explains one of her missions:

> 'I generally act as a greeter to those souls who have passed over but have no clue where to go, especially if they've died from trauma, sudden or violent death. Sometimes they are scared and I'll find them hiding in a dark space, a cave or an energy stream. I make myself seen, holding a white light around me and ask, "Do you need help?" or "Are you ready to go?"
>
> 'If the person doesn't trust me or is still too frightened to leave their dark space, I ask them if they want to see an angel or a holy figure from their religious beliefs. I am able to call on angel energy if this is what they want. Otherwise, I guide them to the light. I tell them they need to follow the light, which is a luminous bright light that comes from above. As they follow me into the light, their soul disintegrates into the light with a flash.'

Josephine experiences these dreams while in a lucid state and describes her role as rewarding and life-altering.

I've interviewed a number of dreamers who are engaged in this role as human dream guides. Other parts of their job may also include bringing healing and comfort to those who are ill or in need of help.

> *'I'm flying with the angel of death. I find myself in an elderly man's house, looking down on his body that is lying still in bed. He is about to draw his last breath. The angel gives me a light and telepathically communicates to me to hold it. The old man follows me until he reaches the streaming light from above, where he vanishes into it.'*
>
> **Christina**

> *'My soul presents in different forms – myself as the human that I am, or as energy (golden mist/cloud) or as the infinite space of unconditional love . . . I escort souls from being stuck in the in-between worlds to the place of freedom from earth life bonds and attachments of the life that was.'*
>
> **Betty**

Those of us who have not experienced these dreams may find it difficult to believe this phenomenon. However, people who dream of being able to be of service in their non-physical body, through their consciousness during their dreaming state, report that this is not something out of the ordinary for them and accept it as part of their life.

Religious and Ascended Masters Guides

Religious figures, known as ascended masters, may appear in dreams as Jesus, Buddha, Krishna, Mother Mary or saints depending on your religious beliefs and traditions. This is a common dream, particularly at the time of death. An ascended master who appears as a spirit guide is often an entity that led a physical life and has moved on to a higher spiritual plane. Their primary focus is that of helping all of humanity, so if you are dreaming of an ascended master or enlightened holy being pay attention to what they have to say, as it is an important message for you and for our collective good.

Angel Guides

The word 'angel' comes from the Greek word 'messenger'. Angels are the most mystical dream guides of all; they have captured our imagination as beings that work for the highest good. They are often associated with the monotheistic religions of Judaism, Christianity and Islam, and are said to protect the vulnerable, to look after those who have lost their way, help us in times of danger, protect us from death if it's not our time to die, guide the souls of the dead to the afterlife and offer us messages of hope and healing. In essence, angels are known as holy spiritual beings who serve God by helping people on earth.

According to those involved in angelic intuitive work, angels have their own individuality and characteristics as they each have a purpose, being messengers from God. In order to recognise the angel guides, they are distinguishable by colour, essence and the feelings that they evoke in us.

Colour is a way of symbolising the different types of missions that the angels are on to assist dreamers. By thinking of angels who 'specialise' in different types of work according to their 'colours', people can focus their dreams according to what type of help they're seeking from God and his angels.

The most common angel guides in dreams are the four archangels: Michael, Raphael, Gabriel and Uriel. According to those who work with angelic energy, each of the archangels gives out an energy stream that is unique to them. Here are some common qualities and attributes that are generally believed to be associated with these angel guides. In dreams, angel guides are described in the same way and with the same archetypal energy that people often have in waking life or in a meditative state.

Michael

Colour – blue
Qualities – truth, honesty, justice
Purpose – to protect and take away the negative
General message – must tell ourselves the total truth

Michael is the Angel of Protection and is associated with the colour blue. He is the leader of all the holy angels and can be asked for protection against any sort of physical or spiritual danger. He carries the sword of truth and protection that emits a blue glow. You will recognise Michael easily, as he is depicted in art and sculpture holding the sword, and in some imagery he is shown to be battling Lucifer and throwing him into the abyss or hell.

Michael is known for his exceptional strength, leadership and courage, as he protects, defends and fights for good to prevail over evil. His sword cuts through negativity. As an archetypal symbol, Michael brings us insight into discrimination and the need for justice. He evokes in us a desire to address rights and wrongs in our waking lives.

When Michael appears it may be time for you to stand up for your convictions, take risks to start a new adventure, cut negative patterns and behaviours from your life and overcome your fears. In other words, be a leader in your own life, cut the cords to what's keeping you small and be an inspiration to others.

Raphael

Colour – green
Qualities – wholeness, acceptance, healing
Purpose – to give insight and healing
General message – to face our pain and express our inner feelings

Raphael is the Angel of Healing and is associated with the colour green. He is responsible for the healing of body, mind, soul and spirit. Raphael mends broken spirits and helps you accept the truth.

When Raphael appears it is because the dreamer, or someone else in the world, is needing their wounds healed. The wounds may be physical (manifesting in illness), mental or emotional. As the dreamer you may be asked to take care of yourself in these areas or extend that care to someone else you know.

As an archetypal energy, Raphael brings healing to the wounds we carry. Only we know when we are ready to let go of these wounds and embrace wellness though wholeness. Raphael will help us move from repression of our feelings to free, honest expression and enable us to connect to our deeper feeling nature. By expressing our true selves it will bring us closer to those we love, beginning with ourselves.

Gabriel

Colour – white light
Qualities – strength, persistence, commitment
Purpose – to get the message across
General message – to accomplish our goals through commitment

Gabriel is the Angel of Guidance and Revelation (announcement) and corresponds to the colour white. In the Bible, Gabriel is mentioned in both the Old and New Testaments. In the Old Testament he appeared to the prophet Daniel, helping to interpret his dreams, and in the gospels he appeared to the Virgin Mary, foretelling the birth of Christ.

Gabriel is commonly regarded as the archangel of dreams, premonitions and clairvoyance as he will offer you wisdom and spiritual advice in the form of dreams and visions.

As the communicator angel, Gabriel comes to us when we need help with communicating effectively and when we need to clear away confusion so that decisions can be made about our lives. He is also known to help and guide those in creative communication areas such as writers, artists, actors, teachers and coaches.

As an archetypal figure, Gabriel brings the annunciation of the birth of the divine child in us. We can grow ourselves into that person we want to become and reinvent ourselves over and over. But first we must communicate with our deepest self to break free of old belief patterns, addictions and insecurities that hold us back, and be inspired to create ourselves in an image of who we long to be.

Uriel

Colours – gold/purple/red
Qualities – peace, beauty, wisdom
Purpose – to promote wisdom and spiritual truth
General message – to appreciate life and beauty

Uriel is known as the Angel of Wisdom. In art, he is often depicted carrying either a book or a scroll, both of which represent wisdom. Another symbol connected with Uriel is an open hand holding a flame or a flaming sword, which is a symbol of God's truth. As such he brings transformation in our lives.

Uriel may be visiting you in dreams when you gain new insights about the best decisions to make in various situations. Perhaps you need to let go of bitterness and resentment, or have a renewed hope when all faith is lost. Those who dream of Uriel claim that he comes to them when an adversity needs to be turned into blessings and adjustments need to be implemented in order to bring about positive change. He is said to create harmony and resolve conflicts, and is the angel of nurses, doctors, counsellors and teachers.

As an archetypal figure, Uriel brings understanding so that we may be able to let go of our repressed fears, anxiety and anger. This process will empower us to have greater wisdom and insight from our higher self and discover our true potential.

Angels of Death

Azrael or Azriel means 'helper of God' and is known as the angel of death. He is best known for helping dying people make the transition from earth to the afterlife, and comforts those who are grieving the death of a loved one. Religious tradition says that at God's command the angel of death detaches the soul from the body and returns it to God. Azrael is often depicted in art as fighting the grim reaper, however, this is not how he may appear as a dream guide.

As discussed, Archangel Michael is associated with death as he acts as a guardian and conductor of souls who make their transition to the afterlife. He is known as a warrior and defender of the people who battle Satan (Lucifer) and his evil minions. You may see Michael or Azriel in dreams when souls pass over and they get stuck in between life and death, especially after suffering trauma or sudden death.

As archetypal symbols, the angels of death are our personal escorts into the afterlife – our transition from life to death requires our psyche to have a formidable bodyguard to keep us safe (from our greatest fear – being dead) and provide justice and a safe passage for us to be able to come to terms with our mortality.

How to work with angel spirit guides

In their book *Dreaming With the Archangels: A Spiritual Guide to Dream Journeying*, Linda and Peter Miller-Russo write that archangels may work during your dreams to help you solve problems if you invite them to do so before going to sleep: 'You should awaken with a dreamworld memory that contains the solution (or a seed to the solution) to your problem. Sometimes you will not remember having a dream at all. Yet the answer to the problem will come to your conscious awareness later in the day.'

Ask for your spirit guides and angels to help light your way through the images your dreams have shown to you.

Animal Spirit Guides

Individual animals represent qualities and characteristics that our dreams want us to focus on in ourselves. Once we bring those animal attributes into our consciousness, we can begin the journey to understanding ourselves at a deeper level.

Here are some common animals that act as guides to those who have passed on or as messengers to those who are grieving their loved ones.

Bees. Images of bees were once found on ancient tombs, and are believed to be sacred insects that are able to travel between the natural world and the underworld.

Birds. Birds are popular as guides as they assist the flight of the soul from the body. Eagles, owls, ravens and cranes are some of the more common birds that are seen in the afterlife dreams.

Dogs. These faithful companions in life continue their relationship with us after death.

Dolphins. They appear when the transitions to the afterlife involve a journey across water.

Foxes. The cunning fox is a familiar figure as a wise guide of the spirit world.

Horses. Horses were once regarded as carriers of the soul, and we associate the horse with movement and safety.

'Medicine' in Native American practice and in the tradition of animal medicine refers to the healing aspects that a particular animal brings to our consciousness – how it supports, strengthens, empowers or revives both the spiritual and the physical body. Once we are aware of what a certain animal represents, we can begin to create changes in our life according to that awareness.

Spirit or power animals appear in our dreams as protectors, guides and aspects of our instinctual self we have lost, rejected or kept hidden. They appear to remind us of who we are and what characteristics we need to become fully functioning and balanced in our lives. Because they are connected to nature much more closely than we are, their wisdom about Mother Earth needs to be respected and heeded.

Each spirit animal is associated with traditional and shamanic practices and appears in our dreams with their own character meaning. They act as a guardian spirit, providing protection and knowledge. A totem animal is used for personal guardianship or as an ancestral emblem of a family or clan in many indigenous societies including the Australian Aboriginal and the American Indian cultures.

The animal delivers messages from the spirit realm that you need to pay attention to in your current life. There are countless animal guides and they have individual symbolic characteristics. The roles these animal spirits will play depends on what you need to hear at the time.

The shadow animal appears in dreams when you need to learn an important lesson. This totem presents the things we fear the most, or lessons that we refuse to learn.

The life animal awakens you to your spiritual potential and teaches you important life skills. It comes into the world with us at our birth and stays with us throughout our lifetime.

The medicine animal brings 'medicine' to help you heal and to bring you comfort in times of crisis, be it physical, emotional or psychological. It is sometimes known as the messenger totem, as it brings our attention to a particular situation or danger and then leaves.

The journey animal comes to you as a guide when you are beginning something new and setting off in a new direction. A journey totem will stay with you until you have resolved a particular issue or completed a mission and then it will move on.

Generally animals in shamanic custom are those found in the areas of ancestral lands of the specific people. In American Indian traditions, it is the medicine-wheel animals that have a great significance. The most commonly known ones are eagle, wolf, buffalo and bear, but there are many others.

A shaman's role is to enter the conscious dreams (lucid) where they can see the future and communicate with spirits or totems. A shaman can, at the same time, enter your dream or 're-enter' to clarify its meaning and bring back medicine for healing.

Roberta's soul retrieval

Roberta experienced a soul retrieval in which a shaman used trance techniques to induce an altered state in her, which mimicked a hypnagogic (the state immediately before falling asleep) stage in sleep. He suggested she meet up with her spirit animals and verbalise under hypnosis which animal she encountered on her journey.

> 'I walked into a field and saw an ox with a plough. I took off the plough and bridle. The poor ox doesn't know what to do now without these restraints and so he moves along and sees a herd of buffalo. He'd love to be part of the herd, to roam free and move with the seasons, eating naturally from the environment. The ox is very surprised that this was possible. The leader of the buffalo greets the ox and teaches him the ways of the buffalo. The ox is invited to remain with the herd as long as he wants.
>
> 'Ox is finally happy. He now belongs to a herd and no longer does he need to work with the plough, but wander the plains in the company of the buffalo.
>
> 'The ox then goes back to the plough and asks buffalo to stamp on the plough with him until it is broken in tiny pieces.
>
> 'The shaman asked me to light a match and burn the bridle and yoke to the ground until it was reduced to ashes, then dance around the fire with the ox, buffalo and the other creatures of the plains. All this was done under the shamanic induced dream state.
>
> '"What gift does the ox give you?" the shaman asked.
>
> '"A bell. A bell from around its neck," I answered.

'The shaman wanted to know why the gift was a bell. I didn't have to think for long. "Every time I forget who I am, I will ring it and not feel alone."

'That was my medicine – buffalo/bison medicine. It is a symbol of spirituality and prosperity. To me, an ox who was shackled to a yoke represented my approach to life – working harder and harder to achieve prosperity but only making small progress when subjected to the elements, the modern equivalent being the world of financial and economic downturns. The buffalo was the sacred abundance I needed to integrate in my life in order to free myself from the pressure.

'I felt a transformation on waking up, feeling that the stagnant energy of being overworked, overwhelmed and not making progress in my life has moved.'

Roberta

In our dreams about animals, without Shamanic techniques there is a lot to be learnt about our needs, which we are made aware of from animal dream symbols and metaphors. The medicine we retrieve from animal dreams is the medicine that is unique to us, which will enable us to begin a healing process. Here are a few examples from my clients who used the power of animal dreams to understand what needed to be healed in their life.

The animal chase dream

'I dreamt that a polar bear and a lion were chasing me on bicycles in our local streets. They were trying to shoot me. Then the lion cornered me in a garage, but he didn't really want to kill me. He said he'd better pretend to kill me so the polar bear would think I was dead. So I lay on the ground and the lion spread red cordial over me to look like blood.'

Bianca

Dream Insight

Chase dreams are classic anxiety dreams. Killers, wild animals, shadows – all of these are your actual 'fears' that are chasing you/hounding you/ wanting to take hold of you. Usually something triggers this fear in our conscious mind and when we go to sleep our unconscious mind dreams it in images.

Ask, what aspects of yourself are you afraid of?

Polar bear represents a threatening or menacing person in real life or it could be that aggressive part of yourself. Bears are also associated with nurturing their young – they are fiercely protective. Is this you? Do you have qualities of that animal in yourself that you don't like?

The lion and his clever trick of protecting you could be the aspect of yourself that is resilient, courageous, strong and outwitted the fierce bear.

The dream is telling you that whatever is scaring you in real life you have the skills, courage and wit to overcome it.

Animals in a cage

'I used to dream a lot when I was younger that I had to look after a lot of animals in a cage. The cage would always be in my backyard at the house I grew up in. The animals would always be a mix but vividly I recall the snakes and kittens. Just as I would get them all in, I would realise there was a hole in the cage and one was getting out, or had gotten out. I would try to round them up again and get them in, block the hole, chase the ones that had gotten out. But they were never always in.

'Recently I dreamt this again, for the first time in years, maybe ten years. But this time the animals were all kittens and puppies, tiny tiny little ones, no bigger than the palm of my hand. I had to look after these babies and feed them and keep them in the cage so they wouldn't get out and die. One or two kept getting out. The lasting impression is that they were so tiny and fragile I had to keep them safe. I looked out, and saw that one had gotten out through a gate and died. My remorse and feeling of responsibility was overwhelming. I hadn't looked after it!!

'I have always interpreted this dream to be symbolic of my feelings of being responsible for everyone and everything.'

'In the recent one, I felt that the little kitten or puppy that got out represented just one of the things I was juggling – another bad relationship with a person who is closed off and emotionally withdrawn and push-pull. I have been

working to end the relationship and I felt the animal that died represented it.'
Caroline

Dream Insight

You are right about this. Sometimes, the helpless young animals represent parts of us that need to be cared for and nurtured, including our plans, our vision for the future, our goals and beliefs.

How to Work With Spiritual Guide Dreams

Before going to sleep, meditate, incubate and set the intention so that you are ready to meet your spirit guide. If you don't have an image of a spirit guide that appeals, think of it as getting in touch with your higher self through meditation. Meeting your dream guide is a way of establishing a connection between your mind, body and spirit and connecting with the spiritual realms of the cosmic/collective unconscious.

Write the dream and the messages in a journal upon waking or talk it over with someone you trust. Keep records of all your dreams and date them. You will be surprised to discover their relevant insights.

Whatever your beliefs and whatever your spiritual views, spiritual dreams carry important messages and it may take time for them to seep through into your subconscious. When this happens you will experience through a deep knowing or perhaps a flash of insight that offers you a solution to an old problem.

Put the message into action in your waking life. Learn all about your spirit guides for growth and healing. If it's an animal guide, learn how to work with its medicine and understand the physical animal – its habitat, qualities, skills and existence.

The most important element of dreaming of a spirit guide is how it makes the dreamer feel. If the dream guide has eased your emotional or physical pain, given you a sense of direction, shown you possible futures and, more than anything else, has made you feel less alone in the world, then the dream experience has been a gift.

CHAPTER 12

Unfamiliar Souls and Spirits

UNFAMILIAR SOULS THAT appear as a dream guide come in many forms. They may appear to help the dreamer only once or continue to appear in sequences, evolving and shape shifting as the dreamer grows in awareness and wisdom. Unfamiliar souls who appear to bring a message or warning or offer help or healing have a high vibration frequency with a bright inner light or halo. Psychics and light workers are cautious of those entities that do not have these qualities and therefore may not be offering genuine guidance. If you are lucid dreaming or in astral projection, it is advisable that you ask the entity three times: 'In the name of God (or holy deity) tell me who you are.' According to light workers, they cannot refuse your request.

In Jungian terms, demons or evil entities in our dreams can represent aspects of our 'Shadow', that is, the parts of ourselves we reject. When these entities visit as 'guides' we need to examine our own personal inner struggles.

Unearthly Spirit Beings

Unearthly beings are also known as aliens, extraterrestrials, star nation, galactic guides, Atlantian or Lemurian beings and mythical creatures that may come to us in our dreams from another dimension. They are said to often communicate telepathically with the dreamer and bring specific learning.

Case Studies

'I recall being taken on guided tours of the cosmos with light beings. They take my soul soaring through the cosmos (sometimes at warp speed and being taken to a star constellation

*— sometimes known or taught about, other times anonymously).
I have had encounters with blue star people who are very tall,
wise and pure in their energy presentation. These beings seem
similar to humans in some ways yet far surpass our human
race by the humble, tranquil and peaceful essence they contain.
They have taught me of space and origins of life and light and
love. These star beings I have come to know as Sirians. I have
another race of beings from the stars who love and guide and
support me in life and dream quests.'*

Jayme

*'A translucent figure dropped from the star-coloured shapes
and stood before me. The figure was neither male nor female.
Its form was the same as our body, very lean, and its movement
lightning fast. The figure spoke to me, "I am going to activate
your light body", and with that one sentence jumped into my
body. The moment this happened my entire being changed.
I knew without any doubt that I was able to do anything,
anything that I wanted. I had become like a superhero figure
straight out of Hollywood.*

*'With my one arm stretched in front of me I took off into
the night sky and began flying, my thoughts focused, with
ease and clarity. "What do I want to heal?" I asked myself.*

*'With that one question I flew directly across the valley
to a relationship that has been broken down for some years.'*

Kristin

It could be disputed that these dreams of alien spirits may be part of our
collective unconscious yearning for knowledge of the meaning/creation
of life and how the cosmos works. 'Are we alone on this planet?' is the
perennial question we seek to know as humans. It is reassuring for our
conscious psyche to feel supported and needed and part of the energetic
nature of the universe.

Spiritual dreams, by their very nature, do not possess logic as we
know it on a conscious level, therefore it's important to suspend disbelief
and enter the dream story as an experience, one which is able to impact
positively on our waking lives.

PART 3

Application

THE SPIDER WOMAN, sometimes referred to as Grandmother Spider Woman, is portrayed in Native American Indian myth as the mother who created all life and spins her web connecting all life to each other. According to legend, Grandmother Spider Woman weaved the first dream catcher – a delicate web woven within a ring of willow wood.

The dream catcher was used to protect the sleeping person from nightmares while letting good dreams through. It was believed that the night air was filled with good and bad dreams, and when a dream catcher was hung over the bed, swinging freely, it would catch dreams as they went past. The positive dreams would slip through the small hole left in the centre of the dream catcher, then glide down the feathers to the dreamer. The negative dreams would get caught up in the web and disappear with the first rays of the sun.

The power of the dream catcher was its ability to sift through the ones that were beneficial to the dreamer. As dream catchers, we need to navigate a special web – that of the dreamworld – and know which dreams we will allow to enter.

This third and final part of the book contemplates ways to catch our dreams and how we must each weave our threads to create a magnificent web that will capture the messages from our dreams. It's an ingenious trap that will feed our psyche and bring to the surface all that needs to be worked through for our health and well-being. It is this application and attention to our dream work that will make a difference in the way we live our lives and dream our dreams.

> 'The dream is the small hidden door in the deepest and most
> intimate sanctum of the soul, which opens into that primeval
> cosmic night that was soul long before there was a conscious
> ego and will be soul far beyond what a conscious ego could
> ever reach.'
>
> **– C.G. Jung**

CHAPTER 13

Practical
Dream Work

*'A dream that is not understood remains a mere occurrence;
understood it becomes a living experience.'*
– C.G. Jung

DREAMS ARE A way of listening to the language of the soul. In working with our dreams, we begin an important inner journey into a new and different way of knowing, as we are able to better integrate the psyche's message into our conscious life.

This application of our dreams into our conscious lives mean we are called to action in order to move ourselves forward into growth, from the darkness of the unknown to the light of awareness. Dreams are truly transformative.

*'No Mud,
No Lotus.'*
– Thich Nhat Hanh, Zen Buddhist monk

At some time in our life we will probably find ourselves overwhelmed by challenges and difficult circumstances. We submerge into the dark and murky mud where the lotus flower begins its life. For us to overcome these negative obstacles we need to use all of our inner resources – the mud that holds the lotus roots – as it is in these deepest parts of ourselves that we find fertile conditions that will make growth and transformation possible.

Being in the mud, in a state of decomposition, darkness and away from life, is where we begin our journey into wholeness and purity.

The lotus buds represent the promise of the strength and beauty that each one has within, and in the right conditions can bloom and therefore transform. And so each of us is asked to take this hero's journey into the underground, the mud of our subconscious, trusting that at the very end there is promise of sunlight and self-awareness. The journey of the lotus is a symbolic journey of the transformative cycles of life, much like our dream messages from our subconscious.

Dreams are a way of dealing with and processing heightened emotions. It takes an intuitive approach and sensitivity to gently probe into your subconscious and retrieve the gifts awaiting you.

You are the dream catcher, yet it is not enough to simply catch your dreams like an observer watching a movie. You must ask the questions of the dream, 'What is it that this all-knowing part of self is asking me to look at?' 'How do I use this information to give meaning to my life?'

Through this fascinating process of enquiry, and by focusing on your dreams, your dream recall will improve and you will learn how to understand your personal dream symbols or motifs, characters and events in your dreams. Your curiosity will lead you to learn a little more about yourself. Your experience in this world will be deeper and richer for it.

Dramatic Dream Structure

Dreams follow a similar dramatic structure to classical stories, despite the fact that they are fragmented and are not logical. Emotions and scenes are exaggerated in order to alert you to the things that require more attention in your life. Notice what your feelings are at every opportunity. They are your emotional compass that will point you in the right direction for clues to understanding all the components of the dream. See if you can break down your dream to these four stages to unravel the dream's message.

Setting. Where does the action take place? Look at the mood, the characters, time and place. Is it familiar to you? Morning can be a time that indicates a new beginning or a fresh start. Afternoon is the end or resolution, while night brings the unknown into view.

Problem. If some conflict or opposing scenes arise it's here that the purpose of the dream will be highlighted. What are the relationships you have with the characters in your dreams? These will help you to work out the relationship you have with yourself.

Climax and confrontation. It's the consequences of the problem where a strategy can be formulated. Notice how you are feeling – is the problem solved or do you wake up frustrated before the ending is satisfactorily reached?

Ending. The last scene of the dream is where we can gain understanding of the direction we should follow and integrate in our waking lives.

Dream Interpretation

In the past, dream interpretations have used a traditional 'what this dream foretells' method to help people understand their dreams, and this usually involved people believing that dreams told us about future events. Teeth falling out meant a death in the family and black was an omen of an impending disaster.

However, the modern approach to dream interpretation is based on psychology and is more about 'what this dream means about you' as a way of analysing what's happening in your life.

Many believe in a combination: that some dreams are psychic or predictive and others are about your spiritual journey and everyday life issues. The differences can sometimes be very subtle because dreams are layered, where a symbol or theme can relate to something that happened in our childhood, events that took place during the day, our spiritual or subconscious parts of ourselves, and they can mean more than one thing even within the one dream.

In other words, there is no definitive meaning to our dreams. We are all individual and therefore dreams are a reflection of our personal inner world, reflecting our mental, emotional and physical states from the world around us.

Sometimes we are too close to our own issues, and sharing our dreams with friends and those we trust can give us much deeper insights for peace of mind. However, you are the final authority on your dreams, and you should never give the power of your dreams away by handing them over to other people to interpret without input from you.

Steps to Understanding Dreams

1. Describe the dream. Write down the dream as soon as you wake up, using as many details as possible or share your dream with someone. Note the settings, people and characters, objects, emotions, actions. Write the dream in present tense. This brings you back into the total experience of the dream and recreates it.

2. Bridge the images. Connect the images to specific situations in your waking life. Does the theme remind you of anything or anyone in your life? Find as many connections as you can.

3. Record your emotions during and after the dream.

4. Reflect on your dream. What is the dream asking you to do? Consider acting on the advice of your dream. What lesson have you learnt?

Emotions

The majority of our dreams are anxiety based and reflect what's going on at a subconscious level from our waking-life experiences. It's important to pay attention to your emotions in your dreams. Dream symbols will be exaggerated and experiences amplified so that you will be made aware of the dream's importance. Note how you feel during and after the dream. Common strong emotions include fear, desire, conflict, frustration, anger, feeling victimised or in survival mode. On the more positive side, a dreamer can experience feelings of motivation, creativity, passion, spiritual connection, love, compassion, joy, relief and achievement. In dreams these emotions will manifest through exaggerated or extreme dream scenarios to help you understand those feelings that are hidden in your subconscious mind or perhaps totally rejected in your unconscious mind. When brought to the surface, these emotions are likely to mirror feelings or undercurrents that are vying for your attention in waking life.

Relevance of Recent and Past Events

It's very common for recent events to come up in our dreams – especially those that take place up to two weeks before the dream. Sometimes it is because our minds are trying to process and organise those events, and other times they offer us relevant symbols to pass on information that we need.

Check your daily diary to trace possible conversations, meetings, social events, family and work dynamics, personal relationships, even movies or books that you've recently watched and read – all of these are triggers that influence the content of your dream.

Past events, people and places also come into our dreams frequently. What is it from our past that needs to be examined or resolved? This issue is something that is relevant in your life now. If you dream of a school, ask yourself what happened at that time in your life that is now prominent in the present? Perhaps you had to change schools or were not accepted at school and now this situation is being mirrored in another aspect of your waking life?

Recurring dreams usually mean we have a recurring issue that is being triggered in waking life. Why recurring? The cycle of dreaming the dream with the same theme repeats because we keep choosing the same strategy to solve the problem or perhaps ignore it. Make sure you not only notice the pattern but also the differences between the dreams, no matter how subtle. You'll know you're making some progress once the recurring dream cycle begins to change or, at best, ends.

If You Can't Remember Your Dreams

1. Take a sincere interest in your dreams. If you are interested in your dreams, there is a very high probability that you will remember them.

2. Set a clear intention throughout the day to remember a significant dream. You might want to re-read some of your previous dreams to start connecting to the subconscious imagery or alternatively meditate on a question you'd like answered. You may wish to write the question on paper and place it under your pillow.

3. The way you wake up is very important so that you don't forget your dreams. Within five minutes of waking, fifty per cent of your dream is forgotten. Within ten minutes, ninety per cent is gone. Set a soft alarm to wake you up fifteen to twenty minutes earlier than usual, when you are still in the REM dream state. Better still, avoid using an alarm clock and train your body to wake you instead.

4. When you wake, keep your eyes closed and remain completely still, focusing on the memory of the dream. Recall all the images, emotions and scenes from your dream and jot them quickly in your dream journal.

5. Alcohol, caffeine, recreational drugs and medication diminish the ability to remember dreams, as does vitamin and mineral deficiency, particularly in the vitamin B group. Certain foods affect our dreams and therefore it's best to avoid heavy or spicy foods before bedtime when our bodies have not had time to digest. Interestingly, people who are giving up smoking have longer and more intense dreams, mostly about smoking, as a result of tobacco withdrawal.

Tips for getting a good night's sleep

DO:

Have a warm, relaxing bath before going to bed

Drink a warm drink of herbal tea, chamomile or milk

Meditate or do some deep-breathing exercises

Listen to soothing music

Make sure your bed is comfortable and the room temperature is not too hot or too cold (ideal is around 18 degrees C)

Use essential oils for bath, infusion or massaged into your skin

Use scented candles to prepare your bedroom, but do put them out before going to sleep.

DON'T:

Drink too much coffee or caffeine drinks during the day or in the evening

Smoke too close to bedtime

Eat a heavy or spicy meal just before bedtime

Go to bed hungry

Sleep in a cluttered or airless room

Watch TV or be on the computer before bed

Have bright lighting or light coming from outside.

Dream it Forward

To fully acknowledge a dream means finding ways to bring it into the world and materialise it in some way that has an emotional connection to the dreamer. In this way, you will honour the gift of the dream.

It may mean painting your dream, connecting a song to it, creating an altar with objects from the dream scene or, for those who enjoy creating with their hands, carving or making a piece of sculpture in honour of the dream. If the eagle is your ally in the dream, wear a piece of jewellery, visit a bird sanctuary, find images of the bird and any information on the habits of the eagle in the wild. If a deceased appears, light a candle in their memory, buy or pick flowers and place in front of their photo or visit their place of rest in order to remember them.

It may simply be that you make a promise to yourself to step further into the direction the dream has asked you to. Do you need to take a break? Is your health in need of reassessment? Does your relationship need work?

As long as you ritualise the lessons you've been given in your dream you are respecting the magic of the dream message, and in doing so you will find synchronicities in your waking life that support your inner knowing.

Good essential oils for sleep

Use oils with caution when choosing aromatherapy products. Consult an aromatherapist. Do not use if pregnant.

Relaxing and calming oils for sweet dreams
Lavender, cypress, rose, juniper, clary sage, marjoram, chamomile, neroli, jasmine, mandarin, sandalwood.

For bathing
Add a few drops of either a single oil or a combination (no more than three oils) to a warm bath about an hour before bed.

For inhalation
Put two drops of oil in a ceramic dish, sprinkle on a tissue, and place near your bed. You may use an infuser or vaporiser, but if using an oil burner make sure the candle is out before going to sleep.

For massage or on skin
Don't use pure, undiluted oils directly on your skin. Buy oils that have been mixed with a carrier oil (such as almond).

CHAPTER 14

Dream Methods and Techniques

YOU ARE YOUR own dream interpreter and only *you* know what your dreams mean, as each symbol is unique to your experience. You may wish to further your journey into understanding your dreams using these techniques as prompts that will gently guide you. Each method may trigger something that you'd not previously considered or unearthed from the depths of your subconscious.

There is no 'one' method or technique that works for everyone. As individuals we may prefer one to another, or we may wish to try a combination of some or all dream interpretation styles. As dream catchers, we must delve deeply to retrieve the golden nuggets buried within our unconsciousness.

Freud and Free Association

Sigmund Freud is known as the pioneer of psychoanalysis and used dreams as a method of analysing aspects of people's personalities. Dream interpretation was a way of accessing the unconscious – the part of our mind that we usually repress but which rules our deepest urges, desires and all those things that we are ashamed of or fear.

Freud viewed most symbols in dreams as having to do with sexual desire and repressed childhood influences, and dreams in themselves as being a form of wish fulfilment. So for Freud dreams are about discovering the hidden parts of ourselves that we are trying to avoid or repress and by analysing them be able to help us face and deal with real-life problems.

Freud created a model called 'free association' in which the dreamer described a chain of associations to each important image or element of the dream by saying the first word that came to mind when prompted by a cue word. The dreamer's response to one cue became the next cue word.

This technique in which the dreamer did not have time to think the image through helped bring the real issue (repressed and/or sexual) to the surface.

Using the dream image of 'suitcase', associations could go something like this:

> suitcase – travel
> travel – airplane
> airplane – flying
> flying – sexual release

Whenever I've dreamt of a plane my free association looked like this:

> plane – luggage
> luggage – packing
> packing – travel
> travel – holiday
> holiday – overseas
> overseas – excitement

Associating from the same symbol is likely to be different for every person. In my case, when I come to a strong emotional connection such as 'excitement' then I link it back to the original word – plane. I actually do feel a great sense of excitement when I fly in a plane. In my dream, the image of the plane is my personal symbol for excitement and perhaps some adventure, too. If you travel frequently by plane for work, it may not have the same association for you.

Symbol Amplification

Carl Gustav Jung was Freud's pupil but broke away from his teacher and developed a different theory of both the unconscious and of the purpose of dreams. He regarded the unconscious as a more spiritual aspect of the self and dreams as a gateway entry into understanding that subconscious. Dreams for Jung were a guide to making oneself integrated and whole as well as to providing solutions to issues the dreamer had to deal with.

He believed universal symbols he called archetypes were reflected in our dreams and contained in a collective unconscious. Jung disagreed with

Freud's free association method of leading the dreamer further away from the original dream image. He preferred the technique of returning each time to the image, symbol or element itself as the cue word. Hence the symbols he created called archetypes. This is the amplification of the dream.

Jung believed that this technique of 'mining' each image to dig up all possible associations might lead the dreamer to discover which of these associations was actually most important. It has similar principles to the 'active imagination' method, where the dreamer is aware of a silent observer or a witness (themselves) who participates in integrating the contents of the dream. This is how I've used this method in its simplest form as I attempted to interpret my dream of sleeping in a hammock. I asked myself and answered the questions about my dream object.

Why a hammock?
The hammock is light, portable, reminds me of restful slumber under a palm tree, stress-free existence.

What does sleeping in a hammock mean to me?
It means I don't have to make the bed, wash and iron bed linen, not wait for the alarm to go off in the morning.

Have I ever done this before? Where and when?
I bought a hammock once but only used it a few times. Then the rain and sun got to it and it broke. I never replaced it because I knew I wouldn't get enough use out of it. I was always too busy.

What does a hammock remind me of?
A hammock reminds me of holidays and total rest.

How does a hammock feel?
It feels nicely ventilated, supported and the movement is soothing – as if I were being cradled. Actually, when I was a baby I used to have a cradle that I loved being rocked in and that I would always fall asleep in after a few minutes of gentle swaying.

As you can see, it began with associating a hammock with holidays and being stress-free, and in the last association I began to understand the symbol of the hammock as going back to my baby years when I felt supported, soothed and had no responsibilities. It was clear that my dream about a hammock was more than simply a piece of furnishing in a dream setting – it went much deeper. It's an example of what you can find if you mine deep for those gems of understanding.

If you try this dream technique, the same amount of questioning is used for each symbol in your dream, utilising anything that is relevant to you such as recent events, associations with the word, past memories (as it was in my case).

Another amplification method Jung used was to describe the event/object/symbol as if you've never seen it before. He said, 'Suppose I had no idea what a symbol meant. Describe it to me in such a way that I cannot fail to understand what it is.'

Hot Chair Technique

Friedrich Perls is the founder of Gestalt therapy, which supports the idea that our emotional 'voids' need to be filled for us to become whole.

He believed that dreams contain the rejected, disowned parts of the Self – like the Shadow in Jung's archetypes – but he differed from Jung in that he believed every character and every object in a dream represents an aspect of yourself. *You* are everything in the dream. He rejected the concept that dream imagery was part of a universal symbolic language or archetypes. Instead, he believed that each dream is unique to the individual who dreams it.

His technique involves the dreamer holding an imaginary conversation with the dream characters, symbols or images from the dream. This is to give them a 'voice' to communicate their meaning. I will use the hammock as an example of one object from the dream.

1. The dreamer sits opposite an empty chair and imagines the dream object (hammock) or character sitting across from them.

2. The dreamer directly asks the dream character or object/symbol/image (hammock) a series of questions.

     Dreamer: *'What are you doing in my dreams?' 'Why are you hanging under my lemon tree?'*

3. At appropriate times the dreamer is asked to reverse roles, to sit in the empty chair being the dream character, object/symbol/image (hammock) and express its point of view. It may go something like this:

Object/symbol/image (hammock): *'I thought I'd pay you a visit, since you haven't taken a break in a while. I'm reminding you that your stressful life has consequences.*

'Why the lemon tree? I'm trying to tell you that life sucks sometimes – it can be bitter and you can either stay bitter or you can make lemonade out of lemons. Your choice.'

4. The dreamer is then asked to move back to his own chair, being himself again. This is what the dreamer may respond to the hammock: *'Maybe I do need to take a break, but it's never the right time. I have too many responsibilities. Any suggestions?'*

These role reversals can continue as long as is needed. When a satisfactory level of insight is achieved, the dialogue ends. This dream technique gives the dreamer the 'whole' picture of the dream – from everyone's or everything's perspective. In this inclusive way, Perls encourages the dreamer to see each character, object and the ensuing action in the dream as some aspect of the dreamer's own personality – including those aspects that are rejected or repressed. It's amazing how insightful it can be, and it's useful to at least initially have it facilitated by a professional or the process witnessed by a trusted friend so you can debrief afterwards.

Title, Theme, Affect, Question (TTAQ)

[From Savery, Berne and Kaplan-Williams (1984)]

If you pay close attention, most of our dreams ask us questions ranging from 'How are you going to solve your frustrations with your boss?' to 'Why are you feeling sad?' But by breaking down the dream so that the dream (your subconscious) can communicate with you, you can better understand its meaning. After your dream, write down:

1. Title. Give the dream an appropriate title.

2. Theme. What is the theme of your dream?

3. Affect. What are the emotional aspects of the dream? How does it affect you?

4. Question. What is the dream asking of you? What does it want you to do or bring attention to?

Once you have recorded this four-step process into your dream journal you may wish to add further information, checking in with your diary to inquire into other contributing factors for the dream imagery. This technique is not for you to solve the dream as such, but to spark ideas and questions to delve further into possible meanings.

Word Play

As the language of dreams is in metaphors, one of the ways to gain further insight into your dreams is to listen to the verbal or visual puns and idioms. If you dream that you fall in a hole, it may mean that it's how you are feeling in a real-life situation – stuck and not able to get out. It may be that you fall on a heap of leaves, in which case it could suggest you're 'falling in a heap'. In other words, you are not coping.

Some common idioms

Piece of cake; break a leg; costs an arm and a leg; let the cat out of the bag; hit the nail on the head; when pigs fly; bite off more than you can chew.

Common similes and metaphors

As strong as an ox; as light as a feather; as busy as a bee; as white as a sheet; to eat like a horse; to drink like a fish; to have eyes like a hawk; a heart of stone; dead tired; pull your socks up; apple of my eye; life is a journey; time is a thief.

Dream example

Isobel dreamt that she was a man and her boyfriend was a woman who did not take care of her appearance.

> *'I tried to tell the woman that I loved her, convince her that I would look after her. But I felt I could only get about half of her attention. Her attention was elsewhere. She had so many children. All these children just constantly at her,*

everywhere she went, they went. Pulling at her, demanding her attention. How could she give me any attention with all these children around?'

The old nursery rhyme came to mind when I heard Isobel's dream –

'There was an old woman who lived in a shoe;
She had so many children she didn't know what to do.
She gave them some broth, without any bread,
Then whipped them all soundly and sent them to bed.'
Isobel

After some research into the origins of the nursery rhyme, it appears that it was to remind children what would happen if they misbehaved, in which case their mother could become irratio nal and be capable of dishing out worse punishment. More interestingly, it was a warning to mothers to manage their fertility – the consequences were dire if there were too many mouths to feed and not enough food or care for the children.

Isobel's interpretation of her dream was very insightful. 'All these children were a representation of all my boyfriend's problems – they were an external representation of his emotional demands. That was the first time I saw with some clarity just how troubled and plagued he was, and how he was not able to give me the attention I deserved. It was all about his emotional issues that he was overwhelmed by, represented by the children in the dream who were constantly pulling at the woman and hence him in the real-life situation. That dream was the start of seeing him with some clarity and not blaming myself for the relationship not working.'

Group Dream Work

Jungian therapist Montague Ullman developed a structured method of exploring dreams. Some dream groups or circles use his method as it includes not only the dreamer in the therapy, but each member of the dream group at each session. You may wish to join or start up a dream group yourself in your area.

Each group member imagines a dream that somebody in the group has shared as their own dream, and then tries to 'interpret' its message for themselves rather than for the original dreamer. This allows everyone to gain a personal insight from the dream discussed into other aspects of their lives.

There are four steps:

1. A dreamer from the group volunteers to tell their dream in detail.

2. Others in the group discuss the dream as their own, as if they had actually dreamt it. They use the phrase, 'If it were my dream ...' and suggest what the dream might mean for them. The dreamer listens and does not participate, except to answer any questions clarifying the content of the dream.

3. The dream is officially returned to its original dreamer. Here the dreamer may respond to everyone's input and share their own insight.

4. The dreamer takes on board all that is discussed about the dream and reports back at a later time or date about any additional insights he/she gained from the session.

CHAPTER 15

Explore Your Dreams Further

DREAMS DON'T TELL you what you already know. Your dreams exaggerate to get your attention. They are a reality check that there are many aspects of yourself, and that by acknowledging these aspects it will take you into 'wholeness' – in other words, being aware that you are operating from knowing all of you, warts and all. We need to work with our dreams and integrate those parts of ourselves that are not activated by you, your culture or your family. It's about owning your own Shadow, which contains your unlived life, and one of the ways we do this is by working closely with our dreams.

How to Work Closely With Your Dreams

- Always trust your gut instincts. Feelings and emotions during and after a dream are essential in understanding the nature of the dream and how important it is.

- Does your dream mean exactly what it says? Always do a reality check on your dream first. Your subconscious mind absorbs information from your waking world – your external reality – and incorporates it into your dreams (your internal landscape). Treat this dream as a direct communication to you with a specific message, warning or advice.

- Write the first words that come into your mind that you associate with your dreams. Make sure you keep a dream journal handy by your bedside at all times. Use associations and word play as techniques to look deeper into the meanings of your dreams.

- Keep tabs on yourself. Who are you in the dream? Look at the various characters you see yourself as and note if you are an observer at any time. Are you active or passive? What are you doing and how do you feel about it? Are the actions and attitudes in your dreams a reflection of your actions and attitudes in real life?

- Dream re-entry. By the time we are fully awake, we've forgotten 90 per cent of our dreams. It's worth trying to go back inside the dream and get a fuller meaning or message. It may be that it's a nightmare and you want to change the scene and outcome. Dream re-entry is best after you immediately come out of your dream and are relaxed and still sleepy – not when you are fully awake. What questions will you want to know? Focus on the scenery you want to recapture and dialogue with the dream characters. Pay attention to how you journey back from the dreamscape.

- Create your own dream symbols. Dream expert Robert Moss says that 'a symbol calls for exploration not merely interpretation'. As symbols are the language of dreams, it's important that you develop an awareness of personal and universal symbols (archetypes) from which you can learn to navigate the rich, inner world of your subconscious. Keep a glossary of common and recurring symbols in your dream journal.

- Take note of when you have recurring dreams. What are the most common themes for you – snakes, missing teeth, falling? What about water and fire – the common elements we all share as humans? The meaning of each symbol and recurring dream is different for everyone, and by recording your dreams and delving further you will find a pattern that is uniquely yours. Your teeth falling out might mean you are afraid of ageing, brought on by a trip to the department store where you couldn't find a suitable dress. Or for someone else it evokes fear of losing a job or even an overdue trip to the dentist.

- Using some of the techniques above, explore dream symbols by monitoring recurring images and how they relate to situations in your life. Imagine you have to describe a symbol from your dream to someone who's never seen it before. What are some traditional myths or legends that remind you of the dream symbols?

- Share your dreams with someone you trust – family, friend or partner. It will stimulate more dreaming and perhaps encourage mutual dreams.

- Dream incubation. Ask your dreams to address a certain question in your life. Dreams can't be reliable fortune tellers, but a question about something that already exists (should I see my last date again?) is useful for incubation. It can be a mantra or an affirmation. Write it down and put it under your pillow. Your subconscious will do the rest and your dream is likely to give you a response. Simply trust that it will, and act as if it has done so already. The following section is some further information on how to use this technique to harness the potential of your dreams.

Dream Incubation

Dream incubation is the practice of asking your dreams for guidance and advice on important life questions. This area of your consciousness is ideal to provide useful perspective and information when requested. By simply asking for specific guidance from your dreams, you may receive not only advice but also manifest synchronistic events in your waking life. It is therefore important to have a strong emotional connection to what your are requesting, as your dreams can provide a deep understanding of your life purpose.

Potential benefits of dream incubation

- Guidance
- Advice
- Healing
- Personal growth and enlightenment
- Resolution of problems
- Wish fulfilment

Steps to dream incubation

1. Suggest to yourself that you need to wake up without an alarm. Set your alarm fifteen minutes later to improve your chance of waking up spontaneously. Have a blank page in your dream journal ready for when you wake up.

2. Be clear on the topic you want to focus on. Go over in your mind prior to sleep what issue you'd like clarity or advice on, but don't try

to solve it. This must be something you really want or have a personal connection with, and must apply directly to your current life issues. Is it relationships, emotional well-being, insight, creative inspiration or release from a recurring nightmare?

3. Ask a question that you genuinely want answered or clarified. Formulate open-ended questions such as: What am I missing in my relationship with my partner? Why can't I move on from the disappointment of losing my job? How can I learn to show more gratitude? You may wish to use a mantra or affirmation instead of a question – your subconscious mind will be just as generous in answering a statement as it is with a question.

4. Repeat the question to yourself a few times while waiting to go to sleep. Keep it in mind as you are drifting off. Some people write it down and leave it under the pillow just as they are relaxing into sleep.

5. Record the dream as soon as you wake. Do not judge the content. Be grateful for the guidance the dream has gifted you. Many incubated dreams have obvious meanings as they are mostly literal, but others may require more time to work through.

6. Reflect on the dream over the next few weeks or more. Allow time to lapse between recording the dream and understanding it. Give gratitude for any dream images that came through and know that if the answer is not obvious, it will become clearer in time. If you don't remember the dream but can recall the feeling in the dream, that's something you can work on in the next dream incubation. Trust that the process is working and that your intuition will eventually understand the dream.

7. Put the solution into practice. Once you have the insight from your incubated dream, put it into action. Honour the dream by following its guidance.

How to Improve Dream Recall

Dream recall is vital for lucid dreaming. Making an effort to remember and record your dreams will help your waking mind to connect with your dream memories. The more you practise dream recall, the more you will increase your imagination and sharpen your intuition.

For successful dream recall, you will need:

Motivation. You must regard this practice as valuable so that your subconscious mind can help to connect your dreams with your memory.

Practice. Before you go to sleep, re-read your dreams from the previous nights. This will give you the opportunity to connect with your dream memory and highlight the links with the day's events. As you go to bed, use auto-suggestion and clearly ask yourself to remember the dream. Auto-suggestion is a process in which the subconscious internalises repetitive thoughts as a result of an effort by someone to change their mental associations. Tell yourself that you will awake without the need for an alarm clock. At first, you may want to set your alarm clock fifteen minutes early until you get used to this practice.

A journal. When you wake, keep your eyes closed and remain completely still, focusing on the memory of the dream. Recall all the images, emotions and scenes from your dream and jot them down quickly in your dream journal next your bed once you have recalled them.

Persistence. Try to relax and look forward to dreaming. Focus with dream recall auto-suggestion for a few consecutive nights so that it becomes a habit and a normal process in your subconscious mind.

Lucid Dreaming

> *'To dream consciously is to be aware that you are dreaming while you are dreaming.'*
> **– Robert Moss**

Lucid dreaming is conscious dreaming – being totally awake in your dream and knowing that you are dreaming. This state of awareness has been practised by travellers between worlds in ancient civilisations as well as Tibetan Buddhists, shamans and in many indigenous cultures. For all that time, not much was known about it scientifically. However, lucid dreaming became well known after Dr Stephen LaBerge conducted research on lucid dreaming relatively recently. There is now ample information about the scientific nature of lucid dreams and how we can achieve lucidity or clarity in dreams.

Dream control is not about changing a dream's direction of where it's leading you, but about being aware of where you are and who you are within the dream, which then invites you to take action.

In your dream you may have been driving a racing car that was about to crash and your lucid dreaming allows you to eject the driver's seat, like a James Bond car, to escape. Controlling the dream would mean creating the dream scene in the first place from your own consciousness or ego, rather than allowing the scene to come from your dreaming mind.

Main reasons for lucid dreaming

- Stress relief
- Eliminating nightmares
- Personal self-growth
- Increased creativity
- Fun
- Rehearsal of a real-life skill for improvement

Techniques for lucid dreaming

Improve your dream recall. Make a consistent effort to remember dreams in order to familiarise yourself with your personal dream content. To increase dream recall, clearly ask yourself to remember your dreams in the morning (using the same method as incubation). When you wake up, keep your eyes closed and remain completely still, focusing on the memory of the dream. Bring to mind all of the dream images and how you felt during the dream. Write them down quickly before the dream fades. Remember, it only takes ten minutes after waking to forget 90 per cent of our dreams.

Auto-suggestion. As you go to bed put yourself in a frame of mind to become conscious in your dream or to want dream recall the next morning. Repeat the mantra or affirmation over and over in your mind until it's stuck in your head then let it go, expecting it to happen. An affirmation is a positive statement that states a circumstance or condition that you would like to affirm or attract into your life. Repeating affirmations over time trains our subconscious minds to work toward creating better outcomes.

It is a kind of 'brainwashing', only you get to choose which negative beliefs to wash away and which positive ones you want to bring in. In dreams, where we can access our subconscious, it becomes an easy step to bring the affirmation up to the conscious mind and into our waking lives.

Wake back to bed (WBTB). Waking up after every dream during the night is also known as WBTB. You are more likely to remember dreams if you wake up after each REM cycle, before the memory has a chance to fade away. If you can judge the time of your REM cycle use an alarm clock, or use auto-suggestion. The best method is to get up between 1–3 sleep cycles of ninety minutes each (1.5 or 3 hours) earlier than your usual time. Stay awake for thirty to ninety minutes and return to bed and sleep. Morning naps after a period of being awake are the most productive times for lucid dreaming.

Mnemonically induced lucid dream (MILD). This is an effective and common dream-induced lucid dream that requires visualisation. The idea is to do something that reminds you to perform a reality check so you recognise that you are having a dream in your dream. One method to achieve this is auto-suggestion, which involves the use of mantras. You may repeat aloud to yourself, 'Next time I dream, I will remember that it's just a dream.'

Wake-induced lucid dream (WILD). This involves putting your body to sleep but keeping your mind awake. Remain present as you drift off to sleep, focus on your breath and observe any thoughts that come, just like you do in meditation. The main thing about a wake-induced lucid dream is that it requires you to enter the dream right away into REM phase, bypassing the other sleep phases and perhaps causing you to experience sleep paralysis. Two ways to do this is to use the WBTB technique or an afternoon nap.

Perform reality checks. During the day ask yourself, 'Am I dreaming?' Do this five to ten times per day and look for details of your day that demonstrate the fact that you are indeed awake. You may pull your index finger and observe that it remains on your hand intact, rather than stretching out like a spaghetti strand as it might in a lucid dream. Make this a habit throughout your waking hours and you will soon find that you begin to do reality checks while you are sleeping as well. This activity will help build your dream lucidity quickly.

Be patient and relaxed. Learning to lucid dream requires time and practice. Try some relaxation techniques before going to bed. Don't force the experience. Get to know your various states of sleep and enjoy exploring your very own dreaming habits. Some dreamers learn techniques for lucid dreaming and for others it comes from naturally being open to the experience and refining the process each time.

Mantra magic

Some affirmations or mantras might be:

- All difficulties I encounter are quickly broken down into simple steps.
- Challenges excite and motivate me.
- I let others work out their own problems.
- I am open to receiving divine guidance.
- Creative energy flows through me at all times.
- My inner self always knows what to do.
- My body heals quickly and easily.
- I am ready and willing to release the past.
- I attract only healthy relationships.
- I am my own unique self – special, creative and wonderful.
- My life is a joy filled with love, fun and friendship.
- I only attract positive people into my life.

If you need an answer to a personal issue or dilemma, use the same technique and expect it to happen. You may say, 'How can I be more loving in my relationships?'

Kirsty is a lucid dreamer and this is how she described her long-term experience of lucid dreaming:

> 'Lucid dream by definition means the dreamer has some awareness that they are present within a dream. This is not something I learnt, read about or was taught, but somehow I gained the skill level to lucid dream, that is, have the awareness that I am dreaming, over many years of valuing and paying attention to my dreams. For me this is the key, the secret, to dreaming and gaining access to the world of dreams.
>
> 'I still remember dreams, particularly repetitive dreams that I had when I was as young as two and three years old. To me, dreams always had a dimension or a feeling of "realness" about them. And so from a young age I paid attention to them. I believed in the power of dreaming, in the ability to travel and connect with loved ones here and deceased, through the dream realm.
>
> 'Over the years I have journalled my dreams and will often refer back to them. Upon waking, the first thing I do is connect with my dream. I recall the details and who the characters were, where I was and also the feeling that I had around the dream. In my teens I began to decipher their meanings and interpret what the unconscious message was for me. I then learnt through "asking" for specific dreams that I could program myself to receive a message from my highest self and from my team of guides on particular issues. For instance, I would often ask for guidance, insight and understanding about a relationship, romantic or otherwise, or an aspect of myself that needed to receive healing.
>
> 'It is because of my knowing and my belief that I can gain clarity and insight through dreaming that I am able to recognise myself within the fabric and framework of a dream. I don't always control the dream, but I do hold the awareness that I am dreaming. I believe this comes from the value I place each night before I go to sleep on the power and the importance of dreamtime.'

Kirsty

The point of doing 'dreamwork' is to understand the way in which our dreams point us in the direction of greatest benefit to us in our waking lives. Lucid dreaming gives us the opportunity to become our own heroes and to evolve as we overcome obstacles. Bringing these images back into our daily lives and working with the dream themes can be incredibly powerful in helping you to understand the part you play in your world.

The dream catcher legend and history

There are a number of legends and variations within those legends about the dream catcher. The Ojibwe (also known as the Chippewa) are generally credited with originally creating the dream catcher. However, it also became a tradition among the Lakota people, who developed their own legend around it. The main concept of the dream catcher is that it is hung above the bed, where it moves freely in the night air, allowing it to catch dreams that drift by. It is believed that good dreams know their way and are able to pass through the many openings in the webbing of the dream catcher. However, bad dreams are caught in the webbing and destroyed at morning light. In some versions, good dreams slide down the feathers to the sleeping person.

The Ojibwe legend of the dream catcher
Each day a grandmother would patiently watch a spider spin its web over her bed. The old woman's grandson noticed the spider one day and tried to kill it, but the grandmother would not allow this. She told her grandson not to hurt the spider. The spider thanked the woman for her protection, and as a gift offered to spin a web that would hang between the grandmother and the moon so that it would trap bad thoughts or nightmares and keep them away. A more ancient Ojibwe legend of the dream catcher tells of Asibikaashi (Spider Woman), who along with Waynaboozhoo brought the sun to the people. It is believed that Asibikaashi still takes care of her people today; however, since the Ojibwe nation has spread to the four corners of North America, it is difficult to make this journey herself. So mothers, sisters and grandmothers decided to make the weaving webs for the new babies. The shape of the circle in the dream catcher is said to represent

The dream catcher legend and history

how the sun travels each day. The web allows for the bad dreams to be caught and the open circle in the centre is for the good thoughts to come through. A feather in the centre symbolises breath or air, which is a necessity for life. Traditional dream catchers have eight points where the webbing connects to the hoop. This is believed to represent the eight legs of Spider Woman.

Symbols of the dream catcher

There are a number of symbols and meanings in the dream catcher's original form. The circular hoop served as a frame for the web and represented the circle of life. The web itself is shaped after a spider's web and is thought to catch bad dreams. Feathers were originally believed to be a soft ladder for good dreams to slide down and enter the dreamer. They also symbolised the element of air – that which is essential for life. Again, the web of life is emphasised as a motif. Beads have been added to symbolise the good dreams that are trapped there and the single bead in the centre represents the spider that was responsible for making the web (creator of life). Gemstones have also been a recent addition and have replaced feathers, mostly due to feathers being illegal in some parts of the world. Dream catchers with arrowheads as a design feature are believed to represent strength and protection when in the dream state.

The Acorn Theory

James Hillman, archetypal psychologist and author of *The Soul's Code*, says that we are born with a code written into our soul. Like the acorn, which contains the entirety of the oak tree programmed within it, every child has a destiny to grow into. So, the symbols and imagery from our dreams are not random bits of scenery, but have a purpose – they are clues that show us what our destiny is. Our dreams are part of our very own personal *daimon* – that is, the guiding force in us that constantly tries to unite us with our life's calling.

It's important that you honour your dreams. By analysing and participating in your dreamwork, you begin to live more fully in the present in your waking life and, if you are watchful, you may get a glimpse of your personal *daimon* at work while you sleep.

Weaving the Magic of Dreams Into Our Lives

Our inner world comes to us in our dreams because it needs our attention. It is not merely a problem to be solved but a part of our self that needs to be accepted and understood.

Author Anaïs Nin wrote, 'Our life is composed greatly from dreams, from the unconscious, and they must be brought into connection with action. They must be woven together.'

Only when we bring our dream into consciousness and take action to integrate its energy into our ordinary world, make its story a part of our life, do we get the opportunity to be touched by its magic. Dreamwork helps us to make this magic real. In the tapestry of dreams, we are all connected.

As dreamers, it is our responsibility to learn and work with our dreams in our own way. We must make our own intimate relationship with our symbols and not get too caught up in the absence of logic. Our subconscious is mysterious and tends to blur the edges of how we see ourselves in the world. Perhaps the unknown is greater than the known. Our job is to follow the threads that our dreams lead us by and see where they take us.

That's the magic of dreams.

Dream Guide A-Z

'I've dreamt in my life dreams that have stayed with me
ever after, and changed my ideas:
they've gone through and through me,
like wine through water,
and altered the colour of my mind.'
– Emily Bronte

DREAMS CAN MEAN many things to each of us at any given time – they are a personal code and they are different for every individual. It is normal for dreams to be associated with events that happen during the day or with those repressed emotions buried deep within our unconscious. Dreams are also connected to the intuition within our subconscious that is generally not heeded, and even to incidents that took place when we were children and have influenced us since in our attitudes and patterns of behaviour. Your highly intuitive and spiritual nature may be attuned to receiving important information about yourself and others while in the state of dreaming.

Understanding your dreams, therefore, is a powerful way to gain insight into your subconscious mind and bring dream messages into consciousness so that you can gain understanding and healing. This dream guide is simply that – a guide to help unlock symbols in your dreams that are meaningful to you personally and reflect your own inner world.

A

Accident see also Illness/injury and Chapter 1
Accidents bring attention to your safety and the importance of taking extra care of yourself in daily life. Are you feeling exhausted? Lacking in concentration and energy? Perhaps you have had some close calls – driving

a little too far outside the lanes or brushing too close against a wall or door handle. Be aware and alert. Your body is telling you that you need to rest and concentrate. Is there an accident waiting to happen on a physical or emotional level?

Address

If you dream of a childhood address it suggests that you should 'address' some past issues – either of that particular time or any significant past times when emotional events took place. Something in your waking life has triggered this recollection of past experiences. Look at finding a new way of dealing with these issues. Is it time for you to move on? Note the street number and name. It may relate to your birthday or the name of the street e.g. Easy Street may be a message to take it easy at work or that life will become more 'easy'.

Aliens see also Chapter 11

An alien may indicate that you are experiencing something that is foreign to you or that you are feeling out of place. Do you feel alienated from family and friends?

Alley see also Roads

The setting in a dream can give you an indication about your inner landscape and where you're at in waking life. If the alley is clear and bright then you have a reasonably easy road ahead, despite some narrow misses. An alleyway that is cluttered, dirty with a dead-end is a warning of conditions to come or how you're viewing your present circumstances, either in your private or working life. If the place seems familiar but is unknown to you, perhaps you are not solving a recurring situation. Are you trapped? Are you lost? How you feel about being in the alley is a good indication of how you should interpret the dream.

Angels see also Spiritual guides and Chapter 11

Throughout history, angels have been described as 'messengers' from a divine source. They represent goodness, protection and divine grace. To dream of angels is a good omen, forewarning you of some change in your situation. Their appearance could be a warning of things to come and to keep faith during trying times ahead.

Animals see also Chapter 11

Animals are believed to represent our own instinctual nature, habits and personality. To see domestic or pet animals in your dream, it suggests you are familiar with those habits and behaviours that the animals represent. Wild animals are more likely to represent the wild and unpredictable parts of our personalities. Each animal is unique to the dreamer's own relationship or association with that animal. For example, a dog can be considered a loyal companion, a disease carrier, an aggressive foe or even a menu item. When you dream of a dog, these perceptions will influence the message of the dream.

In indigenous cultures, animals are important totems and guides that carry a message and healing or 'medicine' components. Their meaning is quite different to the general understanding of meaning in dreams as symbols of our nature. When an animal totem or helper comes to us in dreams, their medicine will take time to integrate.

When you dream of animals, be aware of what that animal means to you and what characteristics you associate with it. Usually, it has to do with our instinctual drives. You unmask the personality trappings that make up your public and social persona and are left with basic, deep, instinctual drives that are connected to the more natural world.

Helpless animals in need or rescue indicate parts of you that have been neglected or stored away for future use. Look at the specific animal in the dream to determine what parts of you need to be freed or given permission to do what they love (e.g. birds need to fly, dogs need loyalty and family).

In its *positive* aspect, the animal will give you insight about what needs to be worked on and changed in your life and give access to deeper knowledge about your nature.

In its *negative* aspect, the animal will make us aware of the threat we are dealing with in our own nature or in those around us. Hostile animals generally represent a person, problem or situation that is troubling you in real life. The dream shows you the threat and how to protect yourself so that on waking you can work out a strategy to deal with it.

Questions to ask yourself about the animal in your dream:

• What qualities do I personally associate the animal with?
• What qualities do I need to adopt/control?

- What parts of me need to be nurtured?
- What parts of me or those around me do I feel threatened by?
- What is the message the animal brings me?

Here are some typical associations with common animals in our dreams, both positive and negative. I have included idioms that will bring up more associations for you and an overriding lesson or message to the dreamer based on the most commonly recognised characteristic of the animal in the dream.

Ants

Ants are commonly regarded as hard-working and resourceful. Their organisational skills, diligence and persistence are remarkable, and so in dreams they may represent these qualities that you take for granted or find monotonous. You may need to continue to work hard and consistently to achieve your goal. Teamwork and asking for help are also key factors to your success. If the ants were annoying in your dream, it could be time for you to change or sort out your lifestyle, habits or work.

Idioms: ants in your pants, antsy, working (hard) like ants

Lesson: Patience/teamwork

Baby animals

Baby animals suggest your need to be nurtured. Like babies in dreams, they may also represent new ideas, projects and beginnings that need to be taken care of in order to encourage growth and development.

Idioms: as weak as a kitten, puppy love, as meek as a lamb

Lesson: growth

Badgers

Badgers are commonly associated with persistence and tenacity and are known to fiercely protect their territory. If you have a friendly encounter in your dream it suggests that your perseverance and determination will pay. If you feel threatened by a badger, consider whether it's someone you know in real life who intimidates you and causes you a great deal of stress.

Idiom: to badger someone

Lesson: willpower

Bats

Bats are no longer considered negative symbols of bad luck; however, due to their nocturnal habits of flying noiselessly and unexpectedly they make us feel wary. More frightening for many of us are vampire bats, which feed on blood. We generally associate them with danger and uncertainty. Bats can represent our creative potential and a deeper perception of what's going on around us. As they hang upside down, it may suggest it's time to look at things from another perspective.

Idioms: as blind as a bat, like a bat out of hell, batty

Lesson: perspective

Bears

The bear's aggressive, over-'bearing' and threatening stance when upright suggests a situation that's much bigger than we could possibly handle. Is there someone in your life who is domineering or menacing? Are you feeling bullied and overpowered? What challenges are undermining your confidence? If you are facing a fierce bear or are being chased, ask yourself how much more you can bear of this negative emotion in your waking life. Bears also represent mothering and protection. One wouldn't want to mess with mother bears by threatening the cubs. They are also a special totem animal for American Indian culture and are known for their deep wisdom.

Idioms: like a bear with a sore head, bear down, bear the brunt, hungry as a bear

Lesson: self-confidence

Bees

We associate bees with being busy, productive, industrious and cooperative. Their 'swarm' mentality means effective group work, harmony and protection for the individual. It may be time for you to be part of teamwork, encourage family members to connect more and generally take advantage of any group energy.

The buzzing noise of a hive, however, can make it difficult to hear your own thoughts and stand out as an individual. If you want to break out of the mould, it's difficult to do so when you're under the group pressure and expectations. Watch that you're not always too busy to take care of yourself.

Idioms: busy as a bee, a beehive of activity, make a beeline, having bees in one's bonnet

Lesson: dedication

Birds

Birds have always been connected to flight and therefore associated with freedom. Traditionally they are thought to bring messages through their song and sound, as well as their vantage point from high above. They are often interpreted as the symbol of our soul's longing and aspirations. A bird that is injured or unable to fly suggests that some area of your life needs attending to before you will be able to 'move on'.

Idioms: a little bird told me, free as a bird, bird's-eye view, birds and the bees, the early bird catches the worm, the bird has flown, eagle eyes, nest egg, feather one's nest, hawk (ruthless person or offer of sales in street), watch someone like a hawk, sitting duck, lame duck, chicken feed, wise as an owl

Lesson: perception/freedom

There are many types of birds with individual associations. Here are the most common species:

Bluebirds are for positive and loving thoughts and experiences, so look at how you can adopt a positive outlook on life.

Eagles are the most majestic of birds, representing power, authority, perfect hunting skills and precision. The eagle is considered a highly spiritual animal in shamanic traditions. Are you making wise and strategic choices?

Hawks are swift and accurate when swooping on their prey. Look at long-term actions and from a vantage viewpoint to avoid potential pitfalls.

Owls appear as symbols of an ending or at the passing of a loved one. They represent wisdom and intuition or psychic abilities.

Ravens and crows are symbols of the mystical side of life. They appear at endings and new beginnings and denote spiritual progress to come.

Water birds such as herons, cranes, ducks and swans connect with our emotional and subconscious nature.

Bulls

As an astrological sign, Taurus, the bull, represents determination, passion and strength. Are these qualities you are in need of in your real life? Do you need to be more grounded and pragmatic? On the negative aspect, if you fight or flee from a bull it may symbolise negative, destructive and impulsive emotions you may be experiencing.

Idioms: like a bull at a gate, like a bull in a china shop, take the bull by the horns, bully

Lesson: determination

Cats

Cats represent our feminine nature with their refined qualities of independence, intuition and sleek appearance. Their hunting skills make them powerful predators and this duality make them an interesting domestic companion – making people often wary and distrustful of them. Ancient Egyptians worshipped cats and the Romans even considered them household gods. Black cats were once regarded as evil, treacherous and the witches' familiars. If you dream of cats, be aware of what qualities you admire/dislike in a cat and whether the dream is asking you to adopt some of its characteristics.

Idioms: catty, play cat and mouse, cat calls, copycat, catnap, let the cat out of the bag, curiosity killed the cat, a cat on a hot tin roof, raining cats and dogs, like cat and dog, when the cat's away the mice will play

Lesson: independence

Cows

Cows represent warmth and nourishment. Dreaming of a cow may suggest that you are in need of emotional or physical nurturing or you simply want to live in a more idyllic farm setting.

Idioms: cow juice, cash cow, holy cow, sacred cow, till the cows come home

Lesson: nurture

Crocodiles

The crocodile is a primitive reptile that relies on its cunning and powerful jaws to snatch its prey. As their attack is unexpected and lethal, crocodiles are thought to represent major obstacles or problems that hinder your progress. If you are attacked, it suggests you are feeling shaken by an impending situation. The crocodile could represent a new responsibility, a new role, a job layoff or problem with a client or workmate. Don't be intimidated and don't go on the attack to solve the issue. Focus on a resolution with support from others.

Idiom: crocodile tears

Lesson: adaptation

Deer
Deer are recognised for their timidity and gentleness. They are also able to move with grace and speed. Dreaming of seeing a deer suggests that you may have to care more gently about yourself, the environment and those around you. You may feel that you're innocently being 'hunted' down through work demands or relationships. It's time to step out quietly and practise compassion.

Idiom: deer caught in a headlight

Lesson: gentleness

Dogs
Dogs have been domesticated mostly for companionship and for their assistance in hunting, guarding, defending and working. They can be loyal and devoted companions or in some cultures are considered dirty scavengers. If you are a dog lover, your dreams will make associations with all the positive aspects of dogs. Are these qualities what you want to see more of in your own nature? Are you being a good friend? Are your friendships in need of a review? If you dream of a dog biting you, it may represent your aggressive traits or of those around you. It may all be a loud bark with no bite, so look carefully at the situation.

Idioms: top dog, underdog, dog tired, a dog's breakfast, a dog's life, dog eat dog, cat and dog, let sleeping dogs lie, can't teach an old dog new tricks

Lesson: loyalty

Dolphins
Dolphins were once regarded as sacred. Their intelligence, compassion, friendliness and intuition are commonly admired. When dreaming of dolphins you are accessing your deepest intuitions and creativity, but you must release your emotional blockages and tension first.

Idioms: playful dolphins, dolphin pod

Lesson: communication

Elephants

Elephants are the largest land mammals and we make the obvious associations with their sheer size and strength. In dreams we can't help but notice them. They represent memory and family ties, reminding us of who we're meant to be and what we are doing to stay on track. Their wisdom and patience are what makes these graceful creatures symbols of good luck and prosperity in some cultures.

Idioms: a white elephant, a memory like an elephant, big enough to shade an elephant, jumbo size, elephantine

Lesson: think big/knowledge

Fish

Fish are associated with good luck and prosperity in Eastern cultures. The astrological symbol of the fish is also the Pisces, the many qualities of which include creativity and self-expression. Dreaming of fish suggests we are getting in touch with our deeper emotional selves. Look at your emotional life and be gentle on yourself if you feel out of your depth, a fish out of water (not belonging) or living in a fishbowl (feeling criticised). What/who are you fishing (searching) for and are you using the right bait or lure to catch them?

Idioms: fishing for a compliment, a different kettle of fish, bigger fish to fry, drink like a fish, big fish in a small pond

Lesson: self-awareness

Foxes

Foxes are regarded as intelligent, cunning and resourceful. They are likely to represent a part of our own personality that will use these qualities when facing challenges. They can also be a warning to beware when dealing with someone who behaves in a sly or cunning manner in your waking life.

Idioms: fox, outfox, sneaky as a fox in the hen house, foxy, crazy like a fox

Lesson: stealth

Frogs

Frogs are a symbol of transformation due to their metamorphosis from their tadpole state – changing from something small to something of greater value, such as the frog turning into a prince. They are known as our ecological barometer – alerting us when waters and the environment are polluted. When you see frogs in your dream consider if you require some form of cleansing and what you need to clear out to be able to breathe more freely.

Idioms: frog in your throat, fine as frog hair, raining frogs, ugly as a toad

Lesson: renewal/transformation

Horses see also Chapter 4

Horses represent vitality, a driving force, free spirit, energy and speed. You may dream of horses when you are yearning for these qualities to manifest in your life. Horses are associated with strength and travel, as they have been used for transport in the past. Depending on the dream scenario, the horse could represent repressed or vigorous sexual energy. There may need to be a balance between the instinctive and tamed parts of your personality. What part of your nature is being highlighted? Do you wish to break free from restrictions enforced on you? Racing, betting and horseshoes are also associated with risk and luck.

Idioms: as strong as a horse, put the cart before the horse, straight from the horse's mouth, horse sense, wild horses couldn't drag me away, horsing around

Lesson: power

Insects

Insects are associated with all those annoying little things that 'bug' us and drive us crazy in our waking lives. Their bite can be toxic, and in swarms they create a great deal of havoc and may even threaten our health. What do you associate with the habits of these insects? Who/ what represents small annoyances in your waking life?

Idioms: happy as a flea in a doghouse, no flies on me, a fly on the wall, wouldn't hurt a fly, mosquito bite

Lesson: mindfulness/awareness

Kangaroos

Kangaroos are untamed, agile and very strong. We associate them with bounding to new places, free and wild. Perhaps we subconsciously want to unleash this wild and unrestricted side of our nature or handle situations with a unique approach. You may be experiencing a sense of disorientation in your waking life right now.

Idioms: kangaroo court, old man kangaroo, jump like a kangaroo

Lesson: balance

Lions

Lions are the classic kings of the jungle and symbols of ego, power, majesty, strength and courage. If you see a lion in your dreams it may suggest that you may need to assert your authority and let yourself be heard (roar). If you run from a lion, you may be feeling you lack courage in your waking life. Surviving a lion attack indicates you will overcome a struggle. Does the lion represent you or someone else in your life? Take care to put your power and ego to good use. It may also stand for the astrological sign of Leo.

Idioms: as strong as a lion, a lion's share, lionhearted, into the lion's den

Lesson: courage

Mice

Mice are known for their quiet, diligent and detail-oriented nature. Are you feeling small, unnoticed (quiet as a mouse) and missing out in general (as poor as church mice)? Mice generally represent small problems with family and friends, and your approach in handling your preoccupation with unimportant details needs closer scrutiny. Don't sweat the small stuff i.e. keep the little things from taking over your life.

Idioms: as quiet as a mouse, as poor as church mice, play cat and mouse, when the cat's away the mice will play

Lesson: scrutiny

Monkeys

Monkeys are the cheeky and playful aspects of our nature. They are considered clever and wise – the three monkeys of see no evil, hear no evil, speak no evil. The dream may be telling you to clown around more and enjoy having fun in social occasions or simply be more quick-witted when it's required. A monkey on your back is about problems that won't let go and you may need to learn to discern and sort out what's really important.

Idioms: monkey see, monkey do, make a monkey of, monkey suit, monkey's uncle, monkey business, a barrel of monkeys

Lesson: curiosity/humour

Pigs

The qualities associated with pigs are usually negative – greed, selfishness and filth. You may see these characteristics in someone you know at a conscious level and you dream of a pig to symbolise those things that disturb or revolt you. However, a piggy bank and a good home life reflect some positive points – a piggy bank stands for a healthy bank balance, and a happy home life is described as someone being 'as happy as a pig in mud'. Look at the action in the dream for your intuitive interpretation of the symbol.

Idioms: fat as a pig, when pigs fly, pig out, as happy as a pig in mud, buy a pig in a poke

Lesson: generosity/integrity

Rabbits

Rabbits are recognised as symbols of fertility and new life, with the Christian Easter celebrations and commercialisation keeping this traditional meaning alive in our psyche. Like hares, rabbits are quick and nimble. Your dream may suggest that you will be coming across new ventures, however, it's important that you pace yourself and stay on course to avoid burn-out.

Idioms: quick as a rabbit, breed like rabbits, pull a rabbit out of a hat, bunny

Lesson: self-control/new growth

Rats

Rats are the ultimate survivors and are commonly regarded as devious, dirty, disease spreading, aggressive, greedy and resourceful. To call someone a rat or to rat on someone suggests someone who's untrustworthy and disloyal. You may need to implement some of these rat qualities in order to settle a situation in your life or perhaps you are surrounded by someone who has these opportunistic personality traits. Don't judge until you understand why they are acting in survival mode.

Idioms: rats abandoning a sinking ship, dirty rat, rat on, rat race, smell a rat

Lesson: survival

Sharks

Sharks typically represent our primal, hidden fears. They make good horror movie subjects because they feed off our primal fears of what we cannot see but know is there. Shark fins in the water could belong to the friendly dolphin, and we panic until we are sure. What are you afraid of that may mean venturing into more dangerous waters? Are you swimming with sharks, that is, people who are unethical and only concerned about how to get to the top no matter what they have to do? The shark is the ultimate predator in water, not having a natural enemy. Be careful who you surround yourself with.

Idioms: shark, card shark, loan shark, swimming with sharks

Lesson: respect

Snakes see also Chapter 4

Snakes have in the past been associated with deceit, trickery, sexual urges and danger. We are all aware that snakes can pose a danger to our life and, by making this connection at a subconscious level, we dream of snakes as being warning symbols. Is it a warning from areas of your life that need to be protected? A snake in your dream will certainly alert you to potential threats that are lurking in your waking life, and it may pay to remain vigilant when your intuition reinforces the dream's images.

Snakes in dreams have also been regarded in high esteem for their healing properties, wisdom, life-and-death cycle and transformation. Symbolically, snakes could represent a hidden threat, as in 'snake in the grass'. A snake shedding its skin may be a symbol of renewal, in which case a snake dream could be seen as a positive omen. What old life are you shedding in favour of a new skin that is more appropriate to your growth? The alchemical symbol of the snake swallowing or eating its own tail is known as the ouroboros. An ouroboros dream, therefore, may indicate a time of change and transformation for the dreamer. The ouroboros represents the perpetual cyclic renewal of life and infinity, eternity, the cycle of life, death and rebirth.

In Kundalini yoga, the snake is the energy centre coiled at the base of your spine. This is the place of creativity and instincts and you may gain insight into your deepest inner knowing. Chinese astrologers consider those born under the sign of the snake as having great wisdom, sensuality and diplomacy, and the snake year is usually one that brings about significant changes.

The staff of Asklepius, the ancient Greek healer, had serpents entwined about it, and the symbol of the medical field itself (the staff with two serpents) is a reference to the healing power of snakes and Asklepius' medical practice.

Other symbols associated with the snake are the male sexual energy (phallic symbol) or your own sexuality. You may need to be more comfortable with this part of yourself. A snake in your dream may be a symbol of an ancient, forgotten wisdom that has been replaced by modern beliefs. Being attacked, threatened or finding yourself in a snake pit suggests basic underlying fears of danger and death. Your personal association with snakes is what will give you a clearer understanding of your dream.

Idioms: a snake in the grass, mad as a cut snake, lower than a snake's belly, snake oil, snake along, snake eyes, snake pit, snaky

Lesson: healing/wisdom

Spiders

Generally spiders weave intricate webs to catch unsuspecting prey, and dreaming about spiders may indicate you feel that you are being manipulated or drawn into a web of intrigue or suspicion. If you are genuinely afraid of spiders, dreaming of them is a projection of your fears, which is possibly triggered by something that is making you scared in real life. Are there conflicts going on around you that you can't control?

Traditionally spiders are connected with creativity as weavers of webs (Arachne in ancient Greek myth was a master weaver and we have the word *arachnids* from the language), and also with powerful female and mother figures. The Spider Woman, sometimes referred to as the Spider Grandmother, is portrayed in Native American myth as the mother who created all life. She is represented as the woman who sits in the middle of the universe spinning her web, connecting all living life to each other. The dream is encouraging you to search your heart and reconnect with your own creativity and then share that with others.

Idioms: blow away the cobwebs, web of life, tangled web, spidery veins

Lesson: connection/creativity

Squirrels

Squirrels are organised, efficient and hard working, planning ahead for contingencies and future rewards. Dreaming of a squirrel is a reminder that you feel you need to work hard and save in order to feel comfortable with your life. Be careful not to hoard things or become too possessive. Planning and working steadily towards your goal results in being productive, rather than rushing around and getting stuck in a cycle of busyness.

Idioms: squirrel away, even a blind squirrel finds a nut once in a while

Lesson: preparation

Tigers and other wildcats (cougar, leopard, panther)

Wildcats are regarded as powerful, dignified and solitary predators that are extremely well camouflaged and deadly accurate when hunting. They are a much more dangerous and wilder version of the domestic cat and so the characteristics are similar, only on a much bigger scale. Escaping from one of these big cats could symbolise feeling that you've got away from a potentially destructive element in your waking life.

Idioms: have a tiger by the tail, riding a tiger, paper tiger, eye of the tiger

Lesson: focus

Turtles

Turtles are one of the most ancient symbols in the world and are also widely known for their slow and steady pace. In Aesop's fable of the hare and the tortoise, these attributes were essential in winning the race. Your dream may be telling you to slow down and go at your own pace. If you are having health issues, the turtle prompts you to do whatever you can to care for your body so that you can be comfortable in your own 'shell'. Be your own compassionate friend.

Idioms: turn turtle, turtles all the way down, turtle neck, mock turtle soup

Lesson: protection/compassion

Whales

Whales are the largest mammals that live in water. They represent the balanced energies of the air and water elements. A whale is also said to carry the history of the planet. 'Passing though the belly of the whale' presents a time of darkness and suspension of life as you know it. You may be emerging from a difficult situation or a dark time. The whale offers assurance that a large force remains undamaged within you and that you have the ability to handle difficult circumstances in life.

Idioms: a whale of a time, in the belly of the whale, whale into/away, beached whale, as big as a whale, white whale

Lesson: deeper awareness/cosmic consciousness

Wolves

Wolves have been maligned and misunderstood in European societies in the past. Indigenous peoples called the wolf 'brother' due to the profound teachings it gave humans. Powerful and highly intelligent wolves are social creatures and cooperate in packs for the sake of the group, however, they can be solitary too. If you dream of a wolf it may be telling you to find freedom and passion and return to your authentic self. The wolf may represent people in your life or parts of yourself who threaten you, make you feel vulnerable and seem beyond your control. The dream is telling you to trust your inner voice.

Idioms: keep the wolf from the door, lone wolf, throw to the wolves, to wolf down, a wolf in sheep's clothing, to cry wolf

Lesson: knowledge

Anger

When dreams are compensatory it means that when we don't express our true feelings openly in real life because of our perceived potential consequences, those emotions which cannot be contained come out in our dreams. Are you feeling anger and are afraid to express it? Perhaps you may not be aware that you are feeling this way.

Ants see Animals – Insects

Apartment see also Buildings

Small dingy apartments suggest a bleak financial and overcrowded situation, whereas a spacious one shows potential for improvement in these areas. How you feel being there will give you an insight into your emotional state.

Armchair or sofa; see also Furniture

An armchair is a place of comfort and familiarity. What state the chair is in reflects these aspects in your life.

Army

An army is associated with discipline and obedience. Where do these qualities sit in your life? Is your life a battle? How do you simply 'soldier on' in the face of obstacles?

Attacked see also Chapter 5 – Being Chased or Attacked

If you are attacked in dreams it may reflect those same feelings of being attacked emotionally in your life. Who is attacking you? Identifying the attacker may give you an indication of what's causing you to feel threatened emotionally or even physically.

Attic see House

B

Babies/birth/child see also Pregnancy and Chapter 3

Babies in dreams represent the creation of something new – a new phase in life, a new relationship, a new project or a new beginning. A helpless, abandoned, crying baby or even a small animal indicates that you've neglected or put on hold a creative project or a relationship that needs your attention. Are you nurturing your inner child with some fun and spontaneity? If it's a new career, a lifestyle change or a new creative project, make sure you protect and nurture them so that they can 'grow' into whatever it is that you envisioned.

A forgotten baby indicates that something you began long ago has been put on hold and the dream is jolting your memory to renew your interest. It can also suggest that you are overloaded and need to prioritise so that you don't neglect those areas in life that you care about.

If the baby is ill or distressed you may be feeling overwhelmed by responsibility and unable to nurture and commit to something or someone. It may represent those underdeveloped parts of you that need parenting.

Death during childbirth represents a transformation of one thing ending and a new one beginning. There are changes and transitions occurring in your life.

Badger see Animals

Balloon

Balloons are associated with celebrations and good times. They could indicate you are longing for a change of scenery.

Basement see House

Bathroom see also House

Bathing is a symbol of purification, regeneration and preparation for a new day. Water is also a symbol of our emotions, so if you dream of having a bath it may be a sign that you are washing away feelings or detoxifying.

A typical anxiety dream is looking for a bathroom/toilet, being unable to find it or it's broken or, worse, in public view. If you need to use the bathroom to relieve yourself but can't find it, are you allowing yourself the basic needs of life? You may need more private space and time to do what you need to do.

If the toilet's blocked/broken/overflowing you may need to release something in your life that has served its purpose and it's time to let go of it. Ask yourself what's blocked in your life. What sort of 'wastes' in my life are overflowing around me, affecting my quality of life? What basic needs am I depriving myself of and what negative emotions do I need to release and relieve myself of? Is there an element of shame in this?

Sometimes dreaming about toilets is your body's message that you need to wake up and use the bathroom.

Being exposed to the public while using the toilet suggests that you are feeling vulnerable in your real life and not happy about sharing your personal life in public. However, sometimes it's a good idea to share some of our burdens with others and learn to cope with vulnerability in order to form close friendships.

Bats see Animals

Beach see also Water

You may be due for a holiday and time out in the sun, or that 'life's a beach' and you're feeling happy with your life. A deserted, cold beach may indicate you are feeling emotionally disconnected and lonely.

Bear see Animals

Bed/bedroom see also House

Beds are a representation of rest, of dreaming, comfort, security and intimacy. The condition of the bed is relevant – is it clean? Is it inviting? Is your life a bed of roses or, on the negative side, have you made your own bed and now you must lie in it?

Bees see Animals – Insects

Bicycle

A bicycle is a visual representation of how you are progressing and travelling in life – look at how easy your ride is. If it's bumpy or you fall off, get ready for some challenges ahead.

Birds see Animals – Birds

Birth see Babies/birth/child, Pregnancy and Chapter 3

Black see Colour

Blood see Body

Boat see also Water

A boat symbolises our hopes and fears, as this mode of transport carries us over water (our emotional life). If the water is calm you feel reassured that all is going as it should, but storms and fear of capsizing are an indication that you are not in control and anxieties or fears could potentially overwhelm you. Hold your ground during an emotional conflict storm. If you miss the boat, it suggests you are not feeling prepared for a new opportunity or relationship.

Body see also Colours

The human body is made up of many different parts, and one or more of these may be prominent in a dream. If a particular part of the body is vivid in your dreams, your subconscious is trying to bring your attention to that region. What parts of you do you need to examine more closely? What's not functioning in your life? Do you have a healthy sense of self-esteem? The body dream may also be alerting you to a potential health problem, so make sure you follow up with medical advice if the dream is worrying you and you are experiencing new symptoms.

Ankle
The ankle is both a support and foundation for the body, and if you are dreaming of this body part it could be signalling that you need stronger foundations for your current life's plans.

Arms
Arms suggest embracing all that life brings on a metaphysical level. What are you striving for? Are you being nurturing or nurtured in relationships? If you dream of an arm amputated you may be anxious about losing someone significant to you (losing my right arm).

Back
The back is not only associated with the body, but we use the word 'back' for other definitions such as background, back up, back away, backbone, stab in the back, turn your back, back lash. Is it a warning about the health of your back (lack of support), or does the dream suggest you look at other words connected to 'back' from your real-life scenarios? Look at each meaning separately.

Blood
Blood brings us oxygen and energy, and therefore represents our life force. Blood loss suggests that you are being depleted of energy.

Bones
Bones give us stability and strength. How rigid are you? Do you break under pressure? Broken bones or seeing bones in dreams suggests you need to look deeper into an issue for resolution – bare bones, close to the bone, cut to the bone, feel it in my bones – are some idioms used with bones.

Breasts
Breasts have nurturing and sexual connotations, symbolising content-ment, nurturing and abundance. They are also connected to our mothers and therefore the dreamer may be in need of being mothered by someone who can provide nourishment and love.

Dismembered/loss of limb
Being dismembered or losing a limb suggests that you are feeling fragmented and not connected to those parts of yourself in the dream. If your arms have been cut, think about what you are not 'handling' well

or are unable to embrace and accept. What have I been neglecting or forgetting? (Dismembering is the opposite of remembering.)

Face

The face is the part of ourselves that is mostly seen by others and one that we are mostly critical of. It is our mirror to the world and therefore provides a clue to what's going on in your mind – both in real life and in dreams. How do you present yourself to the world? Are you afraid of being judged? Who can you trust? If you dream of being disfigured, it is possible that your current situation is having a negative effect on your self-confidence. Poor vision or being blinded could suggest that you need to be more aware or adopt new perspectives. The nose suggests knowing through instinct (follow your nose).

Faeces

Faeces are a part of natural bodily function, representing that which we need to release, expel from our system and clean up. It may disgust you to see faeces in your dream, but remember that it is also a great fertiliser. What aspects of yourself do you need to grow?

Genitals see also Sex

Genitals in your dreams represent your personal feelings towards sex, sexuality, the feminine and masculine roles and your attitude to commitment, expression and pleasure. Loss of genitals indicates fears or lack of sexual confidence and inadequacy. Having genitals of the opposite sex suggests your need for balance (yin and yang; Anima and Animus).

Hair

Hair has long been associated with our sexual attractiveness and strength (think of the biblical hero Samson). Wild, tangled hair can symbolise self-critical thoughts. Long, seductive hair suggests the desire for sexual fulfilment. If you have knots in your hair, you may need to untangle your real-life problems.

Hands and fingers

Hands and fingers are connected to creative expression and our ability to control our destiny (we hold our fate in our hands). We use hands to make things happen and communicate. Dreaming of losing these reflect a sense of having lost parts of ourselves, especially in relationships or in roles where we no longer hold or have authority in. Fingers are used for fingerprinting and therefore suggest uniqueness and freedom to express ourselves. Something slipping through our fingers indicates fear of losing something. Universally, our ring finger is linked to commitment.

Head

The head relates as much to the intellect as it does to your overall personality, aspirations and fears. A disembodied head signifies imbalance in your life. If you dream of something happening to your brain it represents that something in your life is affecting your perspective and judgement. How do you process information? A change of thinking is represented by brain surgery.

Heart/chest

Heart or chest is symbolic of romantic love, but also emotional well-being. It represents the way we give love, our capacity for compassion and our inner self-knowing. Dreaming of a weak heart or heart surgery indicates either a health issue or that you are not following your passion. To have heart is also to have courage, so the dream may have a number of meanings personal to you.

Legs and feet

Legs and feet represent our support – our foundation in life. Legs carry us forward into new situations and places. They are our 'drive' and what motivates us. We simply need the right shoes to be comfortable with our identity and life path. If you dream of not being able to move your legs, perhaps you've lost your confidence or have experienced a broken relationship and are trying to adapt to a new status.

Liver/kidneys/bladder

The liver, kidneys and bladder filter impurities from our system in order to eliminate what's not needed. Get rid of what's no longer working in your life. Time to clean up your act.

Lungs

Lungs allow you to breathe, and if you are holding on to past grief you will not allow yourself to breathe in the air of change, friendship, love and forgiveness.

Skin
Skin often represents our feelings. Things get under our skin when we don't express how we feel. If you dream of skin blemishes, being without skin or bugs infecting your skin it may reflect real-life fears and concerns. It may be time to put personal boundaries in place.

Stomach/belly
The stomach/belly is connected to your 'gut' reactions and instincts. Dreaming of the stomach is indicating that you should examine an emotional issue that is troubling you. Nurture yourself.

Teeth see also Chapter 2 – Losing teeth
Teeth are traditionally associated with aggression, vulnerability, ageing and self-expression. Dreams of broken or missing teeth suggest you are feeling vulnerable, unattractive and powerless – that you have little or no control over your life. You may fear that you are losing your voice (metaphorically speaking) or have problems with verbalising what you think.

Throat and neck
The throat and neck are areas of communication. How do you express yourself and speak your truth?

Bomb
You may be feeling explosive inside, keeping your emotions in check or facing an explosive situation. An unexpected event could blow up after a long brewing of deep feelings.

Boss see People

Bride/bridegroom see also Chapter 7 – The Anima and Animus
Seeing either a bride or bridegroom in dreams suggests your desire for harmony and union in some aspect of your life or personality. Examine your relationships and the balance of your own masculine and feminine qualities and roles.

Bridge
Crossing a bridge suggests movement from one state to another, which can be dangerous because you are leaving known territory and exciting

too because you don't know what's on the other side. When two sides are unwilling to compromise we talk about needing to build a bridge to meet halfway. 'Water under the bridge' is to let go of old hurts, and 'cross the bridge when you come to it' means to not act until it's the right time. How you feel in the dream is the key to your emotional landscape. Generally this dream is asking you to make some decisions during a time of potential transitions.

Buildings

Buildings represent the way we feel about our inner environment. What's the current status of your emotional, mental and physical health? Buildings associated with business remind us of our progress, or lack of, in our working life, career and social status. Is the building on solid foundations? How do you fit into the scene? What condition is the building in? All of these highlight the many aspects of your dreams and affect the overall meaning.

Castle

You may be wanting a space where you can be protected and defended against threatening people or situations. Is your home your castle? Is it a sanctuary or is it a place to keep others away?

Church/temple

Sacred or religious buildings offer us respite and help us to reflect on our spiritual lives, our values and ethics. You may be experiencing a desire to develop your spiritual life more fully or need some respite from the outside world.

Hospital

Depending on whether you are a patient or a visitor, dreaming of a hospital suggests you are concerned in your waking life about a health matter concerning you or someone close to you. It also indicates your need for healing and being nurtured before your health is seriously affected.

Hotel

Hotel rooms suggest a temporary stay for work, travel or holidays and may indicate your wish for a change in these areas of your life.

Public building (e.g. museum or library)

What are your social or work relationships like? What is your personal association with these places of knowledge and history in these days of online information?

Tower/lighthouse

Tall structures suggest your need to be protected and feel safe; however, you may not be in touch with your emotional issues. Are you living in your 'ivory tower' separated from reality? A crumbling tower indicates major changes ahead, just like the tarot card of the Tower.

Factory

Look at your current working conditions. Do you feel that you are simply a cog in the wheel? Are you feeling productive? It depends on how you felt during the dream as to whether the dream is indicating boredom in your real life and that you are longing for a change. If the factory is abandoned, consider whether it may represent your hopes and dreams not being achieved.

Bull see Animals

Burglar

If you are being burgled in your dreams, it may reflect your real-life fears of someone intruding on your privacy and taking something away from you. Home, relationships and work areas need to be examined if you are fearful in your dreams.

Buried alive

This terrifying dream is in the same category as being trapped or imprisoned. Take it as a positive indication that others are ignoring your needs and don't take on any more commitments.

Bus

If you are driving the bus, you are carrying a load of responsibilities but you are also in control. Ask yourself if this is satisfying you. If you are on the wrong bus you are conflicted as to the choices you make and what others expect of you. Missing a bus indicates your real-life feeling that you are missing out on something. Waiting for the bus suggests you are frustrated with the time it's taking to achieve your goals or take up opportunities.

C

Car see also Chapter 5
A car is a typical image of the self – your drive and ambition – and the direction your life is going. Ask yourself how you are travelling in life and if you're driving in the right direction of your goals.

Cat see Animals

Caves
Caves represent a sanctuary we can retreat into so that we can rest and regain our mental/physical strength. It is also a symbol of the unconscious, exploring our deepest darkest emotions that are kept hidden from the conscious. The cave is the archetypal place of initiation where you remain until you are ready to emerge as a newer version of you.

Celebrity see also Chapter 8
We associate celebrities with fame and with certain characteristics that are admired by others. They are symbols of our own desire to embody the qualities they are most famous for. What personality traits do you associate with the celebrity in your dream? Do want to be more like them? Perhaps you feel a lack of recognition in your life? What was your relationship with your dream celebrity? If you are enjoying their company it indicates that you feel validation in real life.

Chased see also chapters 2 and 5
Being chased represents your real-life feelings of insecurity and powerlessness. What circumstances do you need to get away from? Take note of who's chasing you. What qualities does that person have to make you feel vulnerable? What aspect of yourself is causing you anxiety?

Child see also Babies/birth/child and Chapter 8 – The Divine Child
Children are symbols of those things that we value or we feel a great sense of responsibility for. If the child is happy, it indicates your sense of harmony and competence; if crying, you may need to find what's making you feel uncomfortable about a situation.

Choking see Body and Food

Church see Buildings

Climbing see also Mountains
If your climb is a struggle, it indicates your current life situation. The dream may suggest you continue to persist until you reach the summit, but if you lose your footing it's best to take a break before continuing the climb.

Clock
Traditional clocks have been replaced with digital displays that come with appliances, mobile phones, computers and more. It's the 'time' factor that reminds us that time is ticking away. Do you need to wake up to something? Finish a job or commit to a personal goal? Check your appointment times, too, as we tend to have this dream when we feel we may miss or be late for an appointment.

Clothing see also Chapter 5 – Being Naked in Public
Clothes represent our persona – the image we are portraying to others as well as the role we play (our identity) at that particular time in our life. Are you anxious to perform in a new role? Do the clothes suggest those qualities – such as elegance, class, casual, well coordinated – that you wish for? Inadequate or inappropriate clothing indicates that you're not comfortable or you are ashamed in a situation or role. Ill-fitting and tight clothes – have you grown out of that identity, or are you being restricted? Being unable to find your clothes for an important event reflects your anxieties of not being prepared or able to meet expectations. Look at what part of the body the clothing covers and the colour. Is it relevant to your sense of self that you project to the world?

Colours
Most of us dream in colour, but as the dream fades upon waking so do the colours and therefore we sometimes assume that we've dreamt in black and white. Colour in dreams is very significant, especially when the symbol is vivid or unusually coloured. A pink elephant, a blue wedding dress or a green sky is our mind's way of bringing these colours to our attention for a reason. Colours carry positive or negative meanings depending on our emotional, physical and mental state. You may be afraid to admit to having certain feelings about situations in your life

or you may not be consciously aware of your emotions. The palette is a reflection of our inner landscape.

It is important to note that dreams can mean so many things to each individual at any given time and could even mean more than one thing within the same dream. These common colours are typically associated with the following images and feelings.

It is said that we have **seven** main energy centres, called *chakras,* that are associated with specific colours and are connected to major organs or glands that rule other body parts. If there is an imbalance or blockage on any level – physical, emotional, mental and spiritual – we will be out of sync and our vitality will be affected. When dreaming of colours, it may be your chakras that need alignment or unblocking.

Red

Red evokes feelings of anger, danger, aggression, passion, power and energy. It is typically associated with blood and therefore the dream is showing you life energy – loss of blood equals death. Are you feeling depleted of energy? Is your health in good shape?

To see red in dreams can mean that you are feeling angry and out of control, or it's a warning. You may turn red with embarrassment (shame) or be unable to control your sexual impulses. We are made aware that red lingerie is 'hot' and sexy, and the 'red light district' is strictly a place for prostitution.

1st chakra: Red – Manifestation

Location: Root chakra at the base of the spine; coccyx

If you are feeling unsettled, you may dream in red images or have pain in the spine and lower back. Red symbolises the earth, and grounding yourself using your survival instincts is a good way to honour the dream.

Message: Your life stability is in a state of transition.

Orange

Orange is the colour of warmth, friendship, kindness, self-respect and positive symbols associated with the sun, the warm glow of the fire, a new dawn or sunset. It gives us a sense of vitality and optimism, and therefore is centred on connecting to our senses and our creativity. Seeing orange in your dreams can also point to difficulty in being social or having intimacy issues.

2nd chakra: Orange – Creativity

Location: Below navel, lower abdomen, sacral, genitals

If you are having dreams with orange colours, you may be dealing with fears relating to the areas of this chakra.

Message: Get creative in new ways so that you don't do the same old thing. Find a new way to express yourself.

Yellow

Yellow is considered a happy colour, symbolising harmony, good mood, energy, awareness and mental stimulation. We connect yellow with the sun, and to have a sunny outlook on life means we are feeling positive. A coward is someone who is yellow and the colour is also associated with deceit, betrayal and sickness. How you feel in the dream holds the clue to its message.

3rd chakra: Yellow – Empowerment

Location: Above the navel, stomach, solar plexus

Yellow is the colour of fire and the place where we feel purpose and power of transformation. This is where we start to put our changes into action and move forward. The dreams that occur here are dreams of struggle within ourselves. You may dream of yellow images and dream that you feel ill, especially in the stomach area.

Message: Have faith in yourself, but also in your higher self.

Green

Green is normally associated with 'newness' – someone is green when they are inexperienced. It's also the colour we connect to nature, the environment, good health, growth and healing. Turning green may also be associated with mould and decay, envy, insecurity and greed, so it's essential that you are aware of this duality. Have you had new ideas or directions that are now sprouting into life? Are you beginning a new project or phase?

4th chakra: Green – Love

Location: Centre of chest, heart

This chakra is associated with love, compassion and healing. It is the central point of the chakra system – the centre of love. It is about our connectedness to all and our ability to love. Our dreams can be filled with many different things at this point because we are tested on our ability to truly love.

If you dream in green images or colour you may have a strong drive to help others, but beware of burn-out.

Message: There are times where you need to lead with your heart rather than your head.

Blue

Blue is commonly recognised as the colour for truth, heaven, sky, sea, peace and intuition, and is therefore a spiritual colour. It is associated with boys and the masculine, and different shades of blue are generally favoured for uniforms. Feeling blue is a negative association with the colour, suggesting depression and sadness. If you dream of someone wearing blue, they may have something to communicate that is truthful and spiritual.

5th chakra: Blue – Truth

Location: Throat

Express yourself through sounds, tones and chants. This chakra is associated with communication, thinking and planning.

You may experience dreams in bright blue images or have a sore throat and be unable to speak. It may be that you lose your voice or choke.

Message: Sing, chant, make sounds or create music. Make it up, be creative with it and express your depths via non-verbalised/structured form.

Purple

Purple contains the tones of indigo (6th chakra) and violet (7th chakra) and often represents compassion, healing and kindness. In history, it was considered a royal colour, and those in high rank and priests were able to wear the rich colour of purple. If you dream of this colour you may be aiming to succeed at your work or be in search of validation.

Deep purple is associated with mystery and a new sense of self-awareness through intuition. Violet has a more spiritual meaning and is connected with spirituality or to a higher power.

6th chakra: Indigo – Vision

Location: Third eye, forehead

The sixth chakra is associated with intuition, seeing beyond the physical and psychic insight.

Message: Envision your desired future joy.

7th chakra: Violet – Transformation

Location: Crown, top of head

The seventh chakra is associated with our link to a higher spiritual realm or to Source/God, which connects us to the divine. It is considered as thought, knowing, understanding and transcendence. When this chakra is active the violet turns to white, which is the ultimate spiritual shade.

Message: You have permission to shine.

Black

Black is not an actual colour. It's a shade or the absence of light, and it symbolises the unknown, the unconscious and the deeper side of yourself. It is synonymous with 'black' and 'shadow' and therefore it may represent an idea, a person, a state of your life or your negative emotions, such as danger, emptiness, death, mourning, despair, depression, fatigue and lack of love. It may simply be that you are hiding something – those rejected or unacceptable aspects of yourself known as the Shadow. On a positive side, seeing black or dreaming in black and white may be pointing you to new directions or to hidden, unexplored potential.

Is there anything lacking warmth of colour (variety) in your life?

Message: What needs to be brought out of the darkness and into the light?

White

White is also a shade and not a colour. It is generally associated with purity, enlightenment, joy, religious figures, spirituality and spirit guides. We use white to symbolise new beginnings in rituals such as christenings and weddings. In cultures where white is worn at funerals, death is regarded as a new beginning or a transition rather than an ending. However, if you dream of white and if you feel it has more of an eerie feeling to it, it may refer to blinding white or bareness where nothing happens. To cover up what embarrasses us is also referred to as 'white out' or 'white wash'.

Message: Is it time for you to become more aware and 'see the light'?

Computer

Thanks to the internet we are all connected via computer technology and therefore it's now become a symbol of information and communication. If there are malfunctions to deal with, recognise that this is a symbol of issues in your life that need to be 'fixed' for maximum functionality.

Court see also People

Are you anxious of being judged? Do you have a guilty conscience or a need to claim justice? Dreaming of being in court suggests that you may be feeling that you or your situation are not being fairly treated and you are seeking retribution or compensation.

Crying

Crying often expresses sadness and hurt, and in dreams indicates that the dreamer has not released some unvented emotion in real life. It may also suggest that their needs are not being attended to.

D

Dam see Water

Danger

Dreams exaggerate impending danger, whether it's a natural or man-made disaster or simply finding yourself in a dangerous situation. This is a reflection of how you see your life at the moment – filled with insecurity and potential threats. If you feel responsible for saving others, it highlights your personal heroic qualities.

Death/dead see also chapters 2 and 6

Death dreams are among the most universal common dreams. Unless someone you know is dying or very unwell, dreaming of death is an ending of something and a beginning of something new. As ancient philosopher and poet Lao Tzu tells us, 'New beginnings are often disguised as painful endings.'

Deer see Animals

Desert

Deserts are dry with little or no water, therefore in a dream setting they denote an absence of emotions and life. It indicates that some aspects of yourself, such as your emotions, need your attention. The landscape in your dream mirrors your inner emotional landscape. Are you feeling barren or devoid of feelings? Do you need reinvigorating? Perhaps you crave to spend time alone without distraction.

Directions

Directions are important symbols in your dreams. Forward or in front represents the future (forward in time), while backward or behind is often a symbol of the past. Up or high indicates a spiritual or intellectual approach to life and downward is about being more instinctive and grounded. On the right indicates logic and reasoning, and to the left are emotional and artistic tendencies. Dark/underground is a symbol of the unconscious/subconscious and light/above ground is our consciousness.

Divorce

Dreaming of being divorced or separated may be a reflection of your concerns about your relationships – not necessarily to do with your partner. Is it time to reassess your relationships? The dream suggests that a split or some distance away from a person, situation or an emotion may be necessary if it is no longer beneficial to your well-being. Losing money or lifestyle is also a major anxiety that may be manifested as a divorce dream.

Doctor see People

Dog see Animals

Door see House

Drowning see Water

E

Eagle see Animals – Birds

Earth

We associate the earth with the nurturing feminine Mother Earth and our life source. To be earthed is to be grounded and supported (terra firma) by the very earth that holds all our experiences. Are you feeling a lack of grounding or connection to your family roots or environment? If you dream of being buried, it's time to adopt a more flexible attitude or upskill so that you remain 'on top' of the heap.

Earthquakes

Earthquakes are the opposite of solid ground and represent emotional upheaval. Perhaps this eruption of emotions may enable you to make major changes from which you can grow, such as career changes, loss of job, selling up and moving away, divorce, retirement or unexpected events where your life's foundations are shattered. Sometimes this dream may be a precognitive dream if you are a highly intuitive person.

Eating see also Food

Eating in dreams suggests that you feel satisfied and your needs are being met. Sharing food represents you sharing yourself with others. There are many idioms connected with food – eat your words, dog eat dog, eat dirt, eaten out of house and home – and all have an association with consuming. Are there negative emotions that consume you? What type of nourishment do you need for your body, soul and mind?

Egg see also Food

Eggs are symbols of potential new life. Perhaps it may be your own potential or that of a new venture, project, life change or phase that has not yet been realised.

Elephant see Animals

Elevators/lifts

Elevators or lifts reflect how well we are progressing with a problem or current issue in our waking life. The movements of the lift and other malfunctions reflect your attitudes and actions, which are either helping you to move towards your goals and aspirations or pulling you off track. Dreaming of a lift that crashes downward or flips you upwards occurs when there are major changes in your real-life role – it may be the added responsibility that creates an imbalance between what you thought was ideal and reality. A lift going up is connecting with our intellectual and rational side; going down is reaching into our subconscious mind for some answers.

Ex see also Sex

Dreaming of an ex partner is not necessarily a subconscious wish to rekindle the relationship. We tend to miss the positive emotional connection and intimacy the relationship provided and often we forget or downplay the negative aspects that caused the separation.

Exams see also School and Chapter 2

Exams and school represent learning and success. Are you being tested in your waking life? Are you qualified to handle any changes and new roles? If you are failing a test or not prepared, this suggests that you may not be feeling prepared or competent in life situations.

F

Faeces see Body and Bathroom

Falling see also Chapter 5

Are you feeling unsupported in your waking life? Perhaps a situation has you feeling out of control at work or at home.

Father see People

Fences

Fences protect our property and keep us at a safe distance from others. They are also about the boundaries we establish in real-life work, family and social situations. What boundaries are you facing in your life? In what ways do you feel confined and/or restricted? You may also be feeling stuck. If you are jumping over the fence, it suggests you are not allowing obstacles to get in your way or limitations to stop you from following your goal. Building or mending a fence is repairing something in your life or placing a positive boundary around your private life.

Fire

Fire is a symbol of urgency, passion and transition. What's urgent in your life right now? Are you feeling 'under fire'? Fire also purifies and therefore cleanses by burning, turning the original material into ashes. In this sense, fire is transformative and represents transition – from base to consumable; from the ashes there is new life and growth. If you dream of being on fire or your child being on fire, consider whether you are going through a transition period – it may be physical changes such as into adolescence or menopause. Other changes can include relationships, moving location, death of a loved one and anything that requires an element of transformation.

Is there a fire that burns within you? It may be that your fire represents a smouldering passion that you'd like to put into action. If the fire is burning out of control, it suggests that you are struggling to control your emotions (all fired up). Fire can destroy and create something new, so ask yourself whether there is an opportunity for regrowth. Be careful not to suffer burn-out, as fires can rage and then burn out quickly.

Fish see Animals

Flood/tidal wave see also Water and Storms
Floods and tidal waves swamp and overpower us, leaving us emotionally battered and disoriented. What is overwhelming you in your waking life and can you survive these new emotional challenges?

Flowers see also Gardens
Flowers are an expression of beauty, perfection and joy. When we give and receive flowers it's an exchange of gratitude, love and appreciation. Note whether you are giving or receiving flowers, as this may indicate your desire for appreciation, respect, approval or admiration.

Blooming flowers represent your hidden potential and becoming more self-aware about your place in the world. Are you a late bloomer? Perhaps a new relationship is about to bloom – with yourself or with others. Faded or wilting flowers suggest the passing of a season or a phase (cycle) or time in our lives that is coming to an end. Life, like flowers, is about transitions, cycles and fragility. Is your life coming up roses? Is it a bed of roses? These idioms suggest the way in which society identifies flowers with lifestyle.

Look at the colour, condition and species of the flowers in your dream to gain greater insight into their presence. There are traditional symbolic meanings of flowers that may assist you in understanding the general association with that individual flower. For example, rose meanings vary according to colour but generally they are a symbol of deep love, balance, passion and intelligence. They can be a message for healing and courage. Only the dreamer can define their own association with the flower.

Flying
Flying represents the desire for escape and freedom.

Fog see Weather

Food

Food is a symbol of our basic needs for physical, mental and emotional nourishment. Its function is to keep us alive and healthy, and to bring enjoyment. In any area of your life where this is lacking, your dream will bring it to your attention. Preparing healthy food suggests that you'd like a more balanced lifestyle. Cooking is all about being creative in the kitchen – the hearth of the home – and this applies to your personal and working life.

We use food to celebrate social occasions and important events – it connects us to others and creates bonds in relationships. A party or celebration represents your search for new ideas, perspectives and social attitudes. If the food is spoilt or indigestible, it denotes that there is a principle that you cannot 'swallow' or be part of. Choking and vomiting food is another type of aversion.

Look at what each food type represents in areas of your life that are associated with basic needs – bread, for example, is a staple food we need for survival and it's also slang for money, as is dough. Some common idioms about food – brain food, fast food, food for thought, junk food, mood food – can assist in highlighting your association with food in the dream.

What needs nourishment in real life? Are you lacking or feeling deprived in any areas of your life? What will make you feel abundant? What 'feeds' you, your soul, your ideas or your life in general?

Forest see also Trees

The forest is a symbol of the unconscious, where one can become lost and confused in hidden areas previously unexplored. In fairy tales the child enters the forest to overcome impossible odds and survives. In this act of survival the child grows and matures into a functioning adult. Basically, we are moving through a time in our life that is making us feel insecure, confused and dissatisfied. It may be that 'you can't see the forest for the trees', meaning that in your waking life you don't see the whole picture/situation because you are too concerned with focusing on one single point or detail.

Fox see Animals

Funeral see Death/dead

Furniture

Furniture services our needs with its functionality, so we use tables and chairs for meals, sofas for relaxing, beds for sleeping and intimacy, and so on. In dreams, furniture is a symbol of our attitudes and values, depending on the outcome of the dream. A wardrobe or cupboard stores hidden memories and experiences; a bare or broken table may suggest your feelings of not having an active social or family life. Examine the association you make with the furniture piece and its function, and relate it to your experiences and attitudes.

G

Games/sport

Games represent the way you interact with social structures, playing the game of life, using strategies and training to work out how to survive and succeed. Solitary games suggest your preference for self-direction, while an interactive game highlights your inclination for competition and challenge.

Various games are a reflection of the ways you navigate through life at a social level. Card games indicate risk and luck, while chess is a game of strategy and patience. Your dream game will give you clues regarding what you feel comfortable playing. It may be telling you that it's time to change the game or go up a level in order to make progress. Conversely the dream may be alerting you to have more fun. Perhaps your psyche is reminding you that it's not whether you win or lose but how you play the game that counts.

Gardens see also Flowers

A garden represents your inner landscape. A lush and well-kept garden is an indication that you are both creative and organised, whereas an untidy or abandoned garden suggests that you are lacking in order, focus and direction and perhaps not dealing with past hurts or disappointments. What needs weeding in your garden?

Gates

Walking through a gate is a sign of a new venture or new path in your waking life. Opening your gate represents allowing things to be possible as you are open to them, but be careful not to 'open the floodgates' as this may contain emotions that overwhelm you. If your gate is closed, perhaps you feel that opportunities are not available to you. What's stopping you from opening the gate and being more receptive to new opportunities or relationships?

Ghosts

Ghosts represent the past. What's haunting you about the past? It may be old ambitions that were not fulfilled, expectations not met, memories or guilt. Is there an unresolved issue between you and the ghost? A resolution is needed if the dream becomes a recurring one.

Gifts

What gifts or talents should you embrace? Perhaps you are the giver of the gift and you feel that you have something to offer. Is it well received? If you are the recipient, accept the gift unconditionally. Being unappreciative could highlight your attitude to something in your life you ought to be more accepting of.

Graves see also Death/dead

Graves, like death, symbolise an ending, and the grave is a testament to that loss. It may be the end of a relationship or phase of your life as you know it and you are grieving its conclusion. Symbolically it represents those things you have buried such as past hurts, emotions, unfulfilled ambitions, talents or relationships.

H

Hair see Body

Hands see also Body

Hands are often seen in dreams, as they have a deeper significance than most other parts of the body. They are universal symbols of activity, generosity, productivity, creativity, an open heart and spirituality (praying hands). We also associate hands with communication – waving, cheering, raised hand for question, aggressive gestures, shaking hands for greeting and more. Many cultures use their hand gestures to enhance their communication skills. If you dream of any problem or injury to the hand it is a sign that you are feeling a lack of control or are unable to perform your regular role.

Hawk see Animals

Horse see Animals

Hospital see Buildings

Hotel see Buildings

House

If you are involved in moving or selling a house or simply have wanted to move, the dream will guide you to what you'd ideally love to live in – without the practicalities of price and location. Take note of how the house feels for you in the dream, rather than simply focusing on the actual design. Those characteristics may help you find your ideal house and location.

Generally the house in a dream is a metaphor for the self and how you feel about yourself and your life. Each room represents different parts of you. Dreaming about a house will convey a great deal about your physical, emotional and personal life. Where is the house located? Is it in good condition or is it in need of repair? What parts of yourself are you neglecting? Where do you fit in? Do you feel happy and secure there? What is the view from the windows? All these details give you clues about where you are in your life and how you are feeling.

If you dream of previous homes or your childhood home, you're not necessarily longing or living for the past. What experiences did you have in the house and how did they become a framework for early behaviour patterns and belief systems? When we dream of our childhood home, our psyche is revisiting emotional issues in waking life that have to do with family values or domestic-related beliefs and how they were formed from those early years.

If any of the rooms are cluttered or cramped with ornaments or the furniture covered in dust, explore the deeper metaphoric meanings. Have you taken on too much responsibility and neglected your needs? Is it time to dust off your old ambitions or interests you put aside long ago? Are there old hurts you need to clean up so that you can feel refreshed and ready to start a new life again?

Attic

Attics are where we keep memorabilia, and therefore it's where our memories are stored away. As it's the highest room of the house (the dreamer's mind) it may suggest that you are exploring your higher self or a spiritual awakening. Looking for 'old clothing' would represent looking for old aspects or past experiences in your life.

Basement/cellar

The basement or the cellar is the subconscious/unconscious mind and all that is hidden away from plain sight, including your greatest fears and repressed parts of your personality. We also store what we don't need in the basement and what is usually not of immediate use, such as our undeveloped selves. It can be seen as psychological space where things are filed away for potential use.

Kitchen/dining room

The kitchen and dining room are where we are nourished and socialise with friends and family. It represents our social nature and it's the place we go to for comfort and relaxation. If there is conflict in a domestic situation, this is the place where it happens – at the hub or 'hearth' (emotional heart) of the home. It's also our place of creativity where we put together ingredients to create recipes and make delicious meals to our taste.

Bedroom

The bedroom is a place of intimacy, relationships and sleep (our unconscious minds). It is where we dress to suit the roles we play and so it can represent aspects of our persona. We use our bed to rest and recover, and it is therefore a refuge where we feel safe and relaxed.

Bathroom/toilet

The bathroom is our most private room in the house where we take care of our bodies – we cleanse, relax, pamper and make ourselves attractive.

It's also a place of releasing and disposing of our bodily functions, so if there is a problem with the bathroom/toilet in your dream it would indicate that you are not processing your feelings or are not having time out for yourself.

Being unable to find a toilet or not having privacy highlights your embarrassment and vulnerability, and you may be finding it difficult to express your needs around some real-life issues.

Garage
The garage is where we store our things and the car parked there is a representation of action and direction.

Hallways/corridors
Hallways and corridors are transit places and represent our real-life transitions and rites of passage. Doors represent change and new opportunities – one door closes and another opens. Windows are like the eyes – they give you perspective and insight, depending on the vantage point.

Stairs
Stairs, like mountains, require climbing and symbolise the effort it takes to achieve your goals. They can also represent striving for increasing spiritual growth.

Secret rooms
Dreaming of a secret room you never knew existed or one that has been rediscovered after being long forgotten is a symbol of our neglected potential. Our subconscious mind is trying to alert us to the fact that it's never too late to find those parts of yourself you've left behind or discarded. This secret room has come into your dreams to remind you of your old hopes and aspirations – it may be that you're now in a new life transition and you can start dancing lessons you'd put off or go back to playing tennis that you enjoyed so much. Perhaps you're changing jobs or retired and would like to explore options that once held great interest for you.

If the secret room is in a dark area of the house and you're feeling terrified at entering it as it's locked or it's forbidden to enter (like Bluebeard's locked doors), it suggests your psyche is afraid of having to face hurtful memories of the past. It may contain repressed and unpleasant memories of events that you haven't fully dealt with or want to revisit.

I

Illness/injury see also Death/dead

Dreams of being ill often represent periods when we are feeling depressed and our health and spiritual strength are not in top form. We talk of 'ailments' when describing symptoms of illness. Ask yourself what's ailing or troubling you. Dis-ease (disease) means not being at ease with your body. Take note from your dream scenes and body parts as it highlights what is making you feel ill at ease in your waking life. If you dream of a child being ill, it's more likely to do with emotional injury than physical. However, do monitor your health or your child's health as our dreams can sometimes warn of health issues before they are diagnosed.

Insects see Animals – Insects

J

Jewellery/valuables see also Loss and Treasure

Jewellery represents qualities in us that we consider worthwhile, and how we are valued by others. Therefore it's about self-image and personal value. Dreaming of jewellery points to what you hold to be of value and importance. A particular piece of jewellery may have a personal meaning for you in regards to an element/facet in your relationship.

To dream of a jewellery box (your self-worth) symbolises how you see yourself, your values and potential. It's all contained within you.

If you can't find your jewellery, it indicates that you've neglected or repressed valuable parts of yourself. What is making you feel undervalued? If the jewellery has a personal meaning for you in real life, it may be pointing you to those aspects of your life that need to be visited. To search for jewels is to search for your true self. To find jewels means you've uncovered latent valuable parts of yourself.

Jewels have always been regarded by the ancients as having powerful, magical and protective properties. A jewel in the crown shows that you have achieved recognition and self-awareness. Look at your personal association with each jewellery piece.

Judge see People

K

Keys

Are you trying to find a solution to your problem? If the key won't open the lock, it means you need to find alternatives and it's best to ask for advice. A key is synonymous with locking and unlocking. Have you been keeping your emotions and feelings all locked up? 'My lips are sealed' is also an idiom meaning discretion and being able to keep matters confidential. In a nightmare we lose our keys, the door won't open or we fumble. These scenarios reflect our real-life anxieties, fears and obstacles that we are trying to escape from. Keys and doorways often appear in our dreams when there are unexpected changes in our lives.

Kidnapping

Kidnapping suggests feeling that you have no control or you are dependent on someone for your well-being. Are you concerned about new and unexpected changes in your life? Is something valuable (a relationship, job, health) at risk of being taken away from you? You may well be feeling that you are being held at ransom and therefore have to compromise your ethics in some way. It is worth noting who the kidnapper is and what their terms are to give you clues into what's really going on at a conscious level.

Killing see also Death/dead

Dreaming of killing someone represents our desire to 'kill off' parts of ourselves, aspects of our personality we don't like or are afraid to release. It could also be pent-up aggression and anger you've been feeling towards a particular person in waking life and this is the safe option to release those murderous feelings.

Kiss see also Sex

A kiss suggests desire for romance, intimacy and the need to be close. It is also a symbol of acceptance or coming to terms with someone or something. Do you need to kiss and make up? It may be time to let go of someone/something and move on to a new stage in your life. The emotions connected to the kiss in the dream hold the key to the best possible meaning.

Kitchen see House

Knife see Weapons

L

Ladders
Ladders in dreams are all about direction in the dreamer's life. If you are climbing up it suggests you are reaching out for new opportunities and making progress. If there are obstacles as you are climbing, consider what is stopping you from climbing your way to the top. Are you afraid to climb the social or corporate ladder? Are you under pressure to do so? Do you want to climb beyond the last rung of the ladder and reach out for a spiritual awakening? Do you feel in your dream that the ladder is a stairway to heaven? Climbing down the ladder or falling off has more of a negative connection to failure, loss of ambition or status and loss of control, as in 'downward spiral'.

Landscapes/places
Landscapes and places in your dreams are a reflection of your own internal landscape. Familiar settings such as work and home mean that you are feeling comfortable inside yourself, unless there is conflict involved in the scene. An unfamiliar environment indicates a struggle with parts of yourself that are seeking self-expression. Cityscapes represent the way in which you cope socially, whereas caves or lonely places suggest your need for inner peace and escape. Shopping areas and markets highlight transactions and choices as you purchase those things that you need or desire. Are you reconnecting with old parts of yourself or your past? Being lost or being in unfamiliar territory mirrors the emotions you may be experiencing at feeling disconnected or alienated in a new situation.

Library see Buildings

Light
To see light in your dream indicates illumination, awareness, insight or guidance. The light bulb has finally been switched on and you have an understanding about a real-life issue. It may be that a light is shed on a situation and that you need to pay attention to some aspect of your life or that something is being noticed for what it really is. A white light often represents inspiration or spiritual guidance. It is common for people who are near death to see a bright light as they are fully focused on life being so close to ending and nothing else.

The absence of light is darkness or a void, representing your unconscious thoughts, your Shadow self, fear and lack of clarity and hope. It is the opposite of being 'enlightened'.

Lion see Animals

Loss
If you dream of losing possessions, such as money, keys, wallet, pets, car, jewellery or children, it suggests that these things are of value to you and their loss indicates that you are afraid of facing financial loss or loss of status in your daily life. What would it mean to lose your worth (money), ID (wallet), car/home (keys), relationships (children, pets)? These fears and anxieties reflect how you are feeling in your waking life. The dream may be asking you to look at what you may potentially lose, and appreciate and value those things that you have. It may additionally be showing you that you are in danger of losing elements that you value unless you change your attitude and habits.

Luggage see also Packing
Luggage symbolises things that we take with us that we feel we need, even though we don't need all of what is packed away. Are you carrying emotional baggage? Do you need to lighten your load so you can travel lightly on your life journey? The dream may be challenging you to leave excess luggage behind if you want to make progress.

M

Machines
Often machinery in dreams represents how our body and our lifestyle are functioning. Are you an automated machine? Do you need to leave your monotonous job? Perhaps your robotic lifestyle is in need of a makeover? If the machine malfunctions, it indicates that you may be experiencing a few disappointments and setbacks in your waking life. Problems with machines such as televisions or computers suggest difficulty in processing or accessing information. You may also be spending too much time online and losing communication skills and connection with people you know or could potentially come to know.

Maps

If you were lost and needed direction you would reach for a map. We have navigational tools on our phones and in our car at hand for every location we need to arrive at. As a metaphor, a map is your direction in life. Being lost, frustrated and unable to follow the map direction suggests that you need more information before you make major decisions.

Masks

A mask hides our true features and therefore dreaming of wearing a mask indicates your need to hide your true self. Why are you using a façade? Who or what are you hiding from? It can also be a source of disguise to conceal your vulnerability.

Mirrors

Mirrors in your dreams reflect your inner qualities and your subconscious self. How do you see yourself? How do you think others see you? You may be concerned about your appearance, ageing, health and what you ideally should look like. The mirror symbolises what we would like to project to others. Breaking a mirror may not be bad luck, but it may indicate that you are breaking away from a stereotype or image you have of yourself.

Money

We would like to believe that dreaming of money means that money is coming to us in real life. Although this is mostly considered to be a wish fulfilment dream, sometimes this type of dream can be showing us what is possible to gain as a reward for our efforts, or simply that we'll win the lottery or at the races. Unfortunately there is a relatively small chance of this dream coming true.

Money in dreams is more than a representation of wealth, success and power. It also relates to self-worth and an exchange of value. What is valuable to us cannot always be paid for in money. Time, health, love and well-being are worth a great deal. Lack of money or losing money is alerting you to the 'cost' of losing something that means a great deal to you. What's costing you at the moment? Perhaps the dream is asking you to redefine or reassess your values.

Banknotes represent power and your potential for success or your actual financial situation. It may also symbolise your creative and emotional life. You're rich in talent and in your relationship. If you are giving money away it may be expressing your goodwill to help others in financial troubles or you may be simply giving them the richness of your wisdom and advice.

Mother see People

Mountains see also Climbing

If you dream of successfully climbing a mountain in your dream it indicates that you have overcome obstacles and reached your goal. A slippery slope suggests that you are feeling insecure as you face struggles at home or at work. Dreaming of climbing a mountain is a metaphor for encountering obstacles in your waking life and the ability to keep going until you reach the summit. If you are afraid of heights, it may suggest that you are not ready for success or that you fear failure (slipping down). Do you have a mountain of work you cannot get under control? Mountains are also known as mystical places and therefore can represent our spiritual journey to reach a higher level of consciousnesses. To look out from the mountain top is to review your life.

Museum see Buildings

Music

Hearing or playing music in your dreams is an expression of your inner self and the way you communicate with others. Is there harmony or discord? How you play is the way that you express yourself and connect with others. Take note of the instruments you play or hear, as they will have a special meaning for you personally.

N

Naked see also Chapter 5

To dream of being naked is to feel vulnerable and exposed in your day-to-day life. Nudity is a symbol of revealing our true (original) selves to others, unable to hide behind the safety of our clothing. Being comfortable naked means 'what you see is what you get' and that you are being honest and genuine in your approach to a situation with nothing to hide.

Numbers

Numbers hold a different significance for each of us. A number can refer to age, amounts of things, dates, time, address and other associations that are relevant to you. These numbers are regarded as universal symbols with the most common associations; however, treat numbers in dreams as codes that are unique to you. Taking a numerology approach: if you dream of a number with more than one digit you may wish to add them to a single digit. For example, 24 can be reduced to 6 (2 + 4 = 6).

1. Number 1 is the beginning and end of all things, the source, wholeness, unity, individuality, self. Check in with yourself and make sure you are balanced and have not spread yourself too thinly.

2. Duality (yin/yang, yes/no, good/bad) balance, choice and relationships. Look at the choices you are making. Are you procrastinating? Do your relationships need work?

3. Creative power. Middle, beginning and ending. The family unit of mother, father, child. Do you feel complete? Are you ready for something new? It may be time to complete that creative project.

4. Balance, life cycle, four seasons, earth, nature elements. Is your 'house' in order? Is your life stable? Look at what needs to be structured.

5. Represents the human body with its five fingers, toes and senses. It's also about movement and motion. Are you stuck? Do you need to move or travel to get away?

6. Balance, harmony and health are the characteristics of this number. Are you living in the moment? Are you spending time with people you love or are you out of balance?

7. This mystical number is associated with victory, magic and healing. Other symbolic meanings include seven days a week, seven stages of man, seven colours of the rainbow and seven chakras. Everything goes in cycles – what is coming up for you now? Look at developing new skills and be ready for new insights.

8. The symbol of the number 8 on its side means infinity and so it suggests regeneration, new achievements and higher consciousness. What new lifestyle changes are coming your way?

9. The number of completion of a cycle before a new one begins (pregnancy and childbirth). You are on the verge of a new adventure – the last number before you complete your cycle. Do you need to go back to your roots before you move forward to your next phase?

10. The law of heaven and earth, ten commandments, balance and unity. If you add 1 and 0 it will give you 1. Is it time for a new beginning?

11. In numerology, 11 is a master number – that is, it is not added up to make a single digit. In dreams the number 11 stands for mastery, spirituality and intuition. Do you have a vision of the kind of life you wish to create?

12. Symbol of cycles and cosmic order. There are twelve signs of the zodiac, twelve disciples of Christ, twelve months of the year. What cycle are you part of right now?

Nurse see People

O

Ocean see Water

Old person see People

Operation see Surgery

Owl see Animals – Birds

P

Packing see also Luggage
Many dreamers experience packing as a recurring dream. It can range from packing suitcases at home for a trip away without the time to pack everything, having too many things to pack, to packing up hotel rooms

that require sorting, putting away and organising. Packing indicates that we are carrying our personal baggage and we feel the burden of it in our lives. Do you have too many personal issues to attend to? Perhaps you are feeling overwhelmed with juggling too many things both at home and at work. If this is a recurring dream, your subconscious is reminding you to let go of some things, lighten your load and prioritise or you will be overwhelmed and weighed down by those demands.

Paralysis/being paralysed see also Trapped/stuck and chapters 1 and 2

In your dream you try to move but your legs won't carry you. You're paralysed. Stuck. You begin to speak but no words come out or they're all jumbled and you choke. This is a common dream that is often referred to as a nightmare because of the lack of control/powerlessness and impending threat as a result of someone chasing you or your inability to cry out for help.

A paralysis dream suggests that you feel that you are not making progress in waking life and that something is holding you back, preventing you from achieving your goal. It may well be self-sabotage – which is why you are making such a great effort to move but are getting nowhere – you're stuck in a rut. Paralysis in a dream is also an indication of natural paralysis when the body needs to remain still during REM sleep.

Party/celebrations see also Wedding

Dreaming of parties and celebrations can indicate the anxiety you experience around these events. Celebrations are positive experiences, celebrating joyful occasions; however, if you are not feeling happiness in your dream, it suggests that you are not feeling at ease in a social environment. It may also mean that you wish to experience joy or that the celebration is coming your way soon. Do you need to celebrate something in your life, no matter how insignificant it may appear to others?

Christmas, New Year and other major ritual celebrations and festivals are usually stressful times when expectations and hype are experienced. What do the events/celebrations mean to you personally and how do they relate to your real-life expectations of others and yourself? Note the emotion in your dream. Ritual celebrations have a specific message – baptism is for beginnings and belonging; graduation is indicative of opportunities and success.

Dreaming of weddings is the most common celebration dream. At a symbolic level, it is about commitment and relationships. Are you ready to go into a partnership or relationship? Your old identity has to merge with the new person, which requires a loss of old identity, and so there may be a sad emotion associated with weddings. It's common to have a death dream at the same time as a wedding dream.

People see also Chapter 8

People in our dreams illustrate aspects of our relationships to others and with ourselves. Archetypal characters are universal as they represent types of people we meet and qualities we possess and those same qualities we associate with others. When dreaming of people, work out what each person represents to you. Use three words to describe each person in your dream and then ask yourself if these characteristics have been evident in your life recently or if perhaps you could benefit from incorporating them.

Mother

The mother figure is an important archetypal figure in our dreams, representing both the nurturing, protective aspects and the possessive, domineering sides of ourselves. Mother is a symbol of the earth – Mother Nature – and all those qualities associated with growth, fertility, fragility and nurturing. Do you need these qualities in your life? Are you over-nurturing others and need more self-care? Perhaps you need to integrate the positive and negative aspects of the mothering role for a more balanced outcome.

Father see also Authority Figures below

The father in your dream commonly represents an authoritarian figure. You may have authoritarian qualities within you that need addressing or perhaps these qualities have dominated your life and you no longer wish to be treated in a paternalistic manner. Other common figures that are associated with authority, power, masculinity and wisdom come in dreams as a king, judge, priest, boss, police or old man. Are you struggling with authority or do you feel inadequate in an area of your life? Your association with your own father or father figure is the key to working out the dream's message.

Child see also Babies/birth/child

Dreaming of a child or baby indicates that you are about to start a new project or life stage and that it requires all the care and attention you can give it.

Family

Seeing your family or yourself in dreams represents the attitudes, values and opinions that were part of your formative years. Your family is your tribal group and as such there are many associations with each member, depending on their role and how you regarded them. An older sibling can symbolise leadership qualities that you want to integrate. A grandparent represents wisdom and tradition. If there's conflict in the family it suggests that there is conflict within you and your ethics, values or attitudes.

Friends

Friends also represent parts of your personality and the qualities you admire in a friendship such as loyalty, support and fun. Are these qualities missing from you or your friends? If so, it may be time to reassess your friendships.

Men/Women see also Chapter 3

A woman dreaming of another woman is a reflection of her own feminine aspects. When she dreams of a man, she is really connecting with the male energies of ambition, logic and action that need to be activated within herself. If the dreamer is a man, the female figure in his dream symbolises the relationship with his feminine side and with the women in his life.

Stranger

Dreaming of a stranger represents those aspects of yourself that you haven't met yet and may be a little bit tentative to explore. If you are a tourist in your dream, it suggests that you look at something in your life from a new perspective.

Authority figures

Authority figures such as fathers, teachers, police, judges, bosses or priests represent the qualities that are unique to their role. It is possible that these qualities can be used in your current situation. Perhaps they bring up negative emotions from the past at a time when you considered yourself powerless as a dependent. The teacher is a symbol of learning and knowledge – perhaps this is an area that you need to explore in more detail in your waking life. Police and judges are part of the legal system and therefore are law enforcers. What do their characteristics mean to you personally? Dreaming of your boss is a common dream, as it reflects your real-life conflict with authority. Each of these figures could be replacing anyone with authority in your life.

Petrol see also Car and Chapter 5

Running out of petrol while driving suggests that you are running out of energy and need re-fuelling. Think of ways to replenish and revitalise.

Pets see Animals

Plane see also Flying

Are you going on a big journey or heading off in a new direction? Planes involve long and quick travel, and represent our path and aspirations in life. A smooth flight signals that you are comfortable with this, while a turbulent one is preparing you for bumps along the way. Flying is also about the desire for freedom, wild sexual abandonment and escape. If you have trouble packing your bags, are getting on the wrong plane, are missing the plane or are simply not being able to take off, consider what obstacles and anxieties are preventing you from reaching your ideal goal. Are you prepared for the new venture? Dreaming of a plane crash may mean that there are changes ahead out of your control.

Pool see Water

Pregnancy see also Babies/birth/child and Chapter 3

Pregnancy is the creation of life that we associate with creativity. Are you dreaming of being more creative or are you contemplating starting a new project? A man who dreams of being pregnant may be in a situation where his creativity is being questioned or rejected. Usually in dreams men give birth to an object rather than a baby – one that is relevant to what they aim to achieve.

If you dream of being pregnant it suggests the birth of something new – a fresh idea, project, lifestyle. Someone else being pregnant indicates that something is not being expressed in you.

Prison

Prison is universally associated with incarceration, punishment and loss of freedom, and may reflect your emotional state in waking life. What's making you feel imprisoned or trapped? Being a prisoner suggests that the law has put you in a confined area for a reason. Ask yourself if you deserve to be 'locked up' or 'locked away'. What's making you feel that way in your life? Metaphorically you may have locked up parts of yourself or imprisoned belief systems, experiences and behaviours. Make sure that they no longer serve you before keeping them under lock and key. If you are experiencing a lack of freedom in your relationships or at work and see your family or boss as the jailer, it's time to recognise this and begin making some progress by claiming your independence.

R

Rabbit see Animals

Rain see also Weather and Storms
Depending on where you live geographically, rain in your dreams can symbolise relief (from drought) or troubled times ahead (it never rains, it pours). Gentle rain refreshes the earth and brings new life and growth to crops and plant life. If you're needing release from pent-up emotions, the rain is suggesting that you shed some tears to cleanse and get rid of emotions held in check.

Rape see Sex

Rats see Animals

Recurring dreams see also chapters 1 and 2
Recurring dreams are dreams or dream themes that are repeated and therefore recur throughout our lives, usually when there is a trigger that sets them off in our current situation. Most recurring dreams are anxiety-based dreams and are often manifested as nightmares. If you're being chased, for example, the detail of where and who was chasing you may change, but the theme of being chased and the feeling associated with it are the same. The recurring dream asks us to examine what's going on in

our life that we are avoiding facing and begin to find a solution. Once the dreamer confronts and resolves the real-life issue, the dream will have a more positive outcome and may stop altogether.

Rescue

If you dream of being rescued, the dream could be telling you that you need rescuing – possibly from yourself or from a situation that you are not in control of. What do you need to be rescued from? If there is water in your dream, it symbolises your emotional life and therefore is related more to a relationship issue. If you are the rescuer, the dream highlights your desire to be noble and heroic and a need for validation. Examine the dream and notice who or what you are rescuing.

Roads

Roads are symbols of our life direction and spiritual journey. We talk about our life's journey or the path we are on and being at a crossroad when we need to make a decision. Looking at the road behind you is to look back at your past; looking ahead is your future. What kind of road are you travelling on? If it's a rocky road, you may have some obstacles facing you; a side track or unpaved road suggests that you may go off track or that it will be more rewarding to have reached your destination your own way. Streets also suggest navigation – you may need to check in or stop and get directions along the way to help you in your present journey. Consider the following associations with roads for further insight: road rage, on the road, one for the road, on the road to recovery, all roads lead to Rome.

S

School

School, college or other educational institutions epitomise learning, and if you are having recurring dreams of being back in school it often reflects performance anxiety in your waking life. Are you keeping up your grades? Do you need to retrain or upskill? The more advanced the level of education, the more complex the information and more pressure for you to perform in real life. It may be time to implement some changes to do with knowledge and learning.

Searching

To search for something often denotes a need to know and understand yourself. What you are searching for in the dream will give you a deeper insight into what those images represent for you. For example, searching for a child may indicate the need to find the inner child within you, or if it's your child you associate the child with something of utmost value.

Seasons

Seasons and weather represent the cycles of life you are experiencing and your moods. How well are you prepared and equipped to get through each one?

Winter is associated with hibernation and solitude; spring is the beginning of new life; summer is activity and growth; and autumn is the harvest and collecting for the winter months. What stage are you at in your present life? Know that the only constant is change.

Sex see also Chapter 4

Freud saw sex as wish fulfilment, but his theory has been disputed by many working in the area of dreams. Dreaming of sex has physical and emotional interpretations. For men, a wet dream is a biological function that involuntary releases semen while they are asleep, usually triggered by a sex dream. For women, they can also experience sexual stimulation and pleasure in their dreams – our bodies crave for a physical release. There is research on hormonal and physical changes and the higher levels of oestrogen that produce more sex dreams. Circumstances surrounding the experience of a sex dream can vary from pleasurable to disturbing and distressing. Symbolically, sexual intercourse indicates a desire for emotional bonding, closeness and intimacy. It is a longing for a deeper communication on a more intimate level that connects you to someone else.

Being unfaithful

If you dream of your partner cheating on you, it may reflect your real-life insecurities that this may actually happen. This is rarely true, as it is a common anxiety dream for those in relationships. It is in our instinctive nature to fend off romantic rivals to protect our interest, so you may feel this is a possible threat in real life. It may be a matter of your low self-esteem – are you feeling vulnerable and unattractive to your partner?

Perhaps he/she hasn't made a point of telling you they find you attractive. Are you finding it difficult to trust in general? If you are the one doing the cheating, you may be needing intimacy or closeness that you are not getting in real life. Do you feel emotionally abandoned or are you simply not satisfied with your partner? You may also be feeling disloyal to your partner in other ways such as spending less time together, working longer hours and so on. Review your communication style and intimacy – it may be a wake-up call to spend quality time together.

Sex with others

Often sex functions as a metaphor for being attracted to qualities that your dream sexual partner represents. Sex with an older person suggests you are looking for nurturing, stability, compassion, wisdom and security. If you dream of having sex with a celebrity, it indicates you wish to have those same qualities of fame and recognition in your life. Sex with someone you work with is a representation of a good working relationship.

Having sex with a stranger or someone you are not attracted to means you are coming across things in your life that you are not consciously aware of, such as emotional connections, closeness and deep emotions associated with intimacy. These qualities may be missing from your life or, conversely, you don't want emotional involvement that requires commitment to complicate your life.

Sex with your ex

Having sex with your ex is not about wanting to act on the desire or even having those feelings for your ex in real life. Usually it represents our previous experience with past romantic relationships and wanting to recapture the 'best' of that experience to integrate into your present relationship. What do you need to feel more loving?

Sadism/masochism

Sadism and masochism in dreams reflect your need to explore the opposite sides of your nature. This is particularly true if you are experiencing frustration and a lack of power in your everyday life.

Castration

For men, dreaming of being castrated reflects the feeling or fear of losing their masculinity. Having sex with a female boss may be a compensation for being made to feel emasculated in real life.

Homosexuality/bisexuality

Homosexuality or bisexuality is about balancing the feminine and masculine aspects of our self – not necessarily sexual, but also from a psychological and emotional perspective. You may have to accept both of these aspects without judgement.

Incest

Incest dreams cause concern to some dreamers as they may represent suppressed memories of incestuous abuse or of wish fulfilment. However, in dreams it is more of a psychological association. You may be involved with the person in the dream because they have similar qualities to family members and are therefore 'familiar' territory. The incest could also represent your need for closer ties with your family. On the other hand, your close relationship with family may be causing you to feel stifled and restricted.

Rape

Rape in real life is more related to violence than sex itself. In a rape dream, the dreamer may be feeling violated and powerless. Look at the balance of power in your life – is it being abused? Are you the victim or the perpetrator? Rape is also a metaphor for someone penetrating your emotional barriers and therefore highlights your sense of vulnerability and exposure.

Sex settings

Nowhere to make love is a common dream in which you search for a place to make love but wake up unable to find privacy. What obstacles are there in your relationship that are preventing you from being close? Do you need to rekindle the passion?

Interruption from intruders (family, boss or phone call) while making love suggests that there are other people and factors intruding in your private life.

Making love in public may indicate a sense of public exposure and that you feel vulnerable about people knowing your intimate details.

Snakes see Animals

Spiders see Animals

Spiritual guides see also Angels and Chapter 11

Spiritual guides are symbols of your spirituality and a desire to connect with divinity. A guiding light or a spiritual guide may appear in a dream when you are undergoing difficult challenges and soul searching. If you dream of holy figures your interpretation will be a personal one depending on your belief system. Generally, any spiritual figure will bring comfort, reassurance and advice during difficult times. Magical beings suggest your need to reconnect with your creative life, and aliens represent new information and knowledge that is yet to materialise.

Sports see Games/sport

Storms

Stormy weather is an indicator of the level of turmoil in your emotional life and powerful changes, depending on how dramatic the weather is. Extreme natural events such as cyclones, tornadoes, hurricanes and tsunamis are signs of sudden and unexpected changes in your life and their effect on you. What strong emotions are surging through you?

The havoc and devastation they wreak suggest that you are feeling out of control in your waking life. Perhaps an escape plan can be devised so that you emerge with as little damage as possible. There is wisdom to be gained after one of these stormy dreams.

Subways see Tunnels

Suffocating see also Water

To suffocate in a dream suggests that you are feeling overwhelmed or lacking control or that you are being emotionally pressured by demands made on you. Check your health and look at alternatives to help you cope with stressful situations.

Surgery see also Body

If you are due to have surgery, this dream is merely a reflection of your fears and anxieties about the procedure. Having surgery represents the process in which parts of our individuality are interfered with. Note what body parts are being operated on – if it's the heart, this suggests that an emotional issue in real life is affecting you and needs to be dealt with. Limbs represent movement and action – are there parts of you/your lifestyle that need to move so that you can be more flexible? At times our bodies register problems with our health subconsciously before they reach our conscious mind or symptoms show up. As with any dream relating to health, consider getting a medical check-up.

T

Teeth see Body and Chapter 5

Telephone

We are more dependent than ever on our phones as they function to keep us connected through text, talking to someone and all the features of a smartphone with camera and internet. No matter where we are, we can turn to our phones for communication, entertainment, information and all those features that give us comfort. Dreaming of a phone not functioning properly or being unable to hear the other person speaking to you suggests that you are having some communication issues in your daily life or that you feel disconnected/frustrated at not being able to give or receive information. Perhaps you are too reliant on your smartphone and you need to reconnect with people by interacting face to face. It is common for bereaved people to experience talking to the deceased on the phone.

Tidal wave see Water and Storms

Time see also Clock

Time of day is relevant in dreams as it tells us about the qualities or time in your life. Morning suggests a new start; afternoon is for close of day and end of a situation; evening/night is mysterious and intimate and can also be foreboding.

Notice the time and the setting and action around it, for instance, is it on a plane ticket or on a timetable? Typically, time is based around movement and travel is one form of movement.

Toilet see Bathroom

Tornado see Storms

Tower see Buildings

Train see Vehicles

Trapped/stuck see also Chapter 5
This dream usually manifests as a nightmare and it represents our inability to escape something in real life and being unable to see a way out of the situation. You may be stuck in a job you don't like or feel trapped in a relationship that is no longer fulfilling. If you are setting a trap or falling into a trap in your dreams, take note of the dream scene as it may give you insight into what or who you are trying to hold on to. Perhaps the dream is warning you not to get caught in a trap.

Treasure
To dream that you found treasure suggests that you have discovered a hidden talent or skill that you did not know you possessed. You will also be helped by a lot of people, which will allow you to achieve your goals.

Trees see also Forest
Dreaming of a tree can symbolise a tree of life, a family tree or the tree of knowledge. It can represent characteristics associated with the symbol, depending on your beliefs and customs. Trees represent our life force and trees are also known as the lungs of the planet. Dreaming of a tree is highlighting your developmental growth and connections to your family 'roots', which hold you in the solid earth as foundations. If the tree is swaying, it indicates that your family or foundations are not as solid as they should be. Branching out suggests new direction, and buds and fruits are different stages of our life. If you are alighting from a branch, you may be feeling out on a limb. Is it a majestic oak tree or a spiny yucca? What characteristics do you associate with these trees? The type of tree and its overall appearance is important to note in the dream so that you can assess its significance in your daily life.

Trucks see Vehicles

Tunnels
Dreaming of being in a tunnel suggests that you wish to explore your unconscious mind. Crawling in the tunnel is a symbol of the birth canal and therefore your psyche wishes to return to the safety of the womb.

Perhaps you need to rebirth your new identity or project? We say there is light at the end of the tunnel when we refer to hope or positive outcomes. It may be that you have tunnel vision and a broader perspective on an issue could be of benefit.

V

Vehicles see also Cars

Our vehicles show direction, power, navigation and innovations. They are totally reliant on humans to create and operate them, and therefore are associated with our ambition, purposefulness and willpower. Each vehicle is built for a purpose and therefore the dream will highlight your needs and wants. For example, a truck is to carry goods – it may suggest that you are carrying a heavy load (burden), or an ambulance indicates a health emergency. Are you taking care of your health needs? Vehicles also give us an option to travel and escape. Trains and buses can be for necessary trips into work but can also offer long distance journeys at a moderate pace where one can enjoy the scenery. Train tracks are directional and therefore a metaphor for our journey and direction in life – both inner and outer journeys. Do you need to escape from the daily grind and find a new life direction?

Volcano

Dreaming of a volcano represents the rising emotional pressure that is ready to erupt in a violent outburst. There may be someone in your waking life that you feel has an explosive personality or your home/work life is like a volcano waiting to erupt. Perhaps it could be that you're suppressing anger and you may need to let off steam in a way that is not destructive.

W

Water

Water is a powerful symbol of the collective unconscious as it is life giving to all living things. Water is life. Water cleanses and purifies and is often seen as a sign of rebirth, spirituality and healing. Many Hindus believe that the water from the Ganges River can cleanse a person's soul of all past sins, and that it can also cure the ill.

We refer to water as a body of water, and our human body is made up of over seventy per cent of water. It is not surprising that water is a powerful symbol in dreams, and we collectively dream of floods, tsunamis, ocean, seas, lakes and ponds.

How you are feeling in real life or emotions you are repressing in your life will appear in dreams as water themes. Is everything smooth sailing at home or are you being tossed about and afraid of drowning? One dream image suggests you are in control of your emotional life and the other indicates feeling overwhelmed and literally 'adrift'. The type of vessel you are on suggests the resources you have in dealing with your emotions. A large cruise ship will withstand the pounding of the waves better than an unsteady raft or a leaky canoe. You may need to take a closer look at your support systems.

If the water is muddy or the waves are pounding and you are afraid of drowning, it represents those swelling feelings associated with feeling swamped during a significantly stressful and confusing period in your life. If you can breathe underwater, you will have faced your deepest emotions without drowning in them. Clear waters symbolise clarity – you will see your way through.

Oceans and seas suggest the vastness and depths of our psyche and our soul. How you navigate or swim in these large bodies of water and their depths will give you insight into your deepest emotions.

Pools, dams and ponds are more contained, suggesting you don't like to delve too deeply in your emotional state.

A waterfall indicates that you need to let go and release repressed emotions.

Flowing water means movement and change, while stagnant and dirty water such as swamps suggests you are stuck or confused. A waterfall is about releasing strong emotions.

Falling in the water suggests that you are not ready emotionally for whatever is going on in your life. You need to get rid of all the past clutter and belief patterns first.

Drowning, big waves, tsunamis, tidal waves or flooding represent your feelings of being overwhelmed. Are you in denial of the emotional stress you are facing? Are there ways to better accept these feelings that often involve vulnerability and lack of control? If you dive under the tsunami and don't run from it, it suggests that you are willing to meet your challenges.

Weapons
Weapons in dreams are associated with aggression, violence and action. They normally indicate that you feel the only option to settle confrontation or disputes is through force or violence. The weapons in your dream may be suggesting that there needs to be a sense of fairness in getting what you want and the methods you use to obtain it.

Weather see also Storms
Weather symbolises powerful emotions and change. It's important to understand what stage we are at in our own journey through life. In all seasonal/weather cycles there is always a rebirth after death (winter to spring). Rain represents both an emotional release and replenishment for the earth (potential growth). When it's sunny in our dreams, all is well and full of optimism ahead. Snow can indicate an emotional coldness and that you may need to thaw out a little. Fog represents a lack of clarity ahead, so it's best to move slowly with caution when making decisions. Wind is a symbol of change and the idiom 'wind of change' reflects its nature.

Wedding see also Party/celebrations
Women are more likely than men to dream about weddings and the dream scenes tend to have more negative components than positive ones. It may be that the bride goes to the wrong church, is late or can't get there, or it's the wrong groom. These anxiety dreams are not necessarily related to women who are in committed relationships or about to get married. Generally, wedding dreams represent commitment and the beginning of a new partnership. If you see yourself as the bride or groom and you are happy, it indicates that you want to be more involved in your current relationship. It may suggest that you are searching for an inner marriage – an integration of the yin and yang, the feminine and the masculine, the Anima and Animus. The marriage in your dream may represent the union of the different sides of your own character.

If your biological time clock is ticking away and you are anxious to get married, this dream may be a form of wish fulfilment.

In some cultures, wedding dreams are interpreted as possible deaths of someone you know. This is true in a way, as women who take on their husband's name have to 'kill' their old identity and reinvent themselves with a new name that requires tedious bureaucratic processes. Marriage is the death of the old life and the birth of a new one, and it is common to have a death dream and a wedding dream in sequence.

Wind see Storms

Windows see House

Winning

Winning the lottery is a wish-fulfilment dream that many people experience and it's a feel-good outcome – in the dream, that is. In reality you may be struggling financially and the dream of winning a lottery is your fantasy of escaping from the stress and burden, hoping against hope that your luck will change. Have your lucky numbers come up? Perhaps you are hoping for that windfall in your new relationship or job. In case you're lucky enough to have had a prophetic dream, jot down those numbers as soon as you wake up.

Witches

Children generally have frightening dreams of witches in their stereotypical appearance – long, pointy nose, warts, wearing black and flying on a broomstick. In adults' dreams, we associate witches with negative feminine power and personality traits. Ask yourself: are you bewitched or bewitching – and which makes you more apprehensive?

Wolf see Animals

Frequently Asked Questions

Here are some of the most commonly asked questions about dreams and dreaming:

Does everybody dream?

Everybody dreams, including mammals, as they have been shown to exhibit the same brain activity as humans during their sleep. People say they don't dream, but this is incorrect; they simply can't remember dreaming. There are many possible causes for this, including use of alcohol, taking certain medications, chronic insomnia, having too much sleep, stress, fear of reliving traumatic events in dreams or it may simply be a genetic predisposition. Stopping certain medications suddenly has been known to cause nightmares. We don't remember all our dreams all the time and we can go through a dry spell when we don't recall our dreams at all. The good news is that it is possible to increase dream recall with dream techniques such as dream incubation, good sleeping patterns and an increase in vitamins and minerals if the body is depleted of these.

We experience our most vivid dreams in REM (rapid eye movement) sleep when our brain is most active and our large muscles relaxed. Our body is paralysed during this time to protect us from acting out our dreams. REM sleep occurs every 60–90 minutes, up to four times a night, and our dreams lasts longer as the night progresses.

What is the average amount of dreams a person usually has in one night?

Although we don't spend the entire night in a dream state, we can have up to ten dreams per night depending on how long the dreams last. Generally, the average person has three to five dreams each night. An average person spends about two hours dreaming, and most of our dreams happen while we are in REM sleep. There are five cycles of sleep

– from light to heaviest – in which we move through during the night. The very last sleep cycle when we are in deep sleep is the REM sleep. This is where most of the dreaming happens and, not surprisingly, it's usually from this cycle that we wake up and remember our dreams. Each cycle of sleep lasts from 60 minutes up to 90 minutes, which is repeated throughout the night.

How can I remember my dream?

Most dreams are forgotten unless they are written down. On average we forget ninety per cent of our dream within ten minutes of waking up. Sometimes a dream can be remembered later in the day or on another day. This suggests that your dream memory is not totally lost but it is very hard to retrieve, and hence why I personally feel that most dreams are stored in our subconscious mind rather than the unconscious. It just needs a trigger or a fragment of the dream to be recalled and one can retrieve the dream or feelings within the dream.

Before you fall asleep, remind yourself that you want to remember your dreams. Keep paper and pen or your mobile phone to record into by your bedside. As soon as you wake up, keep your eyes closed so that you are still connected to the sleep state and don't start planning your day just yet. Write down, record or even talk to your partner about your dream – even if you can only recall fragments or feelings felt in the dream. Once the dream surfaces to the conscious, it can then be remembered and recorded for review.

Do children dream the same as adults?

Dreams often reflect our anxieties and life issues, therefore children's dreams are quite different in content and intensity. Children under five years old don't have dreams with a high emotional content or logical storyline. As they get a little older and the world around them expands to include school, activities and lots of new people in their social lives, they frequently experience nightmares. Teens will experience vivid dreams that focus on killing or death themes and getting lost. This is due to having to come to terms with growing up, as their bodies are changing and they begin to have to face added responsibilities. They virtually need to kill off the child in them (childish body and behaviour) and accept a new body (hormonal changes) with a different level of expectations from authority figures.

Why do we dream?

There are a number of theories to explain why we have dreams. One is that dreams serve as a way for us to cleanse and release emotions that have built up during the day and need to be processed. In this case dreams are a type of safety valve that helps us release negative feelings such as repressed anger and frustration, as well as excess information – a brain dump of sorts. It's also a means to process events, decisions or dilemmas that take place during the day. The subconscious mind will be able to help the conscious mind to sort and file information on how to deal with these issues in a logical way. Another theory is that dreaming is a biological necessity for sleep. If we are prevented from entering the dream state and are woken up, we will become easily irritated and generally perform below average in our daily tasks.

Do dreams always have meanings?

Typically dreams are a reflection of what's going on for you in your waking life. The images always contain some type of hidden meaning – sometimes it's important and other times it's simply mirroring your anxieties in real life. Only the dreamer understands the symbols and meaning of the dream, as it is personal to them; however, there are many universal symbols that we all can relate to.

Most people who work with their dreams, either by themselves or with others, find that their dream insights are meaningful for them. Dreams can help you learn more about your feelings, values, decision-making skills and general outlook on life. It's been well documented that dreams are problem solvers. They are particularly useful for inventors or scientists, who get ideas from their dreams after working on their research in their day lives, and also artists, songwriters and writers who are open to creative insights from dreams.

Why do we have recurring dreams?

Recurring dreams suggest that there is an issue that the dreamer is not confronting or is unable to resolve. Basically, it's an anxiety dream about a situation you may be struggling with and it causes you to have a recurring dream. Essentially, your waking self wants the problem to be solved. Unless you face the issue in real life the dream will recur and possibly become more vivid and persistent. It's a wake-up call to action.

We have these repetitive dreams because a situation or a trigger that has come up in your conscious life is similar to one that came up in the past. The brain uses a metaphor to bring up your unexpressed emotions about that similar situation. It may be a chase dream where you feel unable to move as you are being chased by a threatening figure or object. It may be that a real life event has triggered you feeling vulnerable and unable to get away from a fearful emotional situation (perhaps an old childhood situation such as bullying). The dream imagery therefore parallels that emotional fear and shows it in such a way that you will remember it and at least be aware that something is causing you emotional stress. Once the trigger is understood, the subconscious mind will usually not bother to give you repetitive nightmares.

Do we all dream in colour?

About seventy-five per cent of people dream in colour. Men are more likely to dream in black and white than women. It may be that the action in the dream is more important to remember and therefore colours would be a distraction, whereas women are more visually oriented and it could explain why they pay attention to colours. If in the dream colours are vivid and/or odd for the item they represent, for example, green blood, then the dream is trying to draw your attention to the blood by making it an odd colour, which you are then more likely to recall on waking.

Do our daily activities affect our dreams?

If you suppress your feelings throughout the day, those emotions have a good chance of showing up in your dream. Repressed emotions are the most common reason for having dreams. We normally don't tell people how we really feel about the way they treat us or what irritates us about them – especially in cases where it's your boss or someone you feel that you can't express your true feelings with. In dreams, these repressed emotions come up in symbols and as classic anxiety dreams. If you have suffered a trauma, nightmares are often a way to release the trauma by replaying it in your sleep, although these dreams may occur in the form of nightmares, which can be very distressing for the dreamer.

Are there any differences in the way men and women dream?

Men and women dream in the same way but do not always dream of the same themes. Research shows that men tend to dream more about men, while women dream about both men and women equally. It has been suggested that men find it difficult to acknowledge their softer, feminine side and this is reflected in the dream, which is essentially about an aspect of ourselves. Women find it easier to accept their dominant aspect (traditionally the masculine role, especially in the workplace) as they have moved out of their feminine traditional role of homemaker. Another possible reason is that men are wired to be the hunter-gathers and despite evolution they still feel the need to be the provider and fight off other potential rivals.

Do women have more nightmares than men?

Yes, studies show that women experience nightmares more than men. It may be that they are more sensitive to the world around them in waking life or that they don't feel safe in their environment. Research also suggests it may be that more women suffer from depression (or are diagnosed with depression due to seeking help more readily than men), and anti-depressants bring on more vivid dreaming. However, although we dream more when we are depressed, we are less likely to recall dreams because they take place earlier in the night than usual.

Why do we remember bad dreams more easily than good dreams?

Bad dreams or nightmares are easier to remember because they are usually more vivid and are emotionally charged with fear. Being woken out of REM sleep makes it much easier to recall the events of the dream. It makes sense that if you wake up with a jolt you will recall the contents of what caused you to wake up.

Why is dreaming of death such a common dream?

Dreams of death are not literally about the dreamer or someone dying. They often occur if you've been experiencing some stressful events in waking life. Issues around relationships, jobs, career changes, depression or even illness can bring about dreams of death. Life changes are often represented as death in your dreams. Your dreaming mind uses the death metaphor to bring attention to what's causing you distress and therefore in a metaphoric sense is 'hastening your death'. Generally, dreaming of death is heralding a new beginning after the death or letting go of something (hence, change). Death and renewal is a natural cycle of life and therefore a prequel of what's to come. If you dream of death be reassured rather than fearful. Embrace the change that is awaiting you.

Is it true that if you dream that you die or that you hit the ground in a falling dream, you will in fact die in your sleep?

This is a myth. Many people have dreamed that they died or hit the ground in a fall and they have lived to tell the tale. I am one of these people. Falling dreams are usually a result of feeling unsupported and vulnerable in waking life. It may also suggest that you need to take a leap of faith into a new stage of your life. If you hit the ground and land softly without injuries, the new move that you are about to make will be relatively pain free. Landing in water suggests there will be some emotional turbulence to wade through. If you hit the ground and wake up in fright because of the fall, it's your body protecting you from a perceived danger (see the question above).

Do people share dreams?

It's possible to share the same dream with people you live with or are close to emotionally. This is known as a type of dream telepathy where people have the same dream and recall it when they wake up. (See Chapter 10 for more information.)

Why do we jerk and wake up in our dreams?

Waking up from our dreams as the result of a jerk is known as a myoclonic jerk. If you dream of falling or you sometimes twitch and you wake yourself up, this can be your brain's way of protecting you as it feels that you are in a potentially dangerous situation. Dreams are so real that if you dream of falling off a cliff, the brain sends a signal to your body to start fleeing away from the danger.

Myoclonic jerks occur more often at the early stages of sleep when the body is preparing to 'let go' and 'fall asleep' – and this release is sometimes perceived by the brain as 'falling' because we are letting go of our control over our waking bodies.

Why do we have nightmares?

Nightmares are more common in children than in adults, however, we all experience nightmares in our lifetime. There are a number of reasons why adults have nightmares, including feeling stressed or overwhelmed, experiencing a trauma or post traumatic stress, facing emotional challenges, medication, drugs and illness. If nightmares occur and seem unrelated to waking life experiences, there is research to suggest that some people who are very empathetic and emotionally sensitive experience nightmares more regularly and for no apparent reason. Generally, however, our nightmares reflect our deepest fears and stresses. (See nightmares in Chapter 2.)

Although nightmares can be very frightening when we are having them, they help us to express our worst fears. This de-activating of our unexpressed fears is actually helpful, as we are able to alert our conscious mind and become aware of those fears. Some experts claim that nightmares actually protect our psyche because we play out our very worst fears as practice in our sleep, so when we do experience trauma and tragedy our bodies have already experienced the emotions in the dream and have survived the onslaught. It seems logical to the psyche that we can then cope better with the real-life traumatic event. Seeing nightmares in this positive light, that is, as being the brain's way of protecting us, can be beneficial when experiencing fear and terror in your nightmare.

Can dreams predict the future?

There are many recorded examples of dreams that have predicted future events. Prophetic, clairvoyant, telepathic or predictive dreams can be attributed to mere coincidence by some, however, there has been plenty of evidence to suggest that this is not the case every time. Other schools of thought are inclined to believe that we've picked up specific information subconsciously (e.g. car brakes that aren't as responsive and we then dream of a car accident, which turns out to be true). It may be that you are worried about someone close to you dying and another relative actually dies.

Prophetic dreams can also be explained as some type of synchronicity that arises out of our universal collective unconscious. Put simply, we 'just know' that there will be a natural disaster and people collectively from all over the world can see this in their dreams before it actually happens.

Very few people are gifted with prophetic dreams regularly, while some ordinary people occasionally get a glimpse through their intuitive minds of what's to happen. It is a fascinating field of study and we are learning more about this phenomenon. (See Chapter 10 for more information.)

Can dreams provide solutions to problems?

Yes. It is no coincidence that we use the phrase 'sleep on it' before making a major decision. By giving your conscious mind time to process the decision during sleep time, the subconscious mind often brings up symbols to represent emotions we've not had time to go through in waking life. By bringing up these unexpressed emotions, the dreamer is given the opportunity to reflect on making the right choice not simply based on logic.

There is a plethora of recorded evidence of people who've been inspired and received solutions to their problems in dreams. Scientists and inventors who've researched and worked on formulas and inventions have been known to make major breakthroughs in their dreams through metaphoric images. The benzene molecule is one such example. Scientists believe that this phenomenon is due to our brain reaching a solution in our cognitive unconscious mind *before* we fall asleep.

Who do people represent in our dreams?

Dreams of people are not usually about those specific people but the qualities they represent to the dreamer. Sometimes, however, we do dream about real people but they look different. They can be physically different or even invisible, but you as the dreamer know that it is a particular person and that they are there even if you can't see them. All the dream elements about the person and the emotions the dreamer felt towards the person will give clues as to what that person actually represents to the dreamer. (See Chapter 7 for more information on archetypes.)

What is lucid dreaming?

Lucid dreaming is being aware you are dreaming while still asleep and in the dream. Many people experience being conscious while in a dream. During a lucid dream you are able to some extent to control what you dream. If a knife is being thrown at you in a dream, for example, a lucid dreamer can potentially will the knife to change into a feather and change the outcome of the dream. In this type of dream the dreamer can remember some of the details of their waking life and act on suggestions they've made before going to sleep. It is possible to learn to lucid dream and increase your ability to change dream events as they occur within your dream. (See Chapter 10 for more information.)

How can I interpret my dreams?

Each dream image is unique to the dreamer because dreams essentially reflect what's going on in your waking life, your emotions, your thoughts and the people around you. To decode your own dream symbols you need to understand what symbols in your dream represent to you and, more importantly, the emotion it evokes during the dream and after. If you dream of a snake, are you comfortable being in the company of a poisonous snake or are you terrified? The key is to understand what associations the snake has for you. For most people a snake represents fear as the elements of a snake include being able to kill with a single strike unexpectedly and in a sneaky way. It may be that the snake is a metaphor for feeling that someone or something in your real life is out to get you and you have to be on high alert as there's no indication of where or from whom that threat is coming. Those who are at ease with snakes may simply regard their qualities as being fascinating and containing ancient wisdom. In that case, the dreamer has a different interpretation of the same image depending on their experience with the object. It's important to look at the parallels in your real life to learn how to interpret your own dream symbols.

There are also universal dreams and archetypes shared by everyone, most of which are anxiety-based dreams such as being chased, flying, death, falling, drowning and more. (See Chapter 5.) The common dream elements and themes in these universal dreams give us insight into our waking life issues. It is up to the dreamer to delve further into their daily life and find the parallels that will help them decipher their dream images and messages. Our subconscious mind offers great insights if we are willing to take the time and patiently review our dreams even long after we've had one. Writing the dream down and checking it against our diary is one way to start the process into understanding our dream world.

Author Biography

Rose Inserra is a successful published author of over sixty books distributed both here and internationally. She has been listed in the Notable Books in the Children's Book Council Awards and short-listed for the Environment Award for Children's Literature in Australia. Her best-selling book *Dictionary of Dreams* has sold more than half a million copies and has become a trusted and practical source for people who wish to gain insight into their dreams. Rose also regularly assists people with interpreting their dreams via private consultations, group sessions and seminars, which have resulted in major life-changing moments for them. She is a member of the International Association for the Study of Dreams and has appeared as a guest columnist and speaker in print media and on radio.

Creativity has always been a huge feature of Rose's role as author, editor and coach. Her studies in creativity coaching with renowned creativity coach Eric Maisel Ph.D has enabled her to teach her clients the latest techniques in accessing their creativity. The program has been particularly successful with writers who are blocked or simply overwhelmed with their project.

In her previous working life Rose was a secondary school teacher and taught children's writing at various TAFE institutes and Adult Education Centres.

Rose Inserra's *Dream Reading Cards* and *Dream Journal* are also available through Rockpool Publishing.

For more information about Rose go to: www.roseinserra.com

Acknowledgements

I wish to thank all of my wonderful dreamers who generously gave their time in sharing their dreams with me. There are too many of you to mention individually, but know that I am so very grateful to each and every one of you. Without your dreams for me to interpret there would be no case studies in this book.

A heartfelt thanks to industry professionals who helped me with advice, research and information on spiritual and para-psychological phenomena, dream studies and psychological data. A special thanks to Elizabeth Russell-Arnot for her insightful explanation on the Dreaming.

Much gratitude to Rockpool publishers Lisa Hanrahan and Paul Dennett, who shared my vision for this book and put their faith in me. Thanks also to Katie Evans for her passionate editing work.

Most especially I'd like to thank my husband Peter for his endless patience, support and encouragement during the writing of this book.

Bibliography

Barrett, D., 'University of North Carolina dream collection', 1992

Campbell, J., *The Hero with a Thousand Faces,* Princeton: Princeton University Press 2015

Crisp, T., *The New Dream Dictionary,* London: Optima 1990

Cross, Amanda, *Children's Dream Dictionary*, London: Hamlyn 2002

Dias, B.G. and K.J. Ressler, 'Parental olfactory experience influences behavior and neural structure in subsequent generations', Nature Neuroscience, 17, 89-96, 2014

Domhoff, W., *Finding Meaning in Dreams*, New York: Plenum Press 1996

Freud, S., *The Interpretation of Dreams,* 1997

Garfield, P., *The Healing Power of Dreams*, New York: Simon & Schuster 1991; *The Dream Messenger,* USA: Simon & Schuster 1997

Guiley, R.E., *Dreamspeak,* USA: Berkley, 2001; 'Precognitive Dreams Sept 11', Visionary Living, Inc.

Gunn, C.M., *Simply Totem Animals*, New York: Sterling Publishing 2010

Hillman, J., *The Soul's Code,* New York: Warner Books, 1996

Holloway, G., *The Complete Dream Book,* USA: Sourcebooks Inc 2006

Inserra, R., *The Dictionary of Dreams,* Melbourne: Hinkler Books 2001

International Association for the Study of Dreams, http://www.asdreams.org/

Jung, C.G., *The Archetypes and the Collective Unconscious,* 1953; *Man and His Symbols,* London: Aldus 1964

Kubler-Ross, E., *On Death and Dying,* New York: Simon & Schuster 1969

Moss, R., *Conscious Dreaming,* New York: Random House 1996

Sabini, M., 'Genealogical Dreams', *Dreamtime Journal*, IASD, Winter 2014

Sams, J.D. Carson, *Medicine Cards,* USA: Bear & Company 1988

Savery, Berne & Kaplan-Williams, *Dreams and Spiritual Growth,* USA: Paulist Press 1984

Siegel, A.B., *Dreams That Can Change Your Life,* New York: Berkley Publishing 1990; *Dreamcatching: Every Parent's Guide to Exploring and Understanding Children's Dreams and Nightmares*, USA: Random House 1998

Spurr, P., *Your Child's Dreams,* London: Eddison Sadd Editions 2009; *Dreams and Sexuality,* New York: Stirling Publishing Company 2001

Villoldo, A., *Courageous Dreaming,* USA: Hay House 2008

Index